Yellowstone B   N

A HISTORY OF RAIL TRAVEL TO AMERICA'S FIRST NATIONAL PARK

By Thornton Waite

Northern Pacific W Class Mikado locomotive #1565, pulling a Boy Scouts of America Special Train at Gardiner, Montana, Aug. 1, 1953.
COURTESY KENT E. WATSON

COPYRIGHT©2006 THORNTON WAITE

All rights reserved. No portion of this book may be used or reproduced without written permission of the publisher.

LIBRARY OF CONGRESS
CONTROL NO. 2006933401

ISBN 978-1-57510-129-3

First Printing: November 2006
Second Printing: January 2008

PRINTED IN KOREA
BY DOOSAN CORPORATION

PICTORIAL HISTORIES PUBLISHING CO., INC.
713 South Third Street West, Missoula, Montana 59801
Phone: (406) 549-8488 • Fax (406) 728-9280
E-mail–phpc@montana.com

Preface

The thought and suggestion for this book came from Yellowstone National Park archivist Lee Whittlesey. Knowing about my interest in railroads, he suggested I write a book describing rail travel to the park through all of the entrances. This sounded interesting, and I subsequently began researching the history of the different lines to the park. I thank him for the idea and for his help in writing this book, providing thoughtful suggestions and opening up the files at the Yellowstone Heritage and Research Center at Yellowstone National Park. The research for this book has been a fascinating and rewarding endeavor.

I would also like to thank Jane Daniels of Ashton, Idaho for providing information on the Yellowstone Branch. Many thanks to Marian Schenck for providing valuable information on the Gallatin Gateway Inn, Ruth Quinn for sending me information on Robert Reamer and Todd Guenther of the Pioneer Museum in Lander, Wyoming, for photographs on the C&NW route. Paul Shea, Collections and Programs Director of the Yellowstone Historic Center in West Yellowstone made the Gadamus Collection available for my research, and the staff at the Pioneer Museum in Bozeman was very helpful by providing information and photographs on the Gallatin Gateway Inn. I was able to receive valuable information on the entrance through Cody from the staff at the Park County Archives, and Joe Piersen of the Chicago and North Western Historical Society provided information on the C&NW service to Lander and Kent E. Watson provided his photos of Gardiner, Montana. Bob Wayner also provided valuable information and suggestions, and Stan Cohen, publisher, was extremely helpful, and this book would not have been possible without the expertise of Leslie Maricelli who laid out the text and photographs. Special thanks go to Robert Jones and my sister Corinne, for reading through my manuscript to look for grammatical errors and making sure the text makes sense. I do, of course, take responsibility for any errors and welcome any corrections.

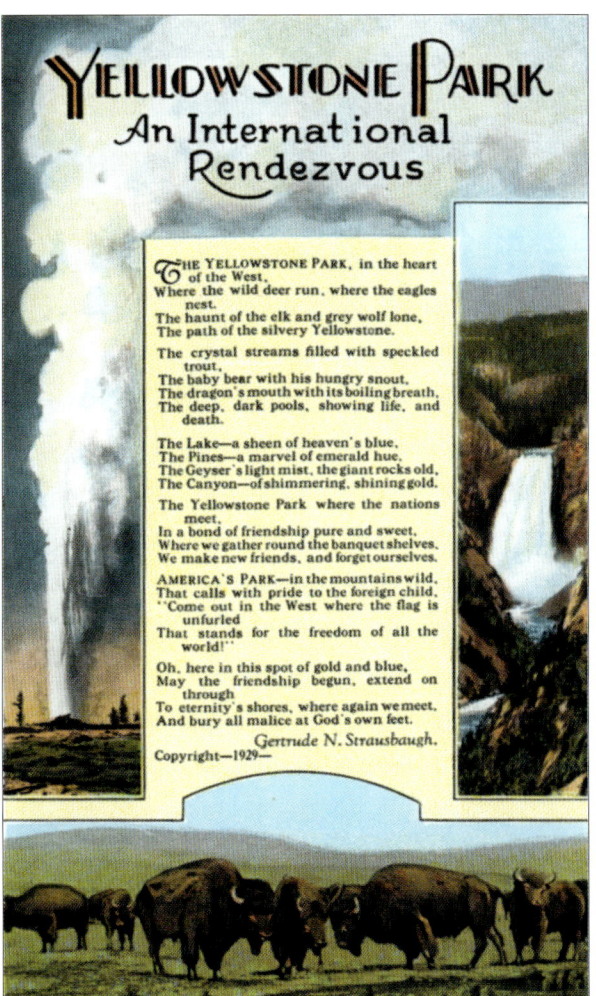

This card was originally printed in 1929 extolling the grandeur of Yellowstone. PHPC

INTRODUCTION

The history of Yellowstone National Park and railroad travel to Yellowstone are closely connected because the railroad was the only practical means of reaching the park for many years. The railroads promoted the establishment and development of the park because they saw Yellowstone as a source of potential business generated by transporting tourists to the park. They worked hard to promote the seasonal tourist business, which took place from mid-June through mid-September. Because of this the history of the railroad service to the park and the impact of the railroads on travel to and through the park is an important part of the history of Yellowstone National Park.

There are five entrances to Yellowstone National Park, all of which could be reached by train travelers when the railroad was used to reach the park. A total of five railroads served Yellowstone National Park and, while they all competed for the tourist travel to the park, they also worked together to provide travelers numerous options to visit the park. The entrances and the railroads are as follows, listed in chronological order in which the railroads began serving the park:

- The Northern Pacific Railway reached the North Entrance at Gardiner, Montana from Cinnabar in 1883. In 1903 the line was extended to Gardiner.
- The Union Pacific Railroad reached West Yellowstone, Montana in the fall of 1907 and started offering service to West Yellowstone in the following spring.
- The Chicago, Burlington & Pacific Railroad reached Cody, Wyoming in 1901 and began offering service to the park through the East Entrance in 1912.
- The Chicago & North Western Railway reached Lander, Wyoming in 1906 and began providing service to the South Entrance in 1922.

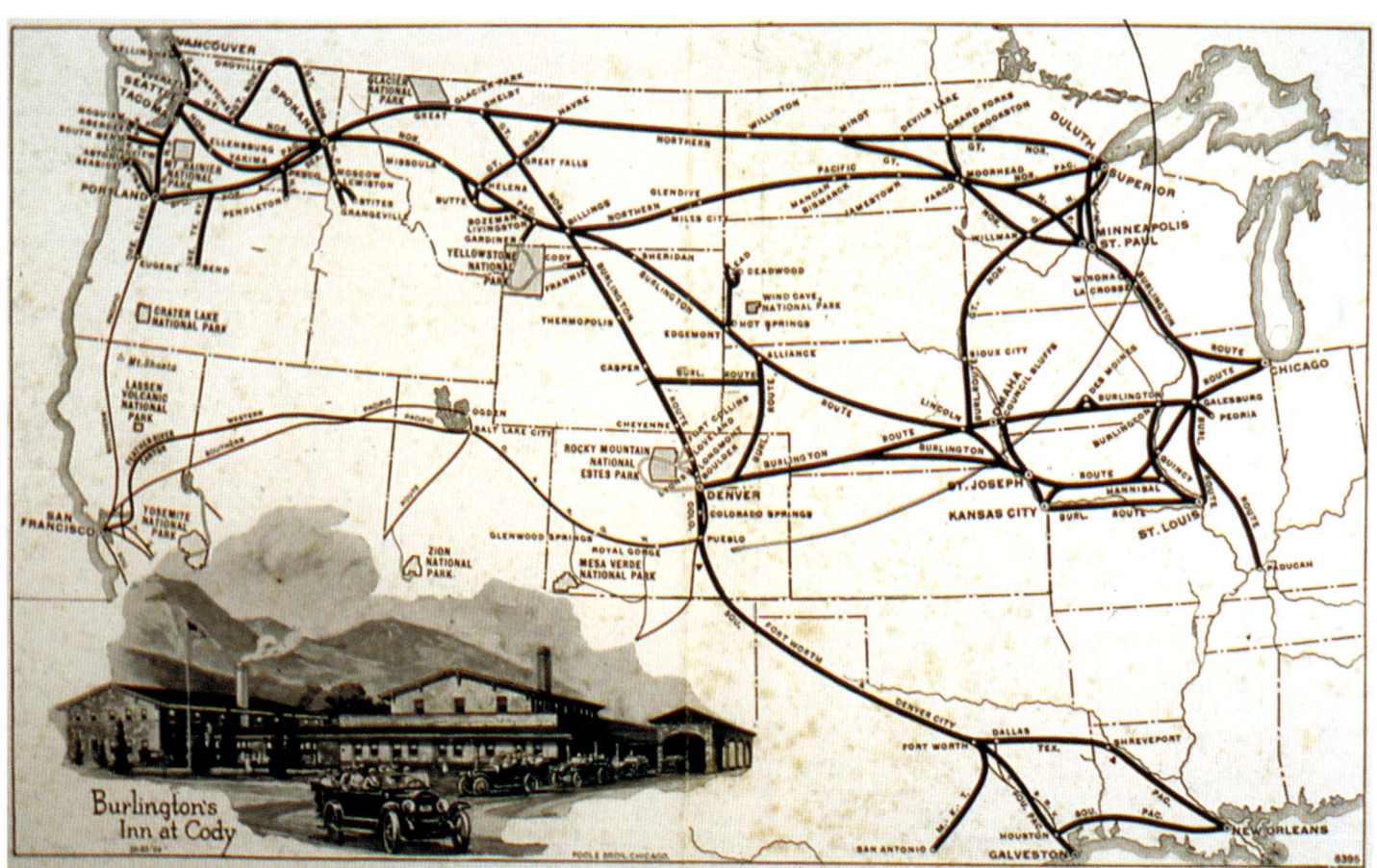

Yellowstone National Park is located in northwestern Wyoming. This map from a 1924 Chicago, Burlington & Quincy Railroad brochure shows how a traveler could reach the park through Cody and Gardiner. Significantly, the map did not show the routes over the Union Pacific through West Yellowstone or through Lander, Wyoming, on the Chicago & North Western, which competed for the tourist business GADAMUS COLLECTION, YELLOWSTONE HISTORIC CENTER

- The Chicago, Milwaukee & St. Paul Railway began offering service to the park through the West Entrance from Three Forks, Montana in 1926. In the following year they offered service from Gallatin Gateway to the West Entrance.
- In 1927 the Northern Pacific Railway began offering the option of riding their train to Bozeman and entering the park through the West Entrance.
- The Union Pacific Railroad began offering service from Victor, Idaho to the South Entrance in 1929.
- The Northern Pacific Railway began offering service through Red Lodge, Montana to the Northeast Entrance in 1937.

The railroads gradually cut back and discontinued service to the park following World War II, and they began substituting bus service to the park entrances from locations distant from the park. After the Northern Pacific discontinued service directly to Gardiner it offered connecting bus service from Livingston, Montana. When the Union Pacific ended service to West Yellowstone it then offered bus service to the park from Ashton, and later Idaho Falls, and the Burlington offered connecting bus service from trains at Deaver and Billings after ending service to Cody. After The Milwaukee Road discontinued service to Gallatin Gateway it again offered connecting bus service from Three Forks.

Significantly, none of the entrances was on the main line of a railroad, and they were all on branch lines[1]. The development of each of these branch lines affected the growth and development of the towns they reached as well as the popularity of the various entrances and routes into the park.

The railroads reaching the park all published colorful brochures and booklets promoting travel over their line to the park. The Northern Pacific Railroad published their "Wonderland" series of brochures from 1886 through 1906. The brochure described the park wonders and how one could reach the park via the Northern Pacific. This is the cover for the 1886 booklet. YELLOWSTONE HERITAGE & RESEARCH CENTER

v

The train services offered to each entrance varied each summer, and the schedules noted in each chapter should be considered to be only an example of the type of accommodations and schedules offered over the years. There was a time when spending the night in a Pullman sleeping car and eating on the dining car was part of the vacation trip, and the railroads all tried to provide the best accommodations possible for the trip to the park.

Although travel to the park by train increased into the 1920s, the increase was not as great as the increase in the total number of visitors to the park. Train travel quickly fell out of favor as it was abandoned in favor of the family automobile. Construction of improved roads, the Depression, and World War II all doomed rail travel to the park, and although the railroads made some efforts to promote travel to the park following the end of World War II, they quickly cut back passenger service to the park as the hoped-for tourist traffic never materialized.

It was not until 1960, when the Union Pacific ended its train service to West Yellowstone, that all rail service running direct to the park boundary ended. Although the railroads continued to offer tours to the park, the bus connections and schedules became so inconvenient and cumbersome that they were soon discontinued.

When Amtrak took over the nation's passenger service on May 1, 1971 most of the passenger trains operated by the railroads were discontinued. This included the Northern Pacific passenger train which ran through Livingston, Montana and the Union Pacific passenger train which ran through Pocatello, Idaho. Starting later in that year, Amtrak inaugurated the *North Coast Hiawatha* through Livingston, Montana. From there Amtrak offered a connecting bus service from Livingston to visit the park, but the train was discontinued in 1979 due to low ridership. The only way to reach the park by rail today is on luxury cruise trains such as the one operated by Grandluxe Rail Journeys (formerly known as the *American Orient Express*). Even this train does not get close to the park and buses are required to reach the park boundary and travel through the park. Instead of having tour groups arrive by train and ride through the park in Yellowstone Park buses today, it is common to see luxury tour buses originating from various points in the country go through the park.

In a later year the Northern Pacific Railway published this brochure, extolling the virtues of the geysers in the park.
YELLOWSTONE HERITAGE & RESEARCH CENTER

Table of Contents

Preface ------- iii

Introduction ------- iv

Chapter One
    Yellowstone National Park, A Brief History ------- 1

Chapter Two
    The Road to Yellowstone National Park ------- 3

Chapter Three
    The Park Tour ------- 7

Chapter Four
    Train Travel to Yellowstone National Park ------- 13

Chapter Five
    Visiting Wonderland ------- 21

Chapter Six
    Yellowstone Park Line, Northern Pacific Railway ------- 29

Chapter Seven
    The National Park Route, Union Pacific Railroad ------- 54

Chapter Eight
    The National Park Road, Chicago, Burlington & Quincy Railroad -- 86

Chapter Nine
    Chicago & North Western Railway ------- 97

Chapter Ten
    The Historic - Scenic Route ------- 113

Chapter Eleven
    Proposed Railroads to Yellowstone National Park ------- 130

Chapter Twelve
    Railroads in Yellowstone National Park ------- 134

Railroad Travel to Yellowstone National Park Today ------- 139

Appendix A
    A Brief Chronology of Yellowstone ------- 140

Appendix B
    Rail Travel to Yellowstone ------- 143

Footnotes ------- 145

References ------- 163

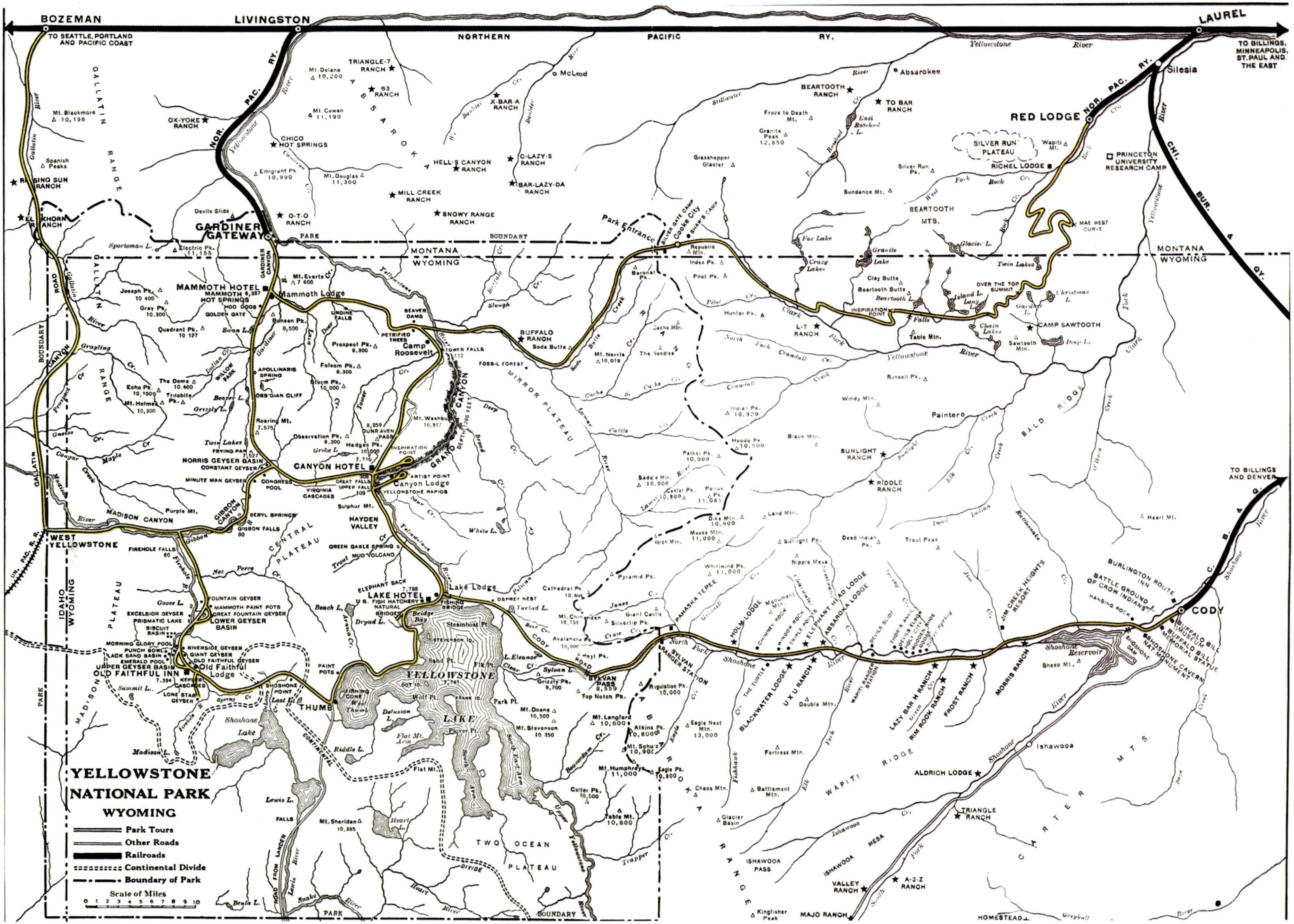
YELLOWSTONE
NATIONAL PARK
WYOMING
Park Tours
Other Roads
Railroads
Continental Divide
Boundary of Park
Scale of Miles
BOZEMAN
TO SEATTLE, PORTLAND AND PACIFIC COAST
LIVINGSTON
NORTHERN
PACIFIC
RY.
LAUREL
TO BILLINGS, MINNEAPOLIS, ST. PAUL AND THE EAST
Silesia
RED LODGE
NOR. PAC. RY.
CHI. BUR. & QY.
PRINCETON UNIVERSITY RESEARCH CAMP
SILVER RUN PLATEAU
RICHEL LODGE
BEARTOOTH MTS.
MAE WEST CURVE
OVER THE TOP SUMMIT
CAMP SAWTOOTH
INSPIRATION POINT
L-T RANCH
Cooke City
SILVER GATE CAMP
Park Entrance
MONTANA
WYOMING
PARK
BOUNDARY
GARDINER GATEWAY
GARDINER CANYON
MAMMOTH HOTEL
MAMMOTH HOT SPRINGS
Mammoth Lodge
Camp Roosevelt
TOWER FALLS
BUFFALO RANCH
MIRROR PLATEAU
GRAND CANYON
CANYON HOTEL
Canyon Lodge
NORRIS GEYSER BASIN
MADISON CANYON
WEST YELLOWSTONE
CENTRAL PLATEAU
HAYDEN VALLEY
LAKE HOTEL
Lake Lodge
YELLOWSTONE LAKE
THUMB
OLD FAITHFUL INN
Old Faithful Lodge
LOWER GEYSER BASIN
UPPER GEYSER BASIN
Shoshone Lake
TWO OCEAN PLATEAU
CODY ROAD
SYLVAN PASS
SYLVAN RANGER STATION
PAHASKA TEPEE
HOLM LODGE
ELEPHANT HEAD LODGE
ABSAROKA LODGE
BLACKWATER LODGE
U X U RANCH
LAZY BAR H RANCH
RIM ROCK RANCH
FROST RANCH
MORRIS RANCH
Shoshone Reservoir
CODY
TO BILLINGS AND DENVER
BUFFALO BILL MUSEUM
BUFFALO BILL MEMORIAL STATUE
SHOSHONE CAVERN NAT. MONUMENT
BURLINGTON ROUTE INN
BATTLE GROUND OF CROW INDIANS
JIM CREEK HEIGHTS RESORT
SUNLIGHT RANCH
RIDDLE RANCH
BALD RIDGE
WAPITI RIDGE
CARTER MTS.
ABSAROKA RANGE
ALDRICH LODGE
TRIANGLE RANCH
VALLEY RANCH
A-2-Z RANCH
MAJO RANCH
HOMESTEAD
ISHAWOOA PASS
ISHAWOOA MESA
GALLATIN RANGE
MADISON PLATEAU
IDAHO
WYOMING
CHICO HOT SPRINGS
O-T-O RANCH
OX-YOKE RANCH
RISING SUN RANCH
ELKHORN RANCH
HELL'S CANYON RANCH
MILL CREEK RANCH
SNOWY RANGE RANCH
X-BAR-A RANCH
C-LAZY-S RANCH
BAR-LAZY-DA RANCH
TRIANGLE-7 RANCH
63 RANCH
BEARTOOTH RANCH
TO BAR RANCH
Absarokee
McLeod

1938

Chapter One

The "Grand Canyon of the Yellowstone" is 20 miles in length and its greatest depth is 1,200 feet. PHPC

Yellowstone National Park
A Brief History

An Act of Congress established Yellowstone National Park, the country's first national park, on March 1, 1872. Most of the park is in Wyoming, with small sections in Montana and Idaho, and it encompasses 3,471 square miles. The park is well-known for its geological features, notably Old Faithful, and is inhabited by large numbers of animals such as buffalo, elk, wolves, and bears. It is run by the National Park Service in the Department of the Interior and is one of the most popular parks in the country.

The elevation in the park ranges from 5,000 feet to 11,360 feet. The summers are not hot, and the park can get cold in the winter – a temperature of -66 degrees Fahrenheit was measured at the Riverside Ranger Station on February 9, 1933. The snowfall is deep, with an average of 91 inches at Mammoth Hot Springs and more snow at higher elevations.

Yellowstone National Park was established as the nation's first national park in 1872. This map, published by the Colorado & Southern Railroad in 1921, shows the roads and trails in the park at that time. The principal entrances were West Yellowstone, Gardiner, and Cody. The South Entrance and Northeast Entrance were not popular at the time. YELLOWSTONE HERITAGE & RESEARCH CENTER

The park was established before any of the three states, Wyoming, Montana, and Idaho, were admitted to the Union and only a few years after they became territories[1]. When the park was first formed Congress designated Nathaniel Langford as the park superintendent. Langford had worked for and promoted the establishment of the area as a national park and, significantly, his work had been backed by Jay Cooke of the Northern Pacific Railroad. Langford had also run for governor of the Territory of Montana. For these reasons Langford was able to influence the development of rail travel to the park and the construction of the railroad hotels in the park by the Northern Pacific Railroad. Cooke also used his backing of Moran's artistry, in particular his famous painting *The Grand Canyon of the Yellowstone*, to promote the establishment of the park.

Some of the significant dates associated with Yellowstone National Park and the railroads are listed in Appendix A.

Mammoth Hot Springs has always been a popular attraction. This view shows the hot springs with the Mammoth Hot Springs Hotel in the background.
AUTHOR'S COLLECTION

Yellowstone National Park has always been most famous for Old Faithful, as shown in this Haynes postcard. AUTHOR'S COLLECTION

Wildlife was another popular attraction not only for the bears but for the elk, buffalo, and antelope which inhabit the park.
AUTHOR'S COLLECTION

Chapter Two

Silvergate and the Hoodoos.
PHPC

The Road to Yellowstone National Park

Travel to the Park Before the Railroad

When the members of the Hayden party traveled to what became Yellowstone National Park in 1871, they traveled by train to Corinne, Utah and then rode by wagon 400 miles north to Bozeman. From there they went up the Yellowstone River to what is now Gardiner and then into the park[1]. Their trip and subsequent reports of the wonders in the park led to the first tourists to the area, and the road through Gardiner was the standard route into the park for many years.

Professor F.V. Hayden mentioned several routes to the park in his subsequent report on his trip to Yellowstone National Park. The recommended route was to take the Union Pacific Railway from the east or the Central Pacific from the west to Ogden. From there one could travel on the Utah Northern Railroad to Franklin in southern Idaho. A stage line then forwarded the traveler to either Virginia City or Bozeman in Montana. Guides, equipment and outfits could be rented in either of these places to go into the park. A second choice would be to purchase an outfit at Ogden and forward it to Market Lake. The traveler would take the train to Franklin and then the stage to Market Lake. From there he would take his outfit north to Henry's Lake, where he could connect with the Virginia City wagon road to the park. A third choice would be to go to Rawlins on the Union Pacific and from there travel to Camp Brown and then to Yellowstone Lake, although this route was unsafe due to Indians.

A fourth alternative would be to go on the Missouri River route to Fort Benton and from there by stage to Helena and Bozeman and then into the park. It was also possible to travel from the railhead of the Northern Pacific at Bismarck and then to Fort Benton, although this was a tedious route. Another route would be to take the wagon trail from the mouth of the Mussel Shell River on the Missouri to the Crow Indian Agency. From the "British Possessions" one could take a road following the Hell Gate and Bitter Root rivers from Walla Walla[2].

None of these routes was easy, and the first tourists to the park had to be determined travelers. In the late summer of 1871 the first known park tourists, a party of six men, including Calvin Clawson, and one tailless dog arrived at the park from the west. The group traveled from Deer Lodge to Virginia City and through Raynold's Pass to Henry's Lake. From there they went into the park via the Madison River. They rode horses since there were no wagon roads[3]. Following their reports of the trip into the "Wonderland," the citizens of Virginia City saw that there would be a rush of tourist traffic into the park and wanted to profit from it. In 1873 they raised $2,000 to extend the wagon road, to be known as the "Virginia City and National Park Free Wagon Road," past Sawtell's Ranch at Henry's Lake into the new park, providing an alternate route to the toll road which reached the North Entrance to the park. Five hundred people used this new road to visit Yellowstone in the first season[4]. Stagecoaches were not able to travel in the park until 1880[5], when the roads and stream crossings in the park were improved enough so that the coaches could travel over them.

The first recorded instance of commercial stage travel to the park took place on October 1, 1880, when Marshall & Goff's Passenger and Express Line carried two passengers and some freight from Virginia City to Marshall's Hotel in the park. Significantly, these passengers were Robert and Carrie Strahorn. Robert was a promoter for the Union Pacific Railroad, and Carrie recorded the trip in her book, *Fifteen Thousand Miles by Stage*[6].

Clearly, the rough and long roads were inadequate for tourist travel to the park, and everyone knew a railroad was needed. Reaching the park boundary was a minimum of a one to two day ride from the nearest railroad. A railroad which reached the park boundary, and possibly even went into the park, was what was required so that travelers could enjoy the park scenery.

There was consideration of a railroad to Yellowstone National Park as early as 1871, when Captain Barlow of the War Department wrote the U.S. Congress that it would be possible to build a line south from Yellowstone Lake to the Snake River[7]. In the following year R. Hering, a surveyor for the United States, wrote that a line could be built to the park and Jackson Hole[8]. Another geologist on the same survey expedition reported on the same route in the following year. In 1871 Calvin Clawson, wrote that "the valleys of the Snake and Madison must inevitably in time be the route of a railroad connecting the Northern and the Union Pacific roads[9]. In 1883 Wyoming Territorial Governor Hale complained that much of the Territory was inaccessible, and he suggested a rail line from the Union Pacific line through Washakie to Yellowstone Park to open up the land[10].

In the annual report for the park dated December 10, 1878, the park superintendent described the various routes to the park, all of which were costly and time-consuming. He went on to say the southern route, via Ogden, would be shortened by the "extension of the railroad 70 miles to the crossing of the Snake River at Eagle Rock[11]," from where the stage coach ride was only 150 miles via Henry's Fork Lake. The Northern Pacific was also to be extended "from Bismarck to the Yellowstone, near the mouth of the Powder River," and this would shorten the 600-mile river route to a 250-mile railroad trip.[12]

Although the Utah & Northern Railway, successor to the Utah Northern Railroad, did reach Eagle Rock in the following summer, it was not until 1883 that the Northern Pacific reached Livingston and Cinnabar. The Northern Pacific built its line from Livingston to Cinnabar in 1883, and it wasn't until the beginning of the Twentieth Century that a rail line reached the park boundary, when the Northern Pacific extended its line from Cinnabar to Gardiner in 1903. As the years passed the railroads built additional lines to reach the park, either directly to the park boundary or in conjunction with travel on roads[13]. The railroads opened up the park to tourists and the park became a popular destination since travel had become faster and more convenient.

Wildlife, and bears in particular, were a popular draw for tourists. They were publicized in the advertisements and in the postcards for sale in the park. One attraction was the feeding of the bears at the hotel dumps, as seen in this Haynes postcard.
AUTHOR'S COLLECTION

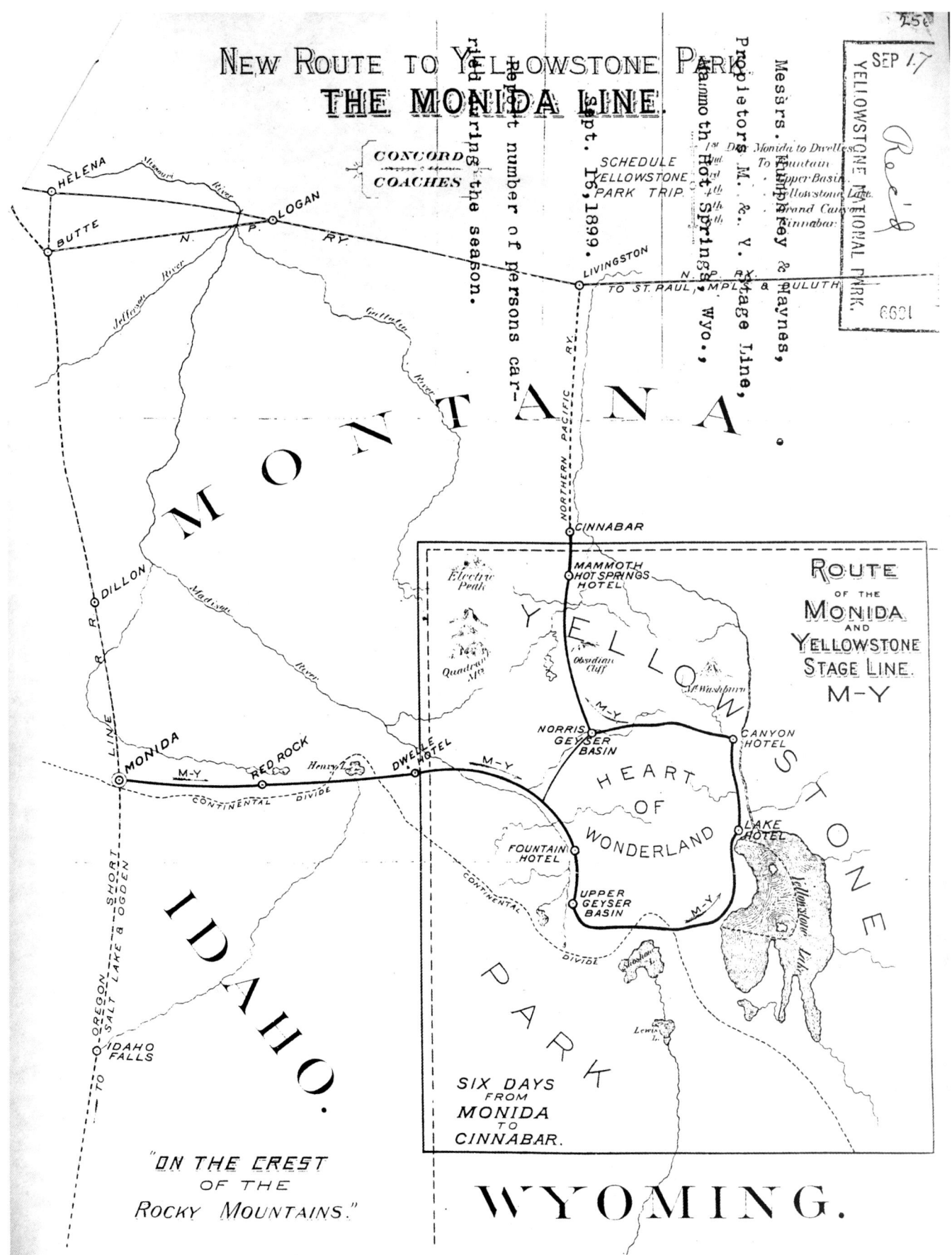

Before the railroads were built, it was difficult to reach Yellowstone National Park. This map shows the stage route of the Monida & Yellowstone Stage Line from the Oregon Short Line to Dwelle Hotel on the west boundary, and the tour route through the park. YELLOWSTONE HERITAGE & RESEARCH CENTER

MONIDA & YELLOWSTONE STAGE LINE
HUMPHREY & HAYNES,
From the Oregon Short Line Railroad,
THROUGH YELLOWSTONE PARK

W. W. HUMPHREY,
MONIDA, MONT.

ADDRESS
Monida, Mont. June 1st. to Oct. 1st.
St. Paul, Minn. Oct. 1st. to June 1st.

September 16 1899

Captain Oscar J. Brown,

    Acting Sup't, Yellowstone National Park,

        Mammoth Hot Springs, Wyo.

Dear Sir:--

    Replying to your favor of September 13th we beg to say that we have carried from Monida through the Yellowstone Park to Mammoth Hot Springs during the season of 1899, from June fifteenth to September fifteenth, four hundred fourteen (414) people; that we have carried from Norris, through the Western entrance of the Park to Monida one hundred forty-one (141) people who had entered the Park from the North and made the Park tour. Sixteen (16) of the people that we brought to Mammoth Hot Springs returned by our stage to Monida, making a total of (157) one hundred fifty-seven from Norris out.

        Yours truly,

           Humphrey & Haynes,

        per _____

In the 1899 season the stage company reported they had carried 414 people from Monida, on the Oregon Short Line, to Mammoth Hot Springs. The Monida & Yellowstone Stage Company was organized in 1898 by Frank J. Haynes and Wm. H. Humphrey to provide stage service from Monida into the park. YELLOWSTONE HERITAGE & RESEARCH CENTER

Chapter Three

Old Faithful, favorite of Yellowstone geyserland. PHPC

The Park Tour

Once the tourists arrived at the park they wanted to visit the sights. Horse-drawn stages or buggies were the initial means of providing travel through the park unless one rode a horse[1]. A typical tour would take several days to travel through the park, and reliable and comfortable transportation was an essential element of the park tour.

The railroads did not directly own or operate lodging accommodations. Instead they relied on the hotels in the park for lodging, and with the exception of the Chicago, Burlington & Quincy and The Milwaukee Road they did not build hotels at their terminals. The Milwaukee Road and the Chicago & North Western both operated their own buses for a few years, but for the most part the railroads relied on a separate company to transport passengers to and in the park. Over the years there were numerous stage companies and camping companies which provided these services. They were consolidated into the Yellowstone Park Transportation Company in 1916, at the same time motorized vehicles replaced horse-drawn stages[2]. Since the park was only open in the summer months, it was sometimes difficult for these companies to be able to make a profit due to the short summer tourist season and the businesses were not, as a rule, very profitable.

One of the first companies offering transportation through the park was the Yellowstone Park Improvement Company, organized in 1883 by Carroll Hobart, Rufus Hatch, and Henry Douglas. They were guaranteed a monopoly on the park concessions, but after starting construction of various facilities in the

Concord stages were the common mode of travel in the park before the automobile. The tourists could rent "dusters" to keep the road dust off their clothes. The travelers in this postcard had arrived on the Northern Pacific Railway at the Gardiner station and were traveling by coach along the Gardner River to the hotel at Mammoth Hot Springs. AUTHOR'S COLLECTION

A view of a Concord stage used to travel to and through the park, seen at Mammoth Hot Springs. Riding them could be an adventure, especially when they had tourists on the top. AUTHOR'S COLLECTION

A popular, low-cost way to visit the park was to stay at the Wylie Permanent Camps. AUTHOR'S COLLECTION

The park roads were initially gravel or dirt, as seen in this postcard showing the road from West Yellowstone. Some artistic license has been taken, since the roads were normally rutted and muddy. AUTHOR'S COLLECTION

This view of a group of tourists in the park was published in an advertising booklet and shows what the roads were like at that time. The gear-jammers, or drivers, entertained the tourists, describing the sights along the way and telling tall tales. GADAMUS COLLECTION, YELLOWSTONE HISTORIC CENTER

The park tour included an overnight stop at the Lake Hotel, located on Yellowstone Lake. The tourists rode in the motor buses with the tops rolled back when the weather was pleasant. AUTHOR'S COLLECTION

Automobiles were allowed in the park starting on August 1, 1915. The stages were quickly replaced by the more convenient motor buses. This bus has just picked up passengers at the West Yellowstone station for their tour through the park. AUTHOR'S COLLECTION

9

park the company went bankrupt in 1885. The company was bought out by the Yellowstone Park Association in 1886[3].

The Northern Pacific Railroad organized the Yellowstone Park Association in 1886, and officials included Charles Gibson, Nelson Thrall, and Frederick Billings. The company built numerous facilities in the park, including the Old Faithful Inn[4]. In 1891 the Yellowstone Park Association lost the transportation franchise and the Yellowstone National Park Transportation Company was incorporated in 1892 to provide transportation in the park. The Yellowstone National Park Transportation Company bought out other transportation companies and received exclusive privileges for the transportation of passengers of the Northern Pacific Railroad. The Yellowstone Park Transportation Company took over the Yellowstone National Park Transportation Company in 1898[5]. This new company was founded in 1898 by Harry Child and his brothers-in-law Silas Huntley and Edward Bach. These men were also involved with the Yellowstone Park Association, which ran the hotels in the park.

With the mandatory replacement of horse-drawn vehicles by motorized vehicles in 1917, the Yellowstone Park Transportation Company purchased 117 White touring cars for the 1917 season[6] with financial backing from the railroads, replacing the stagecoaches used in previous years. It absorbed the other stage companies in the park, including the Yellowstone & Western Stage Company, the Cody-Sylvan Pass Motor Company, and the camping company stages.

A standard route through the park became popular. The Department of Interior even published a "Manual for Railroad Visitors" with schedules for the tour routes through the park[7]. In 1929, the tours ran from June 20 through September 19, and they give an indication of the possibilities available when rail travel to the park was at its peak. The Yellowstone Park Transportation Company offered tours of several durations, with 4-1/2 days being the most popular. The tour package for 4-1/2 days, including 4 nights lodging, 14 meals, and transportation, was $54 in addition to the train fare. The railroads encouraged stopovers at a nominal additional cost. There were numerous possible routes, as follows:

- In and out via Gardiner (Northern Pacific)
- In Gardiner, out West Yellowstone (Northern Pacific/Union Pacific)
- In Gardiner, out Cody (Northern Pacific/Burlington)
- In Gardiner, out Gallatin Gateway and Bozeman (Northern Pacific/Milwaukee or Northern Pacific)
- In West Yellowstone, out West Yellowstone (Union Pacific)
- In West Yellowstone, out Gardiner (Union Pacific/Northern Pacific)
- In West Yellowstone, out Cody (Union Pacific/Burlington)
- In West Yellowstone, out Gallatin Gateway and Bozeman (Union Pacific/ Milwaukee or Northern Pacific)
- In Cody, out Cody (Burlington)
- In Cody, out Gardiner (Burlington/Northern Pacific)
- In Cody, out West Yellowstone (Burlington/Union Pacific)
- In Cody, out Gallatin Gateway and Bozeman (Burlington/Milwaukee or Northern Pacific)
- In Cody, out Lander (Burlington/C&NW)
- In Gallatin Gateway and Bozeman, out Gallatin Gateway and Bozeman (Milwaukee or Northern Pacific)
- In Gallatin Gateway and Bozeman, out Gardiner (Milwaukee or Northern Pacific/Northern Pacific)
- In Gallatin Gateway and Bozeman, out West Yellowstone (Milwaukee or Northern Pacific/ Union Pacific)
- In Gallatin Gateway and Bozeman, out Cody (Milwaukee or Northern Pacific/Burlington)
- In Lander, out Lander (C&NW)
- In Gallatin Gateway and Bozeman, out Lander (Milwaukee or Northern Pacific/C&NW)
- In Lander, out West Yellowstone (C&NW/Union Pacific)
- In Lander, out Cody (C&NW/Burlington)
- In Lander, out Gallatin Gateway /Bozeman) (C&NW/Milwaukee or Northern Pacific)
- In Gardiner, out Lander (Northern Pacific/C&NW)
- In West Yellowstone, out Lander (Union Pacific/C&NW)[8]

The railroads' principal disadvantage, of course, is that they did not offer the flexibility of the private automobile. Some attempts were made over the years to have a rental agency such as Hertz offer service at the park entrances to the rail passengers, but the Yellowstone Park Transportation Company strongly opposed these efforts[9]. Ultimately, however, it did not really matter since the majority of the tourists preferred the convenience of the family automobile.

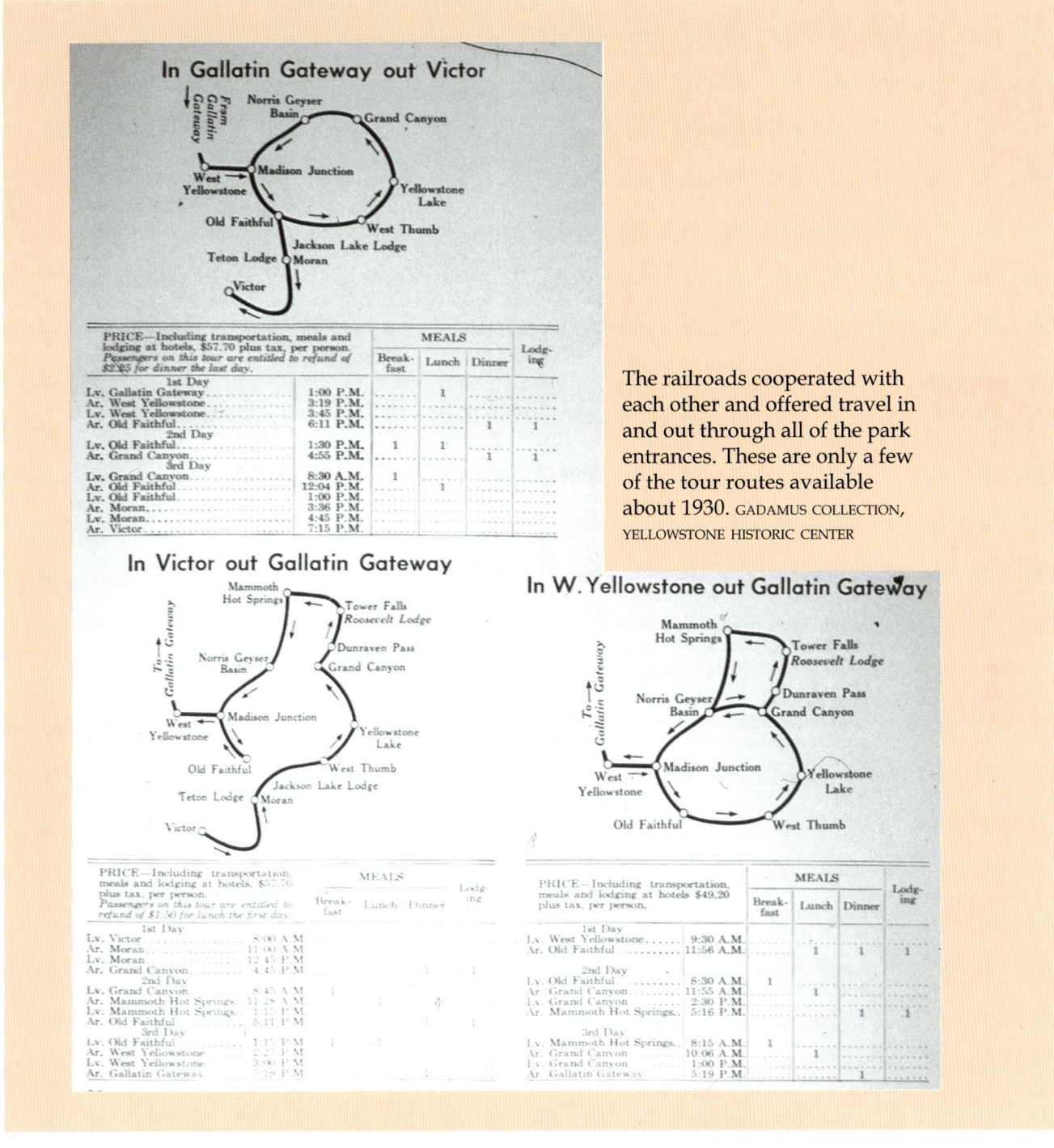

The railroads cooperated with each other and offered travel in and out through all of the park entrances. These are only a few of the tour routes available about 1930. GADAMUS COLLECTION, YELLOWSTONE HISTORIC CENTER

By the late 1930s, when the road from Red Lodge through the Northeast Entrance was opened, the motor buses had been replaced by these buses. The tops could be rolled back so that the tourists could stand up and look at the views. YELLOWSTONE HERITAGE & RESEARCH CENTER

Both the railroads and tour companies offered escorted tours through the park. This flyer for the 1948 season lists the tours provided by Banner Tours to Yellowstone National Park and other western sites. AUTHOR'S COLLECTION

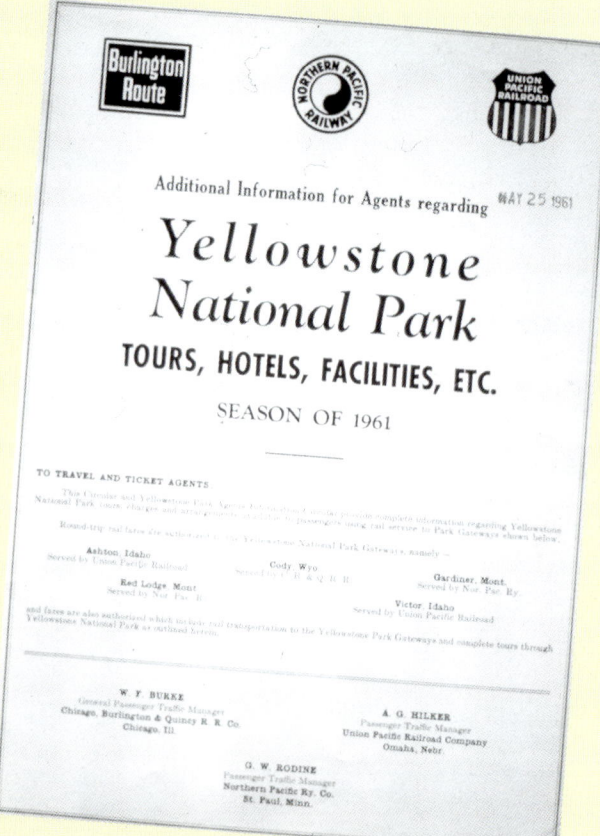

The railroads continued to cooperate with each other through the early 1960s, even though they no longer provided passenger service to the park boundary. They worked together to provide a wide variety of tour routes to and through the park. AUTHOR'S COLLECTION

Northern Pacific W Class Mikado locomotive #1565 pulling a Boy Scouts of America Special Train at Gardiner, Aug. 1, 1953.
COURTESY KENT E. WATSON

Chapter Four

Train Travel to Yellowstone National Park

Traveling by Railroad to the Park

In 1915, before the National Park Service permitted automobiles in the park, one guidebook listed the various ways to reach Yellowstone National Park as follows:

"How to Reach the Park

The most direct route to Yellowstone Park from either Chicago, on the east, or Seattle, Tacoma and Portland, on the west, is the Northern Pacific Railroad, which reaches the Park at Gardiner, Montana. This station is near the northern border, being the end of a spur that leaves the main line of the railroad at Livingston, fifty-four miles to the northeast. It is only a stone's throw to the entrance of the Park from the station, and but five miles to the Mammoth Hot Springs Hotel.

From St. Louis, Kansas City, and other middle-western and southern points, the Park is reached by way of the Chicago, Burlington & Quincy Railroad. This route brings the traveler to Cody, Wyo., from which there is a drive of sixty-three miles to the eastern entrance of the park.

The Oregon Short Line reaches an entrance, Yellowstone, on the west, and provides a convenient means for travelers from Salt Lake City and points in the Southwest.

During the season round-trip tickets are issued by the various railroads, and on special occasions through tickets over these lines allow stopovers in the Park within the time-limit of the ticket. This is generally the case during large conventions and expositions that draw visitors from all parts of the country[1]."

The railroads and routes to reach the park varied over the years, with the competition for the tourists reaching a peak in the 1920s, when five railroads reached the four park entrances which existed at the time[2]. The popularity of the rail routes to the various park entrances is shown in Appendix B. Although park entrances such as Gardiner and Cody had train service year-round, the railroads only offered through Pullman car service from the metropolitan cities from mid-June through mid-September, when the park was open. The Union Pacific simply discontinued passenger service to West Yellowstone in the off-season, offering only mixed train service to West Yellowstone in the spring and fall[3] and allowing the line to be snowed shut in the winter months. The railroads sometimes added additional trains on the lines to the park entrances in the summer months to provide better schedules

13

For many years the railroad was the only way to reach the park. This is the Webb Special train on the Northern Pacific at Cinnabar, Montana about 1896 or 1897. The cars immediately behind the locomotive were used to transport livestock, and were probably carrying horses when this picture was taken. AUTHOR'S COLLECTION

for the tourists arriving and departing the park.

As indicated by the 1915 guidebook description, the railroads provided train service from many of the major western cities, including Portland, Seattle, Salt Lake City, and Los Angeles as well as Midwestern cities such as Chicago and St. Louis. The traffic increased over the following years, although there was a decrease during World War I. In the summer of 1925 the Union Pacific even provided service to and from Jacksonville, Florida. A determined tourist from that city traveled over the Atlantic Coast Line, Central of Georgia, Louisville & Nashville, Chattanooga & St. Louis, Wabash, and Union Pacific to reach West Yellowstone[4].

The railroads ran name trains to the park and provided special accommodations on those trains, with open air observation cars on some Northern Pacific trains between Livingston and Gardiner[5], and, for at least one year, on the Union Pacific train between Ashton and Reas Pass[6]. The Chicago, Burlington and Pacific ran the *Buffalo Bill* to Cody for several summers. The Union Pacific ran trains named the *Yellowstone Special* and the *Yellowstone Express*, and the Northern Pacific ran the *Yellowstone Comet*. Drawing on the popularity of the name, *Yellowstone Special* was even used for a brand of flour, and in 1915 the *Yellowstone Special* flour won a silver medal at the Panama-Pacific International Exposition. The flour was sold in the Upper Snake River Valley in Idaho[7], and a grain elevator in Drummond, Idaho, along the former Teton Valley Branch of the Union Pacific, still has the *Yellowstone Special* flour advertisement on the side, although it is faded with age and from the weather.

The railroads even had cars named *Yellowstone*. In 1886 a private car named *Mary C.* was rebuilt by Jackson & Sharp into the *Yellowstone*. The car included a parlor, stateroom, sleeping berths, kitchen, and toilets. A sleeping car named *Yellowstone* was built by the Pullman Car Works, Detroit in 1882 and when it was dismantled in 1905 another sleeping car named *Yellowstone* was built by Pullman in 1907. Another car named *Yellowstone Park* was built by Pullman in 1926. The cars all used the name of the

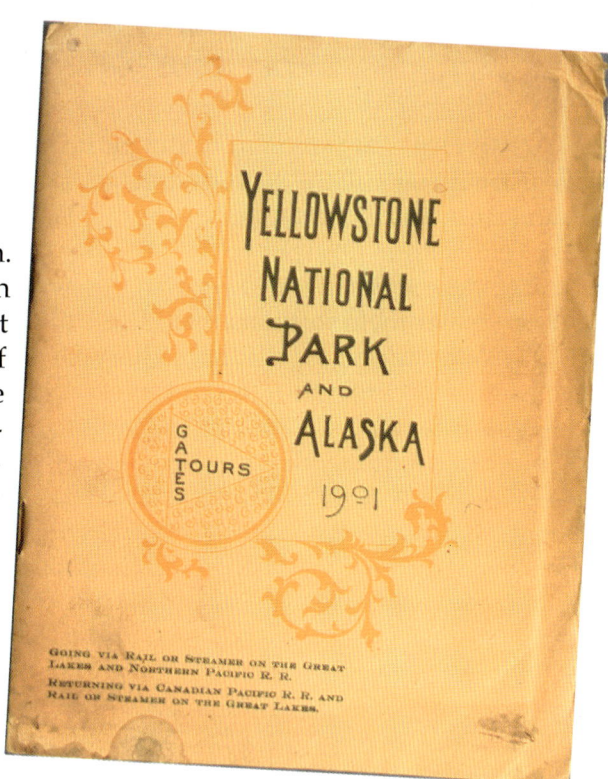

In 1901 Gate Tours offered a tour to Yellowstone National Park and Alaska. This was typical of tours to the park offered over the years by tour companies.
YELLOWSTONE HERITAGE & RESEARCH CENTER

nationally known park, a common practice for Pullman.

Rail travel to the park peaked in the 1920s, even while the number of private automobiles increased at an even greater rate. The railroad ran extra sections of its trains[8] to accommodate the increasing traffic[9]. These trains would run either ahead of or behind the regularly scheduled passenger trains. In 1924 a local newspaper in St. Anthony, Idaho reported that *"The Park trains are running two and three sections every day[10]."* During the Depression years the number of tourists dropped drastically and did not recover until the years just before World War II. In 1940 the Union Pacific reported that its business had almost doubled over the previous year[11]. During World War II, when many of the park facilities were closed, passenger service to the park entrances was either cut back or discontinued, and transportation in the park was limited, with no side tours offered due to gasoline and rubber shortages. In the 1942 season the Union Pacific offered only one train a day to West Yellowstone, arriving in the early afternoon and leaving in the evening. This improved equipment utilization, especially for the Pullman sleeping cars, which were difficult to obtain due to the war effort[12]. This service was not successful because only the hotels, and not the lodges, were open and the bus sightseeing tours were eliminated[13]. The Union Pacific discontinued all passenger service to West Yellowstone in the following summer and did not resume it until the war ended[14].

The railroads optimistically, but cautiously, began offering and improving service following the end of World War II, although there were problems associated with worn-out equipment and difficulties in obtaining passenger and Pullman cars. The railroads noted how the number of passengers increased in the first few years after the war. The Union Pacific reported a slight increase in travel following the end of World War II. In 1946 it had had 2,599 visitors through West Yellowstone, a decrease over 1941 travel, but the decrease was attributed to the lack of tour groups, which had been discontinued during the war. In 1947 the railroad reported 7,751 visitors, increasing to 7,820 in the following year. Visitors through the Victor entrance increased from 238 to 390 in the same years[15]. This was a small increase, but the only increase in rail arrivals at all of the park entrances. Even this modest rise was short-lived as tourists deserted the passenger train for the automobile. By the end of the 1960 season all of the railroads had stopped offering convenient service to the park.

In 1930 the Travel Guild offered a tour to Yellowstone passing through The Milwaukee Road's Gallatin Gateway. This tour was being offered in the first year of the Depression, when all travel to the park was declining. GADAMUS COLLECTION, YELLOWSTONE HISTORIC CENTER

15

Bus and Airplane Travel to the Park

Bus service was provided to the park from the railheads which did not reach the park boundary, but the train was still the preferred means of reaching the park when utilizing public transportation, as evidenced by the fact that the Northern Pacific's Gardiner entrance and the Union Pacific's entrance at West Yellowstone brought in the majority of tourists to the park. Long distance bus service was not practical since the highways were in poor condition and since it took buses so long to reach the park from the major metropolitan areas. The Union Pacific Railroad offered bus service from Salt Lake City to West Yellowstone over its subsidiary Union Pacific Stage Lines in the summer months, but it was never a serious competitor to rail travel.

Air service to West Yellowstone and the park began on June 20, 1936, but it was never very successful. In the first summer daily air service was available from Salt Lake City, Butte and Great Falls. For the period from July 1, 1936 through June 30, 1937 the National Park Service reported that 490 tourists arrived by airplane, compared to 19,962 who arrived by rail and 412,608 who came by automobile[16]. A sightseeing trip over the park on the National Park Airways planes consisted of going over Old Faithful to Grand Teton National Park and return via Lake, Canyon and Mount Washburn[17]. Due to the low level of traffic, the airline scheduled flights over the park for weekends only for the 1938 season[18], and discontinued them in the following season, although Western Air Express, which had merged with the National Park Airways, continued to offer service to West Yellowstone[19]. Flights over the park from Salt Lake City were reinstated in 1940, with a half hour flight evening flight over the Grand Canyon and Yellowstone Falls[20]. Proposals and hopes to have air service replace train service in 1951 did not come to fruition due to the improved highways[21] and the preference for the private car.

Special Trains

In addition to the scheduled passenger trains, the railroads provided special trains to the park. These included trains run to handle large groups of tourists as well as special groups. Over the years there were numerous special trains for groups ranging from the Shriners to the Boy Scouts as well as tour groups and associations which organized visits to the park. In the summer of 1931, for example, the Delaware, Lackawanna and Western ran four special trains from Hoboken, New Jersey to the Park, arriving at West Yellowstone and leaving through Cody. The tour also included stops to see other sights such as Denver and Pike's Peak[22].

The railroads all provided group rates, and sometimes tour groups reserved an entire sleeping car or chair car. One of these special tour groups was Reedy's Tours, under the direction of Frank Reedy, which chartered an entire train from the Southwest to the park, continuing on to Seattle for those who had more vacation time[23]. The company ran this tour for over 25 years, until the decline of tourist traffic in the Depression years.

In 1953 the Boy Scouts of America held their Jamboree at Santa Ana in California and chartered a large number of special trains. En route from Chicago to California many of the trains stopped at West Yellowstone so the Boy Scouts could tour the Park on school buses. Fifty-three of the trains also stopped at the Grand Canyon on the way back[24].

Another special event was the arrival of the private railroad cars owned by railroad officials or other wealthy businessmen. These cars were self-sufficient, and included sleeping quarters, kitchen and dining facilities, lounges and staff. They would either be operated as part of the scheduled passenger train service or as a special train. The use of these cars was often reported by the press, as indicated by the following newspaper report:

"MANY PRIVATE CARS - Private cars have been passing through Pocatello in great numbers since the Yellowstone park opened. Mr. Pontius, general manager of the San Diego & Arizona railroad, passed through the city this morning in private car No. 50 en route to the park. Vice President Ewing of the Pittsburgh & Reading will pass through this evening on P&R car. No. 10 en route to the park.

D.C. Jackling will arrive in Pocatello Tuesday in his private car "Cyprus". The "Cyprus is said to be one of the finest private cars in the county. Mr. Peterman and wife will pass through Pocatello on No. 31 this evening in

In addition to regularly scheduled passenger trains, the railroads operated special trains to the park. The Oregon Short Line operated this special train for its employees about 1912. The banner on the front of the locomotive announces a masked ball that night. AUTHOR'S COLLECTION

In 1927, attendees of the Women's Christian Temperance Union Convention could tour Yellowstone National Park and Salt Lake City on their return trip home. CHICAGO & NORTH WESTERN HISTORICAL SOCIETY COLLECTION

The *Savage Special* was a unique train which ran over the northern Pacific from St. Paul to Gardiner every spring to bring in summer help. The train was full of college students, teachers, and others looking forward to an exciting and eventful summer working in Yellowstone. YELLOWSTONE HERITAGE & RESEARCH CENTER

The Union Pacific's *Yellowstone Special* is seen approaching Big Springs, Idaho, headed towards West Yellowstone on August 6, 1949. The train has eight cars and is traveling at 40 mph. The railroad had to doublehead their trains to get up the grade over Reas Pass into Montana. H.R. GRIFFITHS, AUTHOR'S COLLECTION

In addition to offering escorted tours, the railroads would run special trains for large groups. This is a view from the *Farmers' Special*, taken by Conductor Warren McGee on September 8, 1953, as it went along the Yellowstone River. WARREN MCGEE

private car "Halleck" en route to Victor. They are planning an outing in the Jackson Hole country. M.L. Bell, vice president of the Rock Island, will pass through Pocatello this evening in private car 1911 en route to the park. Mr. Bell and party are coming by the way of Butte. D.G. Geddes and family will pass through Pocatello on August 1st in a Chicago & Milwaukee private car en route to Yellowstone[25]."

Another special train service was operated by both the Union Pacific and the Northern Pacific for many years. Known on the Union Pacific as the "Yellowstone Park Help Special" and on the Northern Pacific as the "Savage Special," the railroads each ran a special train to the park just before the park opened and from the park just after it closed[26]. These trains were used to transport the summer employees to and from their park jobs. The Northern Pacific ran a train from St. Paul, Minnesota, and the Union Pacific ran its train from Los Angeles. Both trains carried around 300 summer employees – teachers, college students, and others interested in an exciting summer job in a national park. Giving credence to the designation on the Northern Pacific of naming the train the "Savage Special," the Union Pacific train had special instructions relating to the trip through Las Vegas. The railroad crew was ordered to lock the train doors shut when the train was stopped to be serviced at Las Vegas since some employees had been known to rush out to do some quick gambling – and miss the train when it left[27].

Presidential Trains

Many United States presidents also visited the park. Due to its closeness to a main line and the park boundary at the time the North Entrance was the one typically used by the presidents. Presidents who visited the park included Chester Arthur, Warren G. Harding, Theodore Roosevelt, Calvin Coolidge, and Franklin Delano Roosevelt.

President Arthur was the first president to visit Yellowstone National Park. In 1883 his staff felt he needed a vacation and arranged a rail tour for a month-long stay at Yellowstone National Park in the summer. The trip was suggested by park supporter Senator George C. Vest of Missouri. The special train left Washington, D.C. on July 30, traveling over the Pennsylvania Railroad to Chicago. The party left Chicago on August 1 and traveled over the Chicago & North Western to Omaha and the Union Pacific to Green River, Wyoming using the private car of Union Pacific President Sidney Dillon. On August 7 the party then took a wagon to Fort Washakie on the Shoshone Reservation. Leaving the fort on August 9, they went by horseback to the park. The party entered the park on August 23 and reached Mammoth Hot Springs on August 31, ending a 350-mile trip.

When the party reached Cinnabar, on the north boundary of the park, on August 31, a special Northern Pacific train was waiting for him. The train went over the new Northern Pacific line to Gold Creek, Montana, where the president helped celebrate the completion of the Northern Pacific's transcontinental line with General Ulysses S. Grant[28]. It returned via the Chicago, Milwaukee & St. Paul and the Pennsylvania Railroad back to Washington, D.C., arriving there on September 7.

Travel to the park had improved by the time President Theodore Roosevelt visited the park in 1903. The president rode the train to Cinnabar for his visit to dedicate the stone arch at Gardiner, since the line to Gardiner wasn't completed. The train was turned around at Cinnabar and the train and crew waited there for two weeks while the President toured the park. The dedication ceremonies for the Roosevelt Arch were held on April 24, 1903, and after the dedication ceremonies the President spent several days in the park viewing the wildlife. Special trains took the residents from Livingston to Gardiner and back for the ceremonies[29].

On June 20, 1923 President Harding started a train trip to Alaska on what was to be his last journey. His special train went to Denver, then to Cheyenne and Ogden, and continued south to Cedar City in southern Utah for a trip through Zion Park. His party then went north through Pocatello to Butte and Helena with a side trip down to Gardiner, where he was able to rest for two days in the park. The President then went up to Alaska to dedicate the completion of the new Alaska Railroad. He died from a heart attack in California on his way back to Washington, D.C.[30]

In 1937 President Franklin D. Roosevelt visited the park. He came with his wife and a large party for a two-day visit on September 25-26.[31] More recent presidents have arrived by air due to time constraints as well as the ease and security of air travel.

This train is believed to be President Theodore Roosevelt's special train which went west to Cinnabar in 1903. The President of the United States traveled by train to reach the park until airplane travel became common.
AUTHOR'S COLLECTION

President Harding visited Yellowstone National Park in 1923 on his trip to Alaska to drive the final spike on the new Alaska Railroad. He is seen here with his wife departing Gardiner following his trip to the park. COURTESY MARIAN SCHENCK

Chapter Five

The railroads published booklets, flyers, and even postcards promoting travel to the park. This postcard showing the Canyon Falls was published by the Northern Pacific Railway to encourage tourists to travel to the park. AUTHOR'S COLLECTION

Visiting Wonderland
Publicity and Promotion of the Park

The railroads offering passenger service to Yellowstone National Park actively promoted travel to the park since it provided passenger revenue, even if it was only in the summer months. There was, however, competition for the tourist trade since a vacationer could visit different national parks on other railroads, including the Grand Canyon National Park on the Santa Fe, Yosemite National Park on the Southern Pacific, and Glacier National Park on the Great Northern. These railroads also built facilities in or near the new national parks and provided attractive and competitive tour packages.

Although the railroads providing service to Yellowstone National Park vied with each other for the business, they also worked together to encourage travel by jointly advertising service to the park. One could arrive at the park on one railroad and leave through another entrance on a different railroad for the return trip home at the same cost as a round-trip on the same railroad[1]. Baggage was transferred between stations while the tourist was in the park.

The railroads all promoted travel to Yellowstone National Park in magazines and printed brochures, and publicized the park at events such as the Panama-Pacific International Exposition in San Francisco in 1915, where the Union Pacific built a small replica of Old Faithful[2]. The Northern Pacific published a series of booklets titled *Wonderland* to describe the wonders of the park[3], and the Oregon Short Line published a series of pamphlets called *Where Gush the Geysers* in the same time period. The railroads even had representatives give lectures using lantern slides showing the sights in the park[4]. In 1913

In 1902 six cents could get a reader a copy of this Northern Pacific booklet promoting travel to Yellowstone National Park. GADAMUS COLLECTION, YELLOWSTONE HISTORIC CENTER

21

Wylie Way Camps sponsored a tour of the park for a party of ten advertising agents who worked for various railroads. The agents received a six-day visit to the park, showing them what travel to the park was like and why they should promote it[5].

In August 1886 the Northern Pacific Railroad ran a special editorial excursion train to Yellowstone National Park under the direction of Northern Pacific general passenger agent Charles Fee. Designed for members of the Montana Press Association, the special train took the members to Gardiner, and from there they went to the Mammoth Hot Springs Hotel, where they were entertained[6].

In another instance the Union Pacific Railroad commissioned a book describing a visit to the park[7], and had movies made for lectures by the Department of Tours, all promoting travel to Yellowstone[8]. In 1890 the Northern Pacific General Passenger Agent Fee published a brochure titled "A Romance of Wonderland", containing a "diary of a woman's trip to Yellowstone National Park"[9].

The Union Pacific had a long series of advertisements from 1923 through 1960 in which cartoon bears were used to promote visits to the park. Other railroads also advertised in newspapers and national magazines to tell the readers why they should choose their railroad to travel to the park. Even the employee magazines would tell the employees why they should travel to Yellowstone, and the articles described the sights and facilities[10]. In 1938 the Northern Pacific sponsored a special summer school for boys, which included a visit to Yellowstone National Park[11]. Probably one of the most unique promotional efforts was by the Burlington to have travelers tour the park on their bicycles. A pamphlet distributed in 1898 told how one could bicycle through the park in *"three days and eight hours - nearly two days quicker than the stage"*[12].

Even when a railroad did not reach the park it would sometimes publish promotional folders on the park. As an example, in 1923 the Rock Island Lines and the Denver & Rio Grande both distributed brochures promoting travel to the park[13]. In 1884 the Chicago, Milwaukee & St. Paul Railway published a booklet titled "The Tourists' Wonderland", describing travel in Yellowstone National Park, using the Northern Pacific's Livingston gateway[14]. This was many years before the Chicago, Milwaukee & St. Paul Railway built its line across Montana.

Tourists could travel on special summer rates for little more than the price of a one-way ticket, and special packages were available for travel to and in the park. In 1905 the Northern Pacific advertised a round-trip ticket from Livingston to Mammoth by train and stagecoach for $5, a round-trip ticket between St. Paul and Gardiner for $45, and the same trip, with 5-1/2 days in the park, was $75[15].

Side trips to the park were encouraged. In 1905, when the Lewis & Clark Exposition was held in Portland, visits to the park increased from 13,727 in the previous year to 26,168, but dropped to 17,172 in 1906. The Alaska-Yukon Pacific Exposition was held in Seattle in 1909 and again visits to the park increased, from 18,748 in the previous year to 32,545, and dropped back to 19,575 in 1910[16]. The majority of these visitors arrived by rail. During the years of the world fairs in the Depression years the railroads made special efforts to have travelers make a side trip to the park[17].

The Northern Pacific had a series of booklets at the beginning of the 20th Century based on Yellowstone Park's being called a "Wonderland." This one, published for the 1906 season, emphasized the wildlife and Grand Canyon. YELLOWSTONE HERITAGE & RESEARCH CENTER

Opening day each year was a special event and a good opportunity for the railroads to advertise their train service to the park. In 1923 the Union Pacific handed out special ribbons stating "First in Yellowstone National Park, West Yellowstone entrance, June 19, 1923" since that entrance opened one

All of the railroads which reached the park competed for the tourist business. The Northern Pacific Railway and the Union Pacific Railroad both had extensive advertising campaigns. From 1923 through 1960 the Union Pacific had a series of over 90 advertisements featuring cartoon bears which promoted travel to Yellowstone National Park. This one, published by the Union Pacific in 1929, had a more serious and scientific explanation for the geysers on the inside. UNION PACIFIC HISTORICAL COLLECTION

The Northern Pacific included the "Yellowstone Park Line" slogan on their timetables. The Gardiner Station and the Old Faithful Inn were on the cover of a timetable from 1907. YELLOWSTONE HERITAGE & RESEARCH CENTER

The railroads encouraged stopover visits to the park when worlds fairs, expositions, or even Olympic Events were held. In 1909 the Northern Pacific encouraged visits to Yellowstone National Park for those traveling to the Alaska-Yukon-Pacific Exposition and the Third Annual Rose Festival. YELLOWSTONE HERITAGE & RESEARCH CENTER

In 1914 the Northern Pacific was advertising their open observation car which ran on the end of the trains between Livingston and Gardiner. The arriving tourists rode this car and saw the scenery on their way to and from the North Entrance to the park. YELLOWSTONE HERITAGE & RESEARCH CENTER

The United States Railway Administration took over the operations of the nation's railroads during World War I. In 1919, shortly before the railroads were returned to their owners, the USRA published this promotional booklet for Yellowstone. Interestingly enough, the Chicago & North Western Railway used the same cover for their promotional brochure in the following year, substituting their name for that of the USRA. YELLOWSTONE HERITAGE & RESEARCH CENTER

In 1926 the Chicago, Burlington & Quincy offered escorted tours to the park and advertised them in this booklet. The tours were provided in conjunction with the Great Northern and Northern Pacific. YELLOWSTONE HERITAGE & RESEARCH CENTER

day before the other entrances officially opened for the year[18]. In 1927 the Oregon Short Line's Pocatello Shop Band gave a special presentation at the Salt Lake City depot when the first *Yellowstone Special* train of the season departed for the park[19].

In the 1920s the National Park Service held special opening day ceremonies at a different park entrance each year, and the railroads promoted and publicized the event. In 1923 the opening celebrations were held at the north entrance arch at Gardiner on June 20[20]. Although no specific mention was made by the park superintendent in his annual report, the Northern Pacific presumably participated in the ceremonies. The ceremonies were again held at Gardiner on June 20 in the following year[21]. On June 18, 1925 the Park Service held the opening ceremonies at West Yellowstone with the full support and cooperation of the Union Pacific. Indians from the Fort Hall Indian Reservation were brought in by the railroad, the railroad's Pocatello Shop Band played, and four state governors spoke at the ceremonies[22]. The governors arrived at West Yellowstone on a special train over the Union Pacific. The next year the opening ceremonies were held at the Roosevelt Arch at Gardiner on June 20.[23]

On June 17, 1927 there were ceremonies at Bozeman to celebrate the Northern Pacific's new gateway from there, and the celebration continued at Gallatin Gateway the same day to celebrate the opening of the Milwaukee's Gallatin Gateway Inn. The formal opening ceremonies were held at Cody, Wyoming two days later, with the full cooperation of the Chicago, Burlington and Quincy Railroad[24].

Opening ceremonies returned to West Yellowstone on June 20, 1928, again with the full support of the Union Pacific[25]. They went back to the Gallatin Gateway Inn in 1929[26]. In 1930 the railroads all agreed

Dude ranches were also popular in the 1920s and 1930s, and this Northern Pacific menu cover on the *North Coast Limited* passenger train combined both Old Faithful at Yellowstone National Park with the dude ranches. GADAMUS COLLECTION, YELLOWSTONE HISTORIC CENTER

The Northern Pacific promoted travel to the park and to the surrounding country. This brochure, published in 1928, encouraged parents to send their children to a special camp sponsored by the Northern Pacific. YELLOWSTONE HERITAGE & RESEARCH CENTER

The railroads sometimes held lantern slide shows at various cities in the country to encourage travel over their line to the park. This was the cover sheet of the script for a show sponsored by the Northern Pacific. YELLOWSTONE HERITAGE & RESEARCH CENTER

26

In 1930 the Colpitts Tourist Company offered a comprehensive tour of the Pacific Northwest from New England, including a visit through Yellowstone National Park. GADAMUS COLLECTION, YELLOWSTONE HISTORIC CENTER

to discontinue the special opening ceremonies, presumably due to the expense, although the Northern Pacific did arrange for movies of the first rail visitors for that season[27].

The railroads also promoted special events in the park. In 1925 the Union Pacific reported on the Buffalo Round-up in the park, which was held during "Old Plains Week." The guests were to be taken from the Canyon Hotel in stagecoaches and the buffalo were to be rounded up by Crow Indians on horseback. The Union Pacific employee newsletter reported that "*The Chicago and North Western and Union Pacific passenger departments are handling details of transportation.*"[28]

In addition to the standard advertisements and promotion efforts, *The Official Guide of the Railways*, which listed the passenger train schedules for all of the railroads in the country, provided information on travel to the park. For several years the *Guide* had a separate page in the back listing the national parks, the stations used to reach each park, and the railroads serving those stations. In 1937 the *Guide* listed the following information for Yellowstone National Park[29]:

Station	Railroad
Bozeman, Mont.	Northern Pacific
Cody, Wyo.	Burlington Route
Gallatin Gateway, Mont.	Chi. Mil. St. P. & Pac.
Gardiner, Mont.	Northern Pacific
Lander, Wyo.	Chicago & N. W.
Victor, Idaho	Union Pacific
West Yellowstone, Mont.	Union Pacific

In 1945 the *Guide* listing was the same, except that Red Lodge, Montana (Northern Pacific) Station had been added[30]. Within a few years the *Guide* no longer had the page listing the national parks since rail travel to the parks had declined so much that it was no longer important.

It is worth noting that in addition to promoting travel to the park the railroads also promoted dude ranches in the area for many years. These ranches were a popular attraction in the 1920s, and a tourist could stay at them separately or as part of the tour through the park. Probably the most unusual use of the dude ranch concept was the C&NW, which provided the option for a traveler to ride by horseback from Lander to the park, taking several days and camping out along the way, in lieu of riding a motor coach to the park.

These promotional efforts were important to the railroads since they provided important passenger revenue, and the railroads had large advertising budgets to distribute the information. The Union Pacific and Chicago & North Western jointly ran a Department of Tours to promote tourist travel over their lines, and the other railroads also provided similar promotional efforts. These departments would arrange travel for individuals or large groups of people. The brochures give a reminder of what travel to the park was like in the days of railroad travel.

Tour companies offered visits to the park after World War II, despite the increasing popularity of the private automobile.
GADAMUS COLLECTION, YELLOWSTONE HISTORIC CENTER

Chapter Six

Original Gardiner Station. PHPC

Yellowstone Park Line
Northern Pacific Railway to Gardiner, Red Lodge, and Bozeman, Montana

The Northern Pacific Railway[1] was not only the first railroad to build a branch line to the park boundary to the North Entrance at Gardiner, but it also provided service to the last entrance which was opened to the park, the Northeast Entrance. In addition, the Northern Pacific was heavily involved in the development of the hotel facilities in the park. Today the rail lines to both entrances have been abandoned and the railroad, now part of the Burlington Northern Santa Fe Railway, no longer has any association with the park.

The involvement of the Northern Pacific with the park dates back to 1870, with the exploration of the park by the Washburn Expedition. According to legend, the party concluded that the natural wonders should be preserved as a national park[2]. Nathaniel Pitt Langsford, who was on the expedition, publicized the wonders he had seen in the park on his return to the East Coast, and Jay Cooke, financier for the Northern Pacific Railroad, hired him as a publicist to obtain financial support for his railroad and to promote the park[3]. Cooke's railroad planned to build within 40 to 50 miles of the north boundary of the proposed park because he realized that the railroad would benefit from tourist travel to the proposed park.

The publicity by Langsford led to a $40,000 appropriation in 1871 for the Hayden Expedition, and Cooke's office manager, A.N. Nettleton, requested that Hayden permit Thomas Moran, an accomplished landscape artist, to accompany the expedition[4]. Moran received some financial support from Cooke for the trip, which resulted in his famous oil painting *The Grand Canyon of the Yellowstone*, which is on display today at the National Museum of American Art in Washington, D.C.

Unfortunately for Cooke, the depression in 1873 forced the Northern Pacific Railroad into bankruptcy and it was 10 years before the railroad was able to build a line across southern Montana. One of the first branch lines the Northern Pacific built was the one south from the main line towards the park boundary. In 1881, when the Northern Pacific was building its transcontinental line across southern Montana and was approaching the park from the east, Northern Pacific President Villard ran a special train so his guests could see the potential for passenger business to the park. In January 1882 the Northern Pacific decided to build a rail line directly to the park boundary and formed a separate company, the Yellowstone Park Association, to operate hotels and make improvements in the park.

Over the years one could travel four different routes on the Northern Pacific to reach the park–via Gardiner, Red Lodge, and Bozeman in Montana and Cody, Wyoming. The North Entrance at Gardiner was not only the first rail entrance to the park but it was also one of the most popular. The Northeast Entrance was reached by the Northern Pacific branch line to Red Lodge, with transportation over this route beginning in 1937, after the Beartooth Highway had been improved enough to make bus travel feasible. Following the completion of the highway through the Gallatin Canyon and the inauguration of the Milwaukee service to Gallatin Gateway, the Northern Pacific scheduled a sleeper between Chicago and Bozeman during the park season. This service through the West Entrance at West Yellowstone was started in 1927 to compete with the new Milwaukee Road line to Gallatin Gateway, and it continued through the early years of the Depression. The Northern Pacific also provided through passenger service to the East Entrance at Cody, Wyoming in conjunction with the Chicago, Burlington & Quincy Railroad, making train connections at Billings. Although the service to Gardiner was one of the most popular and convenient rail routes, the route to Cody was also popular due to the scenic ride to the park. Appendix B is a record of the park visitors who arrived by rail through the various entrances following World War I, and as can be seen, the Gardiner Entrance was the second most popular entrance. The Red Lodge route, although longer, provided a scenic tour to the park, while the route through the Gallatin Canyon was not as popular as the other routes since it was not as scenic as the Red Lodge Route and required a long drive to reach the park.

Today the rail lines to Gardiner and Red Lodge have both been abandoned and removed, but both have interesting histories closely associated with the travel to the park. They provided distinctly different and separate means of reaching the park, and travel on both routes was available as part of the standard park tour packages. The rail line through Livingston and Bozeman is now operated by Montana Rail Link and the line to Cody is still used by the successor to the Chicago, Burlington & Quincy Railroad, the Burlington Northern Santa Fe Railway, for freight service.

North Entrance
Northern Pacific to Gardiner, Montana

The North Entrance to the Park at Gardiner, Montana was at the terminus of one of the first branch lines built by the Northern Pacific. The rail line was built specifically to reach the park in order to

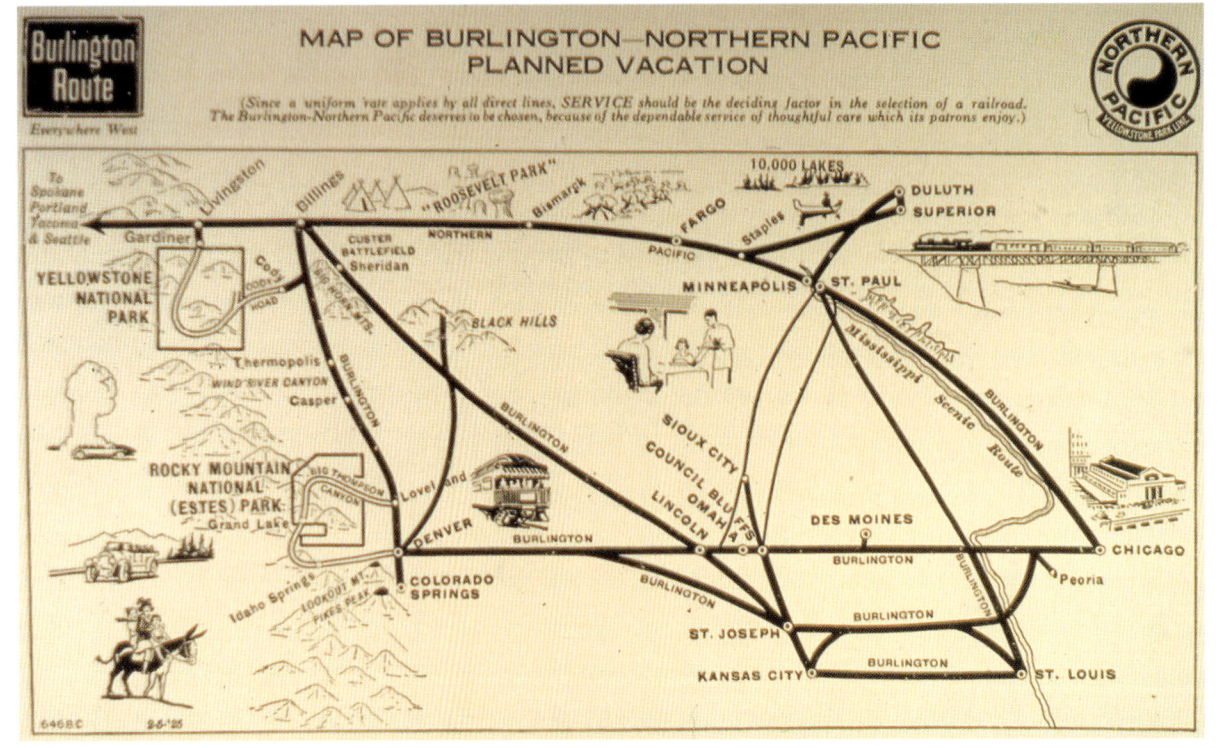

A map showing possible routes between the mid-West and Yellowstone National Park over the Northern Pacific and Burlington lines, including the route to Gardiner. This was published in a 1925 advertising book, and does not show the Red Lodge or Bozeman entrances, which were not yet opened. GADAMUS COLLECTION, YELLOWSTONE HISTORIC CENTER

transport tourists to the park, providing an important source of revenue to the railroad. The success of the line to Gardiner spurred other railroads to build competing lines and routes to the other park entrances. This success also caused the Northern Pacific to become financially involved in the facilities in the park, with the railroad financing the construction of the famous Old Faithful Inn at the beginning of the 20th century. The inn was designed by Ronald Reamer, the architect who also designed the Northern Pacific station at Gardiner.

The Park Branch

When the Northern Pacific Railroad entered receivership following the depression in 1873, the railroad was threatened with the loss of its right-of-way through Montana. If that occurred the railroad would lose the tourist traffic to the park as well as the potential mining business in the Cooke City area. To prevent this from happening, in 1881 Henry Villard, who controlled the Northern Pacific at this time, decided to incorporate an independent railroad under the laws of the Territory of Montana rather than the federal government in order to obtain the necessary right-of-way to the park boundary. S.T. Hauser, a Montana businessman, supported and helped in this effort, and the Rocky Mountain Railroad Company of Montana was chartered in the Territory of Montana on July 18, 1881. The new company was capitalized at $1 million and received financial backing from Villard's Oregon & Transcontinental line. The officers of the line were A.H. Barney, Frederick Billings, Henry Villard, S.T. Hauser, J.T. Dodge, W.F. Sanders, and A.M. Holter, with Hauser the president. The intent behind chartering this railroad was to have the Northern Pacific buy the Rocky Montana line after it had been constructed so that restrictions in the Northern Pacific charter could be circumvented.

The charter for the Rocky Mountain Railroad Company of Montana[5] authorized the construction of the following lines:
- From a point in the Yellowstone Valley near the north line of Yellowstone National Park to the vicinity of Bozeman.
- From Bozeman down the Gallatin and Missouri valleys to the vicinity of Helena.
- From Helena over the Rocky Mountains, down the valley of the Little Blackfoot and up the Deer Lodge and Silver Bow valleys to Butte City.
- From the vicinity of Helena to Fort Benton.

The railroad performed surveys for the Rocky Mountain line between the park boundary, the mining centers at Butte and Helena, and the head of river navigation at Fort Benton. However, before the company performed any construction Congress granted the Northern Pacific the necessary right-of-way across Montana. As a result, they built only the 55-mile section of the Rocky Mountain from Livingston to Cinnabar. Over the years Hauser continued to push the Northern Pacific to use the Rocky Mountain's charter to build a north-south rail line between Butte and Helena[6], with no success.

Hauser, who obtained the right-of-way for the Rocky Mountain line to the park boundary, secured financial backing from the Northern Pacific for the construction of the line. This was only one of seven branch lines that the Northern Pacific constructed in this manner. Two routes to the park boundary were surveyed, one from the Northern Pacific main line near Bozeman and south up the Gallatin River to what is now West Yellowstone, and a second one which went up the Yellowstone River from Livingston through Paradise Valley to Mammoth Hot Springs. The former route, though scenic, would have taken longer and cost more to build, so the directors chose the latter, shorter route after the railroad was incorporated. The surveyors also found a route through the park to the Snake River and down to Jackson Hole[7].

In March 1883 Winston Brothers & Clark were awarded the contract to build the 60-mile line from Livingston south to Mammoth Hot Springs in the park. At the time they were building the Northern Pacific main line across southern Montana. They began grading began in April and laid the first 34 miles of track towards Cinnabar from June 23 through July 21. The track laying to Cinnabar was completed in August of that year[8]. Construction was relatively easy since no major bridges or roadwork were required, and the ties were laid on cinder ballast. It was reportedly the fastest track-laying ever performed on the Northern Pacific since it was so easy, and also because of the fact that the tracklaying crews were available following the completion of the Northern Pacific's transcontinental line[9].

There were, however, several obstacles to the construction of the line. When the railroad reached Fridley the railroad had a feud with F.F. Fridley, the founder of the townsite. The Northern Pacific wanted to name the station Emigrant, and although Fridley objected, that name was used, but it was not "accepted" until about 1911. When the construction crew reached Fred Bottler's ranch, four miles to the south, an agreement for the sale of the land had not been reached, so Bottler turned on his irrigation water, stopping all construction. The legal formalities were quickly attended to. The railroad then reached Yankee Jim's toll road. The railroad wanted to build over the toll road through the canyon, and when Yankee Jim saw the construction crew coming he held them at bay with a shotgun. Again, the railroad quickly agreed to build him a new road. Legal ownership of Yankee Jim's land by the railroad was not finalized until 1923, after he had died[10].

Construction south of Cinnabar was not possible because the railroad could not obtain land from "Buckskin" Jim Cutler. Cutler owned the property the railroad wanted for a station and terminal tracks at Gardiner, and he wanted the Northern Pacific to pay what he felt was an appropriate price for the land, in part since gold had been discovered in the area in July 1883. The Northern Pacific refused to pay what they felt was an exorbitant price and could not obtain title to the land until Cutler died[11].

The Northern Pacific began operating passenger service from Livingston to Cinnabar on August 16, even before it had connected the tracks with the main line[12]. The Northern Pacific operated the line of the Rocky Mountain Railroad on September 16, 1883 under a 99-year contract, ending operations for the first winter on December 10[13]. The first scheduled train began operations on September 1, 1883[14]. On June 20, 1884 there was a daily passenger train between Livingston and Cinnabar, with stage connections to Mammoth Hot Springs.

On October 23, 1884 the Northern Pacific decided to extend the line to Mammoth Hot Springs, but this would have required a tunnel to be built in the park[15]. Although the railroad couldn't build to the park boundary at this time it made surveys to extend the line seven miles into the park to Mammoth Hot Springs and also ran surveys to Old Faithful and other park sites. Due to local opposition the railroad never built the extension to Mammoth Hot Springs. At Hauser's urging the railroad also looked at a branch line from Gardiner to the mines in the Cooke City vicinity, and at the same time Hauser purchased some land in Livingston for a smelter for this ore. Opposition to this proposed line resulted in Congress passing a resolution in 1892 so that no railroad construction could take place in the park boundaries[16].

The Northern Pacific extended the line from Cinnabar to Gardiner starting in 1902. On April 8, 1903 President Theodore Roosevelt arrived at Cinnabar to dedicate the new arch at the North Entrance. Since the tracks and yard facilities at Gardiner had not been completed, the president's train sat on the wye[17] at Cinnabar for 16 days while he toured the park.

Although Roosevelt traveled from Cinnabar to Gardiner by stage coach since the extension was still being completed, it wasn't long before the line was opened to Gardiner. The facilities at Cinnabar were dismantled and replaced by new ones at Gardiner soon after Roosevelt's train left. The railroad closed the Cinnabar station on May 3, and the post office was closed on June 15. The Cinnabar depot was moved to Gardiner, where it was converted into the freight depot[18].

A description of the line to Gardiner gives an idea of what the sources of revenue were along the line, ranging from passengers to dude ranches to livestock and mine products. The Park Branch left the main line at Livingston, at an elevation of 4,494 feet, and went 54.1 miles to Gardiner, at an elevation of 5,287 feet. The line had 72 pound per yard rail except for the last 10 miles, which had 90 pound per yard rail[19]. The line passed through a narrow canyon three miles south of Livingston, known as the "Little Gate of the Mountains," into Paradise Valley. The line then paralleled the Yellowstone River south to Gardiner. Near this portal there were lime kilns built in 1883 for the smelters at Anaconda and East Helena. The siding was originally known as Limespur, but later the name was changed to Tie Spur and then Allen Spur[20].

There was a livestock siding at Brisbin, 10.1 miles south of Livingston, and Pray, at milepost 16.6, had a section house and an-

In October 1892 the Northern Pacific offered tri-weekly service between Livingston and Cinnabar, taking approximately four hours to travel the 54 miles.

In 1901 the Northern Pacific used this cover for their *Wonderland* booklet. The cover included the railroad's yin-yang symbol, and the contents described the sights to see in the park and how a traveler could reach the park over the Northern Pacific. YELLOWSTONE HERITAGE & RESEARCH CENTER

other siding. Chicory, at milepost 20.6, had another siding and section house. The railroad established the townsite at Chicory on August 18, 1883 and tried to promote settlement of this area, with no success. A water tank for the steam locomotives was at milepost 22.5. Emigrant, at milepost 23, had a station and stockpen. It was the busiest point between Livingston and Gardiner and for many years was the last remaining station between the two towns. Passengers for Emigrant would either go to the nearby dude ranches or to Chico Hot Springs, at the foot of Emigrant Peak, which has an elevation of 10,960 feet. The hospital at the hot springs had a nationwide reputation[21].

Three miles south of Emigrant at Merriman the railroad had a rock quarry which was used to supply rocks for the right-of-way. Dailey was at milepost 30.7 and had a siding with a section house and a ranch house used for the station. It once was the site of a sawmill which supplied the Northern Pacific and the Montana, Wyoming & Southern railroads. Point of Rocks was at milepost 33.6 at the end of Paradise Valley. The valley narrowed here and the railroad had to do extensive blasting to build the line, while the highway went up over the hill. Carbella was on the north end of the Yankee Jim Canyon and had a siding for livestock cars. It served the Tom Miner Basin. Sphinx, named for a nearby rock formation, was a mile north of Yankee Jim's cabin and was one of the original stations.[22]

Corwin Springs was at milepost 46.4, and the site of

William H. Jackson took this photograph of the Northern Pacific arriving at Gardiner in 1905. Wagons in the foreground will take the baggage into the park, while the arriving tourists will board stage coaches which are waiting behind the log depot. COLORADO HISTORICAL SOCIETY

the Corwin Hot Springs resort, a popular destination opened in 1909. The resort never lived up to its expectations and when the hotel burned in 1916 it was never rebuilt. The hot springs became part of the Church Universal and Triumphant properties[23]. Tourists for the OTO dude ranch, one of the oldest and most famous in Montana, also arrived at this station.

Electric, 2-1/2 miles south of Corwin and at milepost 49.0, was originally known as Horr. The mines supplied coking coal from the 1880s through 1915. A tram carried coal from the mines at Aldridge to Electric. After labor and production problems closed the mines the town died out, and the post office closed in 1915[24].

Cinnabar was a passing siding even after the terminal was moved south to Gardiner, with the siding being used to hold extra passenger trains in the peak travel season[25]. It had been made a post office on September 6, 1882[26], a year before the railroad reached it on August 30, 1883.

The Town of Gardiner

The town of Gardiner is at the North Entrance to Yellowstone National Park, at an elevation of 5,287 feet, 793 feet higher than Livingston. The town has always been small, busy in the summer and quiet in the winter months. Located in Park County, it was named for Johnston Gardiner, a trapper and mountain man who worked in the upper Yellowstone Valley in the 1830s. The initial attempts to settle in the area were frustrated by the Crow Indians who hunted in the area. When the railroad built towards the park boundary there was a dispute over ownership of the townsite land, which caused a 20-year delay in the railroad reaching the town. Although the railroad was built to Cinnabar in 1883, three miles to the north, it did not reach the townsite until 1902[27].

Gardiner was established as a town when a post office was opened and operated by James McCartney on Feb. 9, 1880. Surveys for the rail line were made in 1881 and in July 1883 gold was discovered at the Gardiner townsite by Robert "Buckskin Jim" Cutler, who claimed the site. With the anticipated arrival of the railroad and the discovery of gold the town population reached 200 in 1883[28]. In that year the town included six restaurants, five general stores, two hardware stores, two fruit stands, two barber shops, a newsstand, a billiard hall, two dance halls, four houses of ill repute, a blacksmith shop, 21 saloons, and a milkman. Because there was no sawmill the structures were tents and log buildings[29].

The town was not surveyed and platted until 1886. The town continued to grow, and in 1887 it consisted of several frame and log buildings and many businesses as well as dwellings in tents. A fire

The Roosevelt Arch was completed shortly after the line was opened between Cinnabar and Gardiner. Travelers from the Gardiner depot to Mammoth Hot Springs passed through the arch. YELLOWSTONE HERITAGE & RESEARCH CENTER

that summer destroyed the entire town[30] and it didn't rebuild rapidly. A Northern Pacific guidebook in 1896 described Gardiner as *"a small collection of log huts and stores..."*[31]

The Roosevelt Arch at the North Entrance provided a more formal gateway and entrance to the park. President Theodore Roosevelt came to Gardiner in April 1903 to dedicate the cornerstone of the new arch at the North Entrance, a short distance south of the railroad. The railroad opened its line to the north edge of the townsite that year, although not in time for Roosevelt's trip. When Roosevelt dedicated the arch on April 24, he gave a speech to 3,500 spectators, many of whom arrived on four special trains run from Livingston[32]. Following the dedication ceremonies Roosevelt spent several days viewing the wildlife in the park. The 50-foot high arch was completed later that year.

Operations on the Park Branch

Operations on the Park Branch to Gardiner were casual for many years. In 1887 one traveler wrote that the engineer stopped the train so he could chase after two prairie chickens he had seen. After bagging one of them the train proceeded. Even in later years the crews would enjoy seeing the wildlife along the route, similar to the trips through Island Park on the Union Pacific's line to West Yellowstone. The train crews liked the relaxed working atmosphere[33].

The railroad normally operated the trains using oil-burner locomotives to reduce the fire hazard, although it was not unusual to have coal burner locomotives when the train was long enough to require a second locomotive. The oil locomotives were also used to reduce the smoke and cinders for the passengers in the open-air observation cars at the rear of the trains[34].

When the passenger trains arrived at Gardiner in the morning the train crews replenished the water for the locomotives from the fire hydrant and the sleeping cars were spotted so that the drawing rooms were on the north side, out of the direct sunlight. After preparing the train for the return trip, the train crews were able to go fishing and rest until the departure of the evening train. Some train crews would place an open gunny sack on the locomotive pilot (also called the cowcatcher) when it left Livingston. When the train arrived at Gardiner the sack was full of grasshoppers, which were used for fresh bait by the crews who would fish during the day. They would return to Livingston that evening with a basket of fish[35]

Passenger Train Service to Gardiner

The first scheduled passenger train to Cinnabar arrived on Sept. 1, 1883, carrying the business car *Montana* with Adna Anderson, Northern Pacific chief engineer and engineer in charge of the Park Branch, and another business car carrying officials of the Louisville & Nashville Railroad who were on vacation. The train also included cars for President Chester Arthur, who was vacationing in the park at the time. He had arrived at the park from the south and was planning on leaving through the north entrance. The presidential train was the first revenue train to leave Cinnabar.

With the completion of the line to Cinnabar the Northern Pacific began to advertise its route to Yellowstone National Park, since it was, for all practical purposes, the only way to reach the park. The most famous advertising campaign was the *Wonderland* series of guidebooks, based on the book *Alice in Wonderland* and the fact that the park was often called "Wonderland." The brochures were printed between the years 1886 and 1906. In 1896 the railroad adopted its famous Chinese yin-yang symbol, with the slogan "Yellowstone Park Line" added above it in 1906[36]. The promotions not only advertised travel over the Northern Pacific to the park but travel in the park, where visitors stayed at the hotels operated by the railroad.

The Northern Pacific ran through passenger cars to Gardiner so that the tourists wouldn't have to change cars on their trip, taking the cars off the main line trains at Livingston and putting them onto a train for Gardiner. Passengers would arrive at Gardiner in the morning and walk across the station platform to their transportation to Mammoth Hot Springs, which was five miles from and 1,000 feet higher than Gardiner. Their tour of the park began at Mammoth Hot Springs.

For many years the trains running between Livingston and Gardiner included an open observation car, which had benches and open sides so that the travelers could enjoy the sights along the Yellowstone River to Gardiner. In May 1913 the railroad rebuilt two fifty-one-foot, five-inch emigrant sleeping cars into the "rubberneck" observation cars used for this purpose. The cars, originally constructed in Febru-

In the summer of 1930, before the effects of the Depression were felt, the Northern Pacific offered two trains a day between Livingston and Gardiner. Through service was offered between Gardiner and Portland/Seattle. *The Alaskan* also offered through sleeping car service between Chicago and Bozeman, another gateway to the park offered by the Northern Pacific for a few years.

The Northern Pacific advertised in magazines such as the *National Geographic*. This advertisement was from a 1933 issue and featured a cartoon bear, since bears have always been an attraction for park visitors. AUTHOR'S COLLECTION

For several years the Northern Pacific ran a name train known as *The Comet* to the park. The brochure's cover included a bear and the Roosevelt Arch, and also referenced the joint travel available with the Chicago, Burlington & Quincy through Cody, Wyoming.
YELLOWSTONE HERITAGE & RESEARCH CENTER

The service to the park through the Northeast Entrance via Red Lodge consisted of one train a day, as seen in this timetable from June 1941. The timetable listed schedules to Red Lodge and to the park.

The Northern Pacific facilities at Gardiner were basic–consisting of a log depot on a balloon track. The balloon track allowed arriving trains to be facing in the right direction for the return trip to Livingston. The depot was at the bottom of the hill below the town and the Roosevelt Arch. AUTHOR'S COLLECTION

Passengers getting off the train at Gardiner would then board the waiting Concord stages for the short ride to Mammoth Hot Springs. AUTHOR'S COLLECTION

The Northern Pacific often had an open observation car on the rear of the trains between Livingston and Gardiner. The train to Gardiner is seen here in front of the Livingston station in 1925.
WARREN MCGEE

ary 1884, were rebuilt at the Como shops at St. Paul, Minnesota. Each of the dark green cars could accommodate 72 passengers on wooden chairs. The sides were open, with a roof to protect the passengers from the weather and locomotive cinders. The cars were placed on the rear of the train to minimize the cinders which would fall on the passengers from the steam locomotives. These observation cars were rebuilt into maintenance outfit cars in 1943, during the war when they were not needed due to the curtailment of travel to the park[37].

The passenger service varied over the years. The trains typically took two hours or more to travel the 54-mile line, traveling at an average speed of 25 mph. In August 1888 the Northern Pacific had a train running between Livingston and Cinnabar, leaving Livingston at 8:00 AM and arriving at Cinnabar at 10:50 AM. Returning, the train left Cinnabar at 3:40 PM and arrived at Livingston at 6:25 PM, taking almost three hours for the 54-mile trip. A timetable from 1890 shows that railroad provided a Pullman car on Train No. 3, *The Pacific Express*, from St. Paul to Livingston, designated the Yellowstone Park Sleeper, returning on Train No. 4, *The Atlantic Express*. In 1893 the train between Livingston and Cinnabar took almost four hours[38], and in the summer of 1895 the railroad was advertising through Pullman service between St. Paul and Seattle and Cinnabar. The through sleeper service was continued to Gardiner when the line was completed to the North Entrance. By 1909 the railroad was running two trains a day between Livingston and Gardiner in the summer months, mid-June through mid-September[39].

Service to the park over the Northern Pacific and the other railroads reached its peak in the 1920s. In 1921 there were four mainline trains which included cars to Gardiner. These trains had through sleeping cars which were switched onto the two daily trains to Gardiner. Originating cities included Chicago, St. Paul, Portland, St. Louis and Seattle[40]. In 1922 the railroad advertised the *Yellowstone Special*, running on the *North Coast Limited* westbound and the *Pacific-Atlantic Express* eastbound. It carried cars to Gardiner from Chicago and St. Paul -Minneapolis and to Cody from Chicago. Other main line trains had cars from St. Paul, Portland, Seattle, and Kansas City. By the next year the *Yellowstone Special* had been renamed the *Yellowstone Park Comet,* possibly to avoid duplicating the train name used by the Union Pacific Railroad to West Yellowstone. The second section of the *North Coast Limited* was designated the *Yellowstone Comet* in the tourist season, with direct Pullman service between Gardiner and Chicago and Seattle[41].

Train service to Gardiner declined with the advent of the Depression, and by 1932 the through car between Portland and Gardiner was no longer listed in the timetable. In that summer there was a daily passenger train between Livingston and Gardiner and a bi-weekly (Monday and Friday) mixed train. By 1935 the railroad was also running a daily bus service between Livingston and Gardiner[42]. In 1940 the timetable showed one passenger train and one bus trip between Livingston and Gardiner each day, with train connections with the *North Coast Limited*[43].

View of a 16-car passenger train in front of the Gardiner station. The train had two engines to handle the long train. WARREN MCGEE

A view of the Livingston depot, which was the gateway to Yellowstone National Park. It was designed by the architectural firm of Reed & Stem, who also worked on Grand Central Station in New York City. The Northern Pacific built the depot at the same time they extended their branch line from Cinnabar to Gardiner. AUTHOR'S COLLECTION

The June 1942 timetable of the Northern Pacific showed standard Pullman sleeping cars running between Gardiner and Chicago and Seattle but by 1943 the sleeping cars had been discontinued due to the war. The Northern Pacific again had service to Gardiner in the June-August 1946 timetable, with the *North Coast Limited* carrying through sleeping cars to Gardiner from Chicago and Seattle, and the daily passenger train to Gardiner from Livingston had been restored. The service to Seattle was discontinued the following year, only to reappear in 1948. In 1949 the Seattle sleeping cars were no longer shown, the cars from Chicago only ran to Livingston, and there were two daily round trip buses between Livingston and Gardiner[44]. The last known passenger trains to Gardiner were three special trains of Girl Scouts, which ran to Gardiner on August 31- September 1, 1955[45].

Connecting bus service operated by Northern Pacific Transport was available between Livingston and Gardiner until the end of the Northern Pacific passenger service in 1970. Connections were made at Gardiner with buses of the Yellowstone Park Company. When Amtrak ran the *North Coast Hiawatha* starting in 1971 it also showed a bus connection to the park at the Livingston depot. The bus service continued through 1979, when Amtrak's *North Coast Hiawatha* was discontinued.[46]

In addition to the passenger service to the park the dude ranches at Emigrant and Corwin Springs brought in travelers on the Gardiner line. In the 1920s Doctor George Townsend opened a nationally renowned 24-bed hospital at Chico Hot Springs, where up to 2,400 patients were treated each year.[47]

In addition to the passenger service, the railroad brought in mining equipment and supplies for the miners and the park, but the freight business was not as significant as the tourist business. Gold had been discovered in the area in 1865-66 and quartz mining began at Cooke City in the 1870s, continuing into the 1880s and later. In 1883 the Anaconda Copper Company built a lime kiln for the smelter at Anaconda and coal for it was mined in Trail Creek. A gold dredge was built near Emigrant in the 1940s and there was a rock quarry used for company construction and maintenance. A coke oven complex was operated at Horr, near milepost 49, but it closed down in 1915 following a labor dispute.

On Sept. 8, 1953, the Northern Pacific ran a special train called the *Farmers' Special* from Indiana and Michigan. It is shown here on the loop in front of the Gardiner station. By this time the Northern Pacific had discontinued scheduled passenger service to Gardiner, and tourists transferred to buses at Livingston. WARREN MCGEE

The Park Branch Today

The Northern Pacific became part of the Burlington Northern in 1970 and the BN continued to operate the line for the dwindling freight business. The Interstate Commerce Commission authorized the Burlington Northern to abandon the Park Branch[48] and the tracks were removed between Brisban and Gardiner in 1976[49] and between Livingston and Brisban in 1981[50]. Only the first mile of line south from the Livingston depot and a wye off the main line are left, and they are used by Montana Rail Link as an industrial spur[51]. The right-of-way between Livingston and Gardiner can still be seen from the parallel State Highway 89.

Gardiner Today

With the ending of passenger service over the Park Branch the Northern Pacific tore down the decrepit log depot at Gardiner in 1954 with the support of the park superintendent. It was replaced by a plain, wood building which was used for the freight service. When the Burlington Northern abandoned the line to Gardiner this building was converted so that it could be used for community functions. Today the Gardiner Community Library, the Gardiner-Park County Water district offices, and the sheriff's office[52] all utilize the building. The area where the balloon track (a track which made a loop back to itself to allow the train to turn around) was located is now used by the local high school.

The population of Gardiner in the year 2000 was 851[53] and the town is still a seasonal tourist center for Yellowstone National Park. The road to Mammoth Hot Springs, which is open in the winter months, makes Mammoth Hot Springs a popular destination. In addition, the road through Gardiner to Cooke City is also kept open in the winter months.

The Depots at Gardiner and Livingston

The Northern Pacific had two noteworthy, unique railroad depots on the Park Branch, at Livingston and at Gardiner. They were totally different from each other and served different purposes, but they both promoted and advertised travel to the park. Outside architect firms designed both of the depots, which was unusual for the railroad since it typically built standard wooden-framed buildings designed by their own engineering teams.

The Livingston Depot

The Northern Pacific built a new depot at Livingston, known as the "Gateway to Yellowstone," in 1902, at the same time the Park Branch was being extended from Cinnabar to Gardiner. The town was both a division point on the main line with major repair shops and the junction with the Park Branch. The depot was built shortly after the railroad enlarged its shops in Livingston. The Livingston Shops, which employed over 1,000 workers until they were gradually downsized in the late 1970s and early 1980s, were a major influence on the town's economy.

The Livingston depot was designed by the midwestern architectural firm of Reed & Stem, which designed over 100 depots for the Northern Pacific, including the ones at Butte, Montana (1906); Bismarck, North Dakota (1901); Ellensburg, Washington (1910); Seattle, Washington (1906); and Tacoma, Washington (1911). The firm also worked on Grand Central Station in New York City with the firm of Warren & Wetmore.

The new, $75,000 depot was designed to be a more impressive building than the existing two-and-one-half-story brick building at Livingston. It used red brick with terra cotta and buff brick trim and was designed in the Italian Renaissance Revival style. Construction started in November 1901 and was finished in time for the park season the following spring.

The depot was a three-building complex. The center section of the building housed the waiting room and ticket agent and railroad offices, the east wing housed a lunchroom, and the baggage building was on the west side. For many years one of the original horse-drawn stages used to travel through the park was on display in front of the depot. The railroad also had promotional posters for the park on display in the depot and in the 1920s had posters for dude ranches which could be reached via its line[54]. With the ending of passenger service to Gardiner after World War II, passengers transferred to buses at the Livingston depot.

A view of the Livingston station taken in 1990, after it had been restored as a museum. It is fenced off from the tracks which are now operated by Montana Rail Link. AUTHOR'S PHOTO

After the cessation of passenger service through Livingston in 1979 the railroad used the building for offices, even while the shops were being closed. The railroad then donated the depot to the city and over $1 million was spent on restoration by the Livingston Depot Foundation. The Livingston depot is now owned by the city and houses a museum known as the Livingston Depot Center, Chamber of Commerce offices, a restaurant, and a rental hall. Montana Rail Link freight trains use the tracks in front of the depot, and the Livingston Rebuild Center uses the former shops to rebuild locomotives.

The Gardiner Depot

The Gardiner depot was a unique log building, built in 1903 when the line was extended from Cinnabar to Gardiner. The building was on a balloon track so that the trains would be facing back towards Livingston when they reached the Gardiner depot. This avoided the numerous switching operations that the Union Pacific had to perform to turn its trains around at West Yellowstone, where a wye was used. The trains stopped at the depot facing east, so that the baggage carts would be lined up with the freight wagons which would take the luggage into the park. The road to the park led directly through the Roosevelt Arch, which had a stone wall made from the same material used to construct the arch. The tracks were on the north side of the arch, at a lower elevation than the arch, so that the road climbed up to the arch. The Gardiner townsite was built to the east above the depot.

The depot was designed to harmonize with the other buildings constructed in the same time period in the park. It had a rustic architectural style using native materials. The foundations and lower course were rough boulders and the upper walls were unpeeled logs. The platform shelters, and the trusses, gables and ceiling were finished in a similar manner.

The depot contained a waiting room with a fireplace, an express office, a baggage room and toilets. It was 40 feet by 87-1/2 feet, and the baggage room, on the east end of the depot, was 23 feet by 36 feet, due to the large volume of baggage. The waiting room, on the west end of the depot, was 36 feet by 36 feet. The express office, 12 feet by 18 feet, and the ticket office, 12 feet by 19 feet, 5 inches, were on the track side of the depot. The men's and women's toilets and women's waiting room, 10-1/2 feet by 13 feet, were on the opposite side of the depot. The interior furnishings also maintained the rustic effect. The log ends were smoothed and finished, and any cut lumber was high grade material. Wherever the wrought iron nail heads were visible they bore the imprint of the company[55]. The railroad made note of the depot in its *Wonderland* guidebook for 1904, saying:

"In 1903, the Northern Pacific having extended the railway from Cinnabar to Gardiner, a railway station was constructed that, with its surroundings, is one of the most unique, cozy and attractive to be found in the United States. From the Bitterroot Valley and mountains, selected pine logs were brought which, with the smooth, richly colored bark on, were fashioned into a symmetric, well-proportioned, tasteful and rustic building, the interior of which, with its quaint hardware, comfortable, alluring appointments, and ample fireplace and chimney, is in keeping with the inviting exterior.

Two colonnades, supported by massive, single log pillars at intervals, under which young and growing pine trees in wooden boxes are found, add much to the beauty of the structure. On the south side of the station, opposite to the railway track and fronting the great park, is a pretty, artificial lake, the water which supplies it being brought in a flume from the Gardiner River, a mile away. Back of the lake rises the high, brown-black lava arch and its sidewalls, the new and striking official entrance to Yellowstone park, costing $10,000, whose cornerstone President Roosevelt laid in 1903. To the left of the station and arch lies Gardiner, a snug little town on the very boundary of the park; just beyond it flows the Yellowstone river, and still beyond and across the stream, rising high above and some miles away, the high Snowy range, a northern continuation of the Absaroka, terminates the view. At the right stand Electric peak and Sepulchre mountain, great, mighty peaks of volcanic origin and grand form.

The whole combination of railway and train, rustic station, lake, town, arch, and landscape, added to the chattering throng of humanity, full of life and laughter as it hustles aboard the line of waiting coaches with their champing, impatient horses, is full of interest and enthusiasm, and a very fitting prelude to the wonderful trip ahead."

There was a separate wood-framed building for the freight business, originally the Cinnabar depot. Many hunters arrived by train in hunting season, so the trains would ship out the elk hides for the successful hunters[56]. Gold was shipped from Gardiner and other stations along the line into the 1940s[57].

The depot was designed by Robert C. Reamer, who also designed the Old Faithful Inn and other buildings in the park. Reamer was born in Oberlin, Ohio on Sept. 12, 1873 and attended public schools until serious headaches forced him to quit at age 12. At age 13 he told his parents he was going to study under an architect in Detroit, and then between 1887 and 1896 he was in Chicago, apparently studying architecture, at which time it is probable that he was influenced by the Prairie School of architecture. By the late 1890s he was in San Diego, where he was a partner with Samuel Zimmer. He designed the San Diego Diamond Carriage and Livery Company building and several cottages in Coronado in the popular neo-Spanish colonial style. While in San Diego he met Harry Child, who wintered in La Jolla, California. Child had financial interests in Montana and was involved in the Yellowstone Transportation Company and the Yellowstone Park Association, which were incorporated to promote the development of Yellowstone National Park. By 1902 Reamer was working on the Old Faithful Inn in Yellowstone National Park at Child's request.

Reamer was only 29 when he designed the Old Faithful Inn in Yellowstone National Park in 1903-04. He used native materials, a popular approach at the time. He designed the east wing in 1913 and the west wing in 1928, each wing having a different architectural style from the original building. Construction of the hotel was necessary to remedy the inadequate accommodations which were being reported in the national magazines. The Northern Pacific spent $140,000 to build the inn and another $25,000 to furnish it, through the Yellowstone Park Association.

The Lake Hotel in the park was designed by him in 1904-05 in the Colonial style, with an addition in 1923-24. He also designed the Canyon Hotel in Yellowstone National Park in 1911 in the style of the Prairie School of architecture, showing the influence of Frank Lloyd Wright. The construction of this 430-room hotel was a challenge, since it was so cold during the winter months that the nails had to be heated in the kitchen so that their heads wouldn't break off when they were hammered. In 1908 Reamer designed Child's personal residence at Mammoth Hot Springs in the park, and he also developed proposals for a new hotel at Mammoth Hot Springs in 1906 and 1909. Reamer created an "identity" for Yellowstone National Park, and developed a pattern for recreational development in the Western national parks, using a unique architectural style of logs, shingles, rough-sawn timbers and local stone. These developments were a marked departure from the traditional eastern resort hotels, which were large and luxurious. He designed at least 25 different structures in Yellowstone National Park and in Montana over the years. Many of these buildings are still used by visitors to the park[58].

After his successful work at the park, Reamer apparently went to work for the New York, New Haven & Hartford Railroad in New England, but there are no records what he did for them. He apparently moved to Boston at this time and in 1913 was listed as an architect for the NYNH&H. One of his designs was for a large hotel on top of Mount Washington in New Hampshire, which was to be built in conjunction with a new railroad which would climb to the top of the mountain, the highest peak in New England[59]. This was proposed in 1912, but due to a poor economy the construction never started.

About 1915 or 1916 Reamer's family moved to Cleveland, and Reamer worked with his brother who was also an architect. Reamer was rejected by the U.S. Army Corps of Engineers in World War I so in 1916 he began working in the Bremerton, Washington naval ship yards. After the war he joined the Metropolitan Building Company in Seattle as chief architect, and he remained in the Pacific Northwest until his death in 1938. Reamer was versatile in many different styles of architecture, which makes his works difficult to categorize[60].

The Northern Pacific built the Old Faithful Inn, located near Old Faithful, as part of their effort to promote travel to the park. It was designed by Robert Reamer. PHPC

The lobby of the Old Faithful Inn. The fireplace is made of 500 tons of rhyolite, an igneous rock, which was quarried nearby. The lodge pole pines of the Park were used for the walls and as support beams throughout the structure. PHPC

The Northeast Entrance
The Northern Pacific to Red Lodge, Montana

"Red Lodge HIGHroad, loftiest of all Yellowstone Park approaches, is the newest attraction of the Yellowstone tour. Opening to railroad travelers with the 1937 season, it has added to Yellowstone wonders the grandeurs of "sky-line" alpine panoramas.

"Altimeter readings show this road to be one of the highest in all the West. For approximately 21 miles it skims the top of the Beartooth Rockies at an altitude of more than 9,000 feet. The pinnacle of 11,000 feet is reached at one point and mile after mile its altitude hovers around the 10,000-foot mark. Two hundred fifty miles of mountain peaks can be seen with half a turn of the head.

"Red Lodge, Montana, on the Northern Pacific, is the starting point of this pre-eminent highway. Yellowstone sightseeing cars connect there with through Northern Pacific sleeping cars from Chicago. For a thrill drive be sure to go either in or out Red Lodge on your Yellowstone tour!"[61]

Red Lodge, Montana, is located 15 miles north of the Wyoming state line on the road to Beartooth Pass and Yellowstone National Park. The Northern Pacific Railway's tourist business through the Northeast Entrance into the park was dependent on the opening of the highway from Red Lodge. This road went over Beartooth Pass and through Cooke City and Silver Gate, Montana into the park. The Northeast Entrance was the last entrance opened to the park, and starting in 1937 the railroad's service to Red Lodge was operated in conjunction with bus service over the scenic Beartooth Pass in the summer months. Red Lodge started as a coal mining town, but with the closing of the mines prior to World War II the businesses turned to tourism to the park.

For many years everyone had felt it was not possible to find a way to the east from Yellowstone National Park across the Beartooth Plateau. It was not until 1882 that General Philip Sheridan found a route, but the terrain was so rugged that nothing was done at that time to build a road[62]. There were proposals for a road as early as 1890, but no work was performed. When a road was finally built from Red Lodge, the elevation was so high that no attempts were ever made to keep it open in the winter months due to the heavy snowfalls.

In the 1860s miners were active in the Upper Yellowstone Valley between Livingston and the northern boundary of the park. In 1870 silver and lead deposits were discovered at Cooke City, north of the park, and the area was soon called the New World Mining District[63]. By 1871 there was a rough trail through what is now the park from the Upper Yellowstone Valley to Cooke City. Only pack animals could travel the "roads" to Cooke City until 1877, when they were improved enough so that wagons could go over them. Over the years there were hopes that a railroad could be built from the east side of

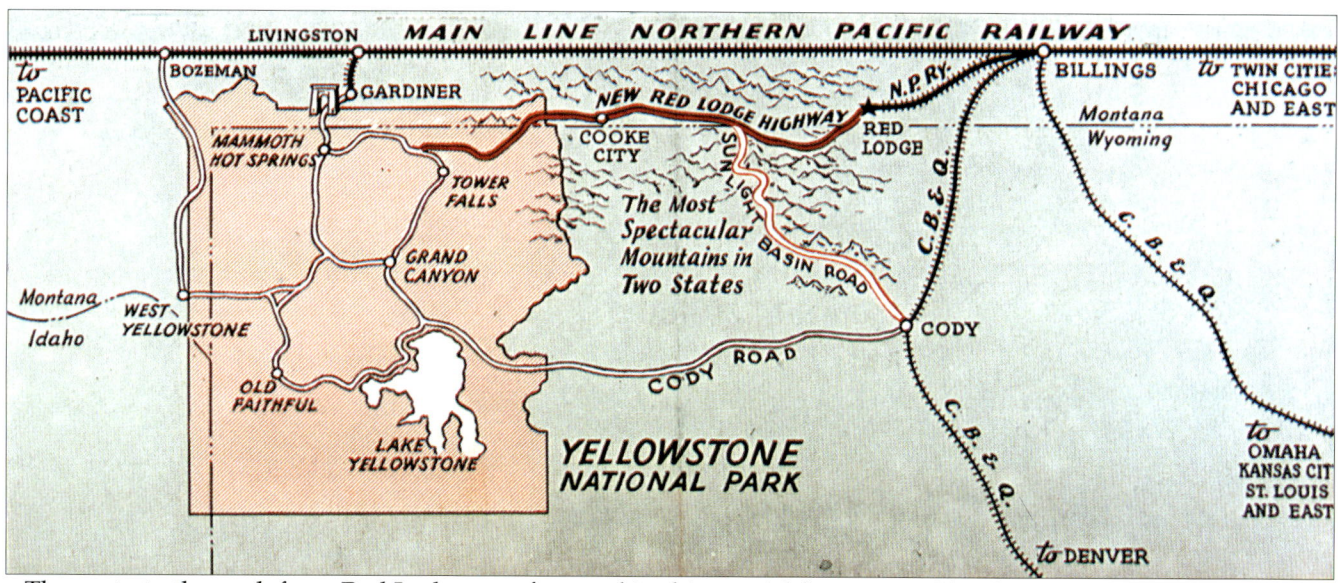

The route to the park from Red Lodge was featured in this special flyer printed by the Northern Pacific when the highway was opened. YELLOWSTONE HERITAGE & RESEARCH CENTER

the park to Cooke City, a route which would have taken the line through the park, but no rail line was ever built due to the terrain and opposition to the construction of a railroad through the park.

The History of Red Lodge

There are many stories associated with the derivation of the name "Red Lodge." According to local lore, the location was originally called Bad Lodge because of spoiled meat which ruined a Crow Indian festival. A more likely story is that the lodges of the Crow Indians were colored using the red clay in the region. An early pioneer insisted that the area was called Red Lodge because there were so many red man's lodges covering the area. Yet another legend has it that it was named after a rock outcrop of reddish colored rock on the mountain to the west of the townsite. Because water comes out of the mountainside through the rock, from a distance it looks like a huge Indian lodge, hence the name Red Lodge[64].

In 1866 a prospector named James "Yankee Jim" George came to the area looking for gold, but instead he found coal[65]. At that time the settlement was known as Rocky Fork because two small creeks joined there to form Rock Creek. Ezra L. Benton of Elmira, New York, was the lone inhabitant at what is now Red Lodge in 1884, and he was the postmaster of the new post office which was established on December 9, 1884[66]. The following year Red Lodge had a population of 11 families and in 1895 it became the county seat for the newly established Carbon County[67]. The county was formed from portions of the adjacent Crow Indian Reservation and Park and Yellowstone counties.

Walter Cooper, Samuel Word, and Samuel Hauser, who was territorial governor, organized the Rocky Fork Coal Company to mine the coal[68] in 1887 with the backing of the Northern Pacific Railroad. The company was also backed by Northern Pacific president Henry Villard and former Northern Pacific president Frederick Billings. They chose the location for the mines because it was on the Crow Indian Reservation, an area off limits to other speculators. The men thought they could persuade the federal government to redraw the reservation boundaries, and this was done in 1887. Mining was immediately started on the east bench and the population increased with the prospect of the construction of a railroad to carry out the coal. By 1891 there were 400 workers in the East Side Mine[69].

When the railroad reached Red Lodge in June 1889 and the town established, the backers of the Rocky Fork Coal Company owned the railroad, the town, and even the sale of electricity. The town quickly grew to a population of over 500 following the completion of what became the Rocky Fork Branch of the Northern Pacific Railroad. The residents were so happy to have the rail line that they proposed to rename the town in Villard's honor, president of the Northern Pacific, an offer he declined[70].

The town was platted in the same year the railroad was completed, and some of the streets were named after Northern Pacific officials and Montana businessmen[71]. The mine managers lived on Hauser Street and although Billings Avenue has been renamed Broadway, other original street names remain unchanged.

Red Lodge was incorporated in the spring of 1892, when the population was 1,180[72]. In that year 1.8 million acres of the reservation were opened for settlers, but between the Panic of 1893 and the fact that the Crow Indians kept the most arable land, the expected influx of farmers did not take place. There were, however, large numbers of immigrants who worked in the mines. They were principally Finnish, Italian, and Irish, an influence which continues to this day.

Cowboys were a strong influence on the town during the first years. Red Lodge was the nearest town for many of the isolated ranches, and after the cowboys drove the cattle to the railhead at Red Lodge each fall they celebrated. The town responded by hiring John "Liver-Eating" Johnson as a constable. He had never carried a gun while sheriff in nearby Coulsten(Billings), and boasted that "I just beat hell out of the ones that should be arrested and turn 'em loose, and I've never had to arrest the same man twice!"[73]

Red Lodge continued to grow, but on May 23, 1900 there was a large fire which burned the business district[74], at an estimated loss of $100,000. The town was rebuilt and the businesses properly insured after the fire. The town was growing and prosperous, with a booming coal mine industry and irrigation opening up the farmland for oats, hay, and sugar beets. A franchise for a street railway was issued in 1914, but it was never constructed[75].

Coal, however, was the predominant economic force in the town, and the mines produced two huge slack piles which overlooked the east and west sides of town. In 1900 approximately 65 percent of the men in Red Lodge worked in the mines. In September 1905 the two mines in Red Lodge produced 2,000 tons of coal a day[76].

By 1910 the population of Red Lodge was 4,860[77] and people lived in houses spread out from the mines. The railroad tracks came in from the north, dividing the town as they went to the mines on the south end of town[78]. The Northern Pacific used the coal from the mines for their steam locomotives and the Anaconda Company used the coal for their smelters. Mining out of the nearby Bearcreek fields began in 1903 and in 1907 the West Side Mine, also known as the Sunset Mine, was opened[79]. With this increase in mining activity more immigrants arrived to work in the mines, and this affected the residential areas in the town. Each nationality settled in its own neighborhood, with separate neighborhoods of miners from Finland, Italy, and other nations.

Strikes and labor unrest led to the closure of the mines in the 1920s and 1930s, hurting the local economy. The Northwest Improvement Company closed the West Side Mine in 1924 and the East Side Mine was closed in 1932 in favor of other mines which could produce the coal more cheaply[80]. The miners continued to work in other mines nearby but coal no longer supported the town's economy. The population dropped from 4,659 in 1920 to 3,026 in 1930, and then dropped more to 2,950 by 1940, and in 1950 it was only 2,730[81].

Many felt that tourism was the town's only possible salvation. By the 1920s, a time when dude ranches became popular throughout Montana, the town was beginning to sell itself to tourists as the "west". By 1930 Montana had over 100 dude ranches, four of them in the Red Lodge area, and Red Lodge began its transition from a mining town to a tourist town. The town had unsuccessfully tried to promote itself as a tourist town in the 1890s, but there was no real attraction at that time since the park was not accessible. Camping in the local Yellowstone Forest Preserve, later named the Beartooth National Forest and today known as the Custer National Forest, was a popular activity for the local residents.

The Road to the Northeast Entrance

There were proposals for a road to the park before World War I, when a local doctor, John Carl Frederick Siegfriedt, organized the Black and White Trail Association. The organization proposed to build a road from Billings to the park, with a side road to Red Lodge. Some road work was done after World War I and a survey to Cooke City was made in 1920[82]. The principal rationale for the road was to improve transportation to and from the Cooke City mines. Although no further work was performed, it did sow the seeds for further promotions and efforts to build a road over Beartooth Pass.

The road from Red Lodge to the park was built at the same time the road in the park to Cooke City was slowly being improved. Even before the park roads were opened to private automobiles there was a petition to operate trucks from Gardiner through the park to Cooke City which was approved subject to the freight company making improvements to the road. There was considerable controversy concerning how much work the freight companies were to do to improve the road. This was about the same time the road from Red Lodge to Cooke City was being completed[83]. Although the Bureau of Public Roads began improving the park roads in 1926 it was not until 1933 that a survey for the Northeast Entrance Road was completed, 68 miles from Red Lodge to the park boundary.

In 1925 Montana senators wanted a road to the Cooke City mines and worked with the park service to obtain it. In 1931 the Leavitt Act was passed to improve roads to the national park approaches, and work was started in 1932, the same year the East Side Mine closed down. The federal government built the road between Cooke City and Red Lodge at a cost of $2,500,000, following approval in 1931[84]. State Highway 212 (originally designated State Highway 32) was built on an Indian trail following steep grades. Part of the road is close to the trail used by Chief Joseph and his Nez Perce followers on their route from Idaho into Montana. Crews working from Red Lodge and Gardiner met at Beartooth Pass, at an elevation of 10,995 feet on the Beartooth Plateau, after carving the road out of the mountain sides. Red Lodge is at an elevation of 5,557 feet, so the road required the construction of several switchbacks.

It took several years to finish the road, which was not officially completed until June 14, 1936[85], and even then the work continued through 1941. With the improved road came increased traffic: from 1936 to 1937 the traffic increased 55 percent through the entrance, to 7,320 vehicles in 1937[86]. In 1935 the park

The road to Red Lodge was a challenge to build with numerous switchbacks required to reach the 11,000-foot Beartooth Pass. YELLOWSTONE HERITAGE & RESEARCH CENTER

The Northern Pacific began offering travel to Yellowstone National Park through Red Lodge following the opening of the Red Lodge-Cooke City Highway in 1936. The road provides a scenic drive to the park over a steep, curving road. The caption on the back of this postcard states it was a "thrilling name, but really not a dangerous curve..." AUTHOR'S COLLECTION

service built a ranger station on the new Red Lodge-Cooke City Highway. Although the road was not completed, automobiles and freight traffic began using it to reach Cooke City and the park in the summer of 1935[87]. It was closed in October so construction could continue and was officially opened the following June. The road to Cooke City from Gardiner and Mammoth Hot Springs was kept open for the first time during the winter of 1938-39[88].

The improved road and popularity of the new road through Beartooth Pass from Cooke City through the Northeast Entrance led the Northern Pacific to coordinate its rail service to Red Lodge with bus service into the park. The first busload came over the 11,000-foot-high highway on June 20, 1937[89]. The bus trip was 69 miles from Red Lodge to the park boundary, and 124 miles from Red Lodge to the Canyon Hotel in the park, passing over the breathtaking switchbacks on the highway.

The Railroad to Red Lodge

Prior to construction of a railroad access to Red Lodge was difficult–it took five days to take a wagon load of coal to Billings. Bringing goods in was also expensive and time-consuming. However, one of the commodities which apparently didn't have any difficulty getting to the town was the liquor for the 16 saloons.

The Rocky Fork and Cooke City Railway Company was chartered on December 30, 1886 by businessmen not associated with the Northern Pacific, but with the backing of the Rocky Fork Coal Company. The proposed rail line was to leave the Northern Pacific main line at Laurel and go south to the coal fields at Red Lodge and then continue on to the Cooke City mining area. The company was capitalized at $700,000[90]. There were delays associated with obtaining permission to cross the Crow Indian Reservation, but that was received on March 4, 1887. On July 29 the Northern Pacific reached a traffic agreement with the Rocky Fork Coal Company and work on the rail line began in the fall. Surveys had started in April, but it was not until October that Dennis Ryan, a St. Paul contractor, began grading the line at the rate of a mile a day. Grading was to have been completed by January 1, 1888 but funds ran out just as work was about to be finished and the company suspended all work for a full year[91]. The railroad promoters left many of the local residents financially strapped since they had cut and delivered railroad ties and were never paid for them. One promoter had to leave town in the middle of the night to avoid being lynched[92].

A new railroad company, the Billings, Clark's Fork and Cooke City Railroad Company, was incorporated to build a 125-mile line from Billings to Rocky Fork (Red Lodge), and on to Cooke City. There was to be a branch along Rocky Fork. The railroad was initially capitalized at $1 million, later increased to $2.5 million[93]. The company received permission by August 1888 to build across the Crow Indian Reservation and stated that the line to Cooke City would be completed by July 1889. This activity aroused the interest of the Northern Pacific and Montana businessman Samuel T. Hauser, and together they purchased the Rocky Fork Coal Company in January 1889 and resumed construction of the Rocky Fork and Cooke City Railway . Northern Pacific Engineer A.J. Merritt finished what little grading remained to be done and in the following month Greene, Keefe & Company began laying the track[94].

The 44.37-mile line from Laurel, a short distance west of Billings, to Red Lodge was completed on April 13, 1889. The railroad ran as a separate entity until July 31, 1890, when control was taken over by the Northern Pacific[95]. The Rocky Fork & Cooke City Railroad was then merged into the Northern Pacific on September 1, 1896 in conjunction with the reorganization of the Northern Pacific Railroad to form the Northern Pacific Railway[96]. The line was initially designated as the Rocky Fork and Cooke City Branch[97] but later was called the Rocky Fork Branch[98] by the Northern Pacific. When it was completed the line climbed 3,000 feet from Billings to Red Lodge. The coal from the Red Lodge mines was used by the Northern Pacific on its lines east into the Dakotas and west to Spokane.

The railroad added much to the community of Red Lodge when the Rocky Fork Branch was completed. The inside of the wye track used to turn the locomotives at Red Lodge was made available by the railroad for a baseball field, complete with bleachers and bandstand. Meetings, band concerts, and rodeos were also held in that field. The railroad also became the staging point for other destinations in northern Wyoming, with stage connections between Red Lodge and other settlements.

Shortly afterwards two additional branch lines were built off the Rocky Fork Branch. One was for a line from Rockvale to the Clarks Fork Coal Company at Bridger, which was being surveyed in September 1897. In May 1898 an agreement was reached with the Northern Pacific to build the line 10 miles to Gebo, near Fromberg, and that line was completed by December 1. By 1901 the line had been extended south to Bridger[99]. Connections were made at Bridger with the Montana, Wyoming & Southern Railroad when it was completed in 1906. Another branch line was built from Fromberg, on the Bridger line, approximately four miles south and west to Coalville.

Over the years there were proposals for other lines to reach Red Lodge. In September 1907 the Red Lodge Board of Trade was considering the construction of the Red Lodge Electric Railway Company from Red Lodge to the Bear Creek mines, a distance of approximately four miles. There were no further reports on the line until 1913, when preliminary surveys were made for an electric line from Red Lodge to Bear Creek and Washoe to a connection with the Montana, Wyoming & Southern Railroad. By September of that year the Red Lodge citizens had raised $20,000 of the $50,000 needed to build the 4.4-mile line[100], but it was never built.

In 1909 the Eastern Montana Electric Railway Company was incorporated to build a line from Laurel to Billings, and from Laurel to Red Lodge, returning to Laurel to form a loop. The line would have been 85 miles long and would have connected the towns of Billings, Laurel, Selesia, Joliet, Fromberg, Bridger, Belfry, Bear Creek, Washoe, and Red Lodge. The company was also considering a branch line from Red Lodge to Stillwater Valley to Columbus, and then through Park City to Laurel, another 80 miles. The line was capitalized at $500,000, with A.C. Logan president. In 1910 the railroad reported it was making surveys from Billings to Red Lodge and that capital to build the line had been obtained. Another report in the same year discussed a survey from Billings to Bear Creek, indicating the railroad also planned to operate streetcars in Billings. There were no further reports on this line, which was never built[101].

There was a report in October 1913 that the Red Lodge Electric Railway had been incorporated to build a line from Red Lodge nine miles to Bear Creek. William Larkin, Thomas F. Pollard, A.H. Davis, Walter Alderson, and J.W. Chapman were backers of the proposed line. Surveys were completed by the end of November and a route established. C.C. Bowlen was the railroad president, J.N. Tolman was the vice president, and secretary was Walter Alderson. The company was capitalized at $225,000. There were no further reports on the line[102]. Despite the talk and proposals for the construction of other rail lines to Red Lodge, none was ever built. At this time the primary purpose for the railroad was the transportation of coal from the mines in the Red Lodge area.

Railroad Service to Red Lodge

The railroad operated freight trains for the mines along with the scheduled passenger trains on the Rocky Fork Branch. The passenger service varied over the years, due in part to the effect of the opening of the Beartooth Pass Highway and the consequent tourist travel to Yellowstone National Park. Travel was initially slow and informal, and in the first years the local Indians frequently rode into town in coal cars and on boxcars, while the few white passengers rode in a caboose on the rear of the freight train. An old wagon with a board served as a taxi in Red Lodge. A trip from Billings to Red Lodge, a distance of approximately 60 miles, took nine hours, and was so slow that passengers reportedly could shoot game from the window, get out to pick it up, and get back on the train – without running[103].

The local farmers shipped out their products every fall on the railroad, and there were times when hundreds of wagons were lined up by the tracks waiting to load the cars. Cattle shipments were also common from Red Lodge, and in 1893 there were 382 carloads of cattle (approximately 8,000 head), 42 cars of sheep (approximately 8,400 head), and six cars of horses (approximately 120 head) shipped from Red Lodge. By 1895, however, the last of the large cattle operations in the area had ended[104].

Initially the railroad operated a daily passenger train to Red Lodge, scheduling it to leave Billings at 6:30 A.M. and arriving at Red Lodge at 11:45 A.M.[105], taking approximately five and one-half hours. It returned to Billings later in the afternoon. The first passenger trains typically had three cars, including an old mail/smoker car which had been used on the mixed train. There was also an old smoking/baggage/express car, and the third car was a passenger car which had vestibules, retiring rooms on both ends of the car, and upholstered seats.

In 1903 the Northern Pacific wanted to break its 99-year lease with the Rocky Fork Coal Company. By simply refusing to carry out coal from the mines the Northern Pacific forced the company to sell out

It is 1939, and train #205 has arrived at Red Lodge with three cars, and a bus is waiting to take the arriving tourists to the park. The Northeast Entrance was the last park entrance to be served by the railroads, and the road over Beartooth Pass was a spectacular ride. COURTESY WARREN MCGEE

in 1902 for $1 million to the Northwest Improvement Company, a subsidiary of the Northern Pacific. The sale was completed on September 2, 1903. With the sale came an improvement in passenger service. By 1910 the railroad scheduled a train to leave Billings at 10:30 A.M. and arriving at Red Lodge at 1:40 P.M., taking just over three hours. The train returned to Billings later in the afternoon[106].

In 1926 the schedule shows that there was a daily passenger train between Billings and Red Lodge with faster service. It left Billings at 9:15 A.M. and arrived at Red Lodge at 11:50 A.M. Returning, the train left Red Lodge at 3:00 P.M. and arrived at Billings at 5:20 P.M. There was a separate train between Bridger and Billings[107].

With the opening of the improved Beartooth Pass Highway in 1937 the Northern Pacific began offering tourist travel to the park through Red Lodge in the summer season and rearranged its train schedules accordingly. The service to Red Lodge was advertised as alternative and complementary to the service to Gardiner, so that a traveler could go in one entrance and leave through the other. A through car between Chicago and Red Lodge was offered this summer[108].

The timetable from June 1941 shows that the railroad offered two different schedules to Red Lodge, one for the winter months, and the other for the summer months, June 20 through September 13. In the summer a train left Billings at 7:15 A.M. and arrived at Red Lodge at 9:15 A.M. Connections were made at Red Lodge with a bus which left Billings at 7:30 A.M. and went through Cooke City to Silver Gate, or the Northeast Entrance, which was reached at 1:00 P.M. Returning from the Northeast Entrance at 1:10 P.M. the bus reached Red Lodge at 4:45 P.M., giving time to board the train which left Red Lodge at 6:00 P.M. and reached Billings at 8:00 P.M. The bus continued through Red Lodge and reached Billings at 6:15 P.M. The reason for having both the bus and train service as the same time is that the Northern Pacific offered through sleeping car service from Chicago to Red Lodge, connecting with their name train *North Coast Limited* at Billings. These accommodations included a 10-section, 1-drawing room, 1-compartment sleeping car in addition to a passenger coach. Through Pullman service was also offered between Red Lodge through Billings to Seattle, Tacoma and Portland[109]. This passenger service was offered through 1941, when World War II put an end to the service. In the winter months, from September 13 through June 19, the railroad ran a motor car between Billings and Red Lodge, along with a bus between the two cities at a different time of the day.

The June 19, 1942 timetable showed daily bus service from Billings to Red Lodge. There was no bus service beyond Red Lodge since the bus service to the park was discontinued during the war. Following the end of World War II the railroad reinstated sleeping car service from Billings, discontinuing it in 1948[110]. After that bus service was provided from Billings through Red Lodge to the park, operated by

Northern Pacific Transport. Connections were made with the Yellowstone Park Company buses at the park entrance. The railroad continued to promote this route for many years until all service to the park was discontinued.

Decline of the Railroad

The Northern Pacific continued to offer connections with the Yellowstone buses for many years after World War II, despite a decline in the number of passengers. After the train service to Red Lodge was discontinued there was connecting bus service from Billings through Red Lodge to the park. The scenic drive over Beartooth Pass was a popular feature of the trip.

After the passenger train to Red Lodge was discontinued the freight service also decreased to the point that the railroad ran a train on Tuesdays only to Red Lodge. Much of the remaining freight was transported by Northern Pacific Transport, a subsidiary of the Northern Pacific Railway[111]. In 1976 the railroad took only 68 carloads over the line, and a mere 17 the following year[112]. By 1979 it was on an as-needed basis[113]. The rail line from Silesia to Red Lodge was removed from service in late 1980[114] and the tracks removed in 1981[115].

After the line to Red Lodge was abandoned Burlington Northern donated the depot to the Carbon County Arts Guild and it was converted into an office and art gallery. The depot, which was built in 1889, is on 8th Street, near the downtown area. The agent's living quarters on the second floor were removed and the depot is now a one-story building[116]. It is now run by a non-profit organization known as the Carbon County Guild. Known as the Depot Gallery, art work is exhibited for sale and classes and workshops are held in the building[117]. The railroad also donated a caboose to display at the depot[118]. The Pollard Hotel is also still standing, less than a block away from the depot. Built in 1893, it was built near the depot for the convenience of travelers.

The second floor of the Red Lodge depot had been removed when this photo was taken. The tracks have since been removed and the depot is now used by community groups. ART PETERSON COLLECTION

Red Lodge Today

The Beartooth Pass Highway is a popular, scenic route, although it is closed in the early fall through late spring due to the deep snows. It is essentially open for three months each year. In May 2005 the area received heavy rainfall, which, combined with the snow melt, set off a series of slides which closed the road, known by many as "The most beautiful roadway in America", and it was not possible to open it when the summer season started, and it was not until the summer was over that the road was re-opened. It will take millions of dollars to restore the road to today's standards. The population of Red Lodge today is approximately 2,000, and the town relies heavily on the tourist industry in the summer months.

The Bozeman Entrance

One of the more interesting, and least popular, routes to the park was over the Northern Pacific Railway to Bozeman, with a bus ride from Bozeman to West Yellowstone. The Northern Pacific apparently introduced this service to compete with the Milwaukee's new line through the Gallatin Gateway, although it was 14 miles longer. Due to the inconvenience and long bus ride it was never very popular and did not last for very many years. The Yellowstone Park Transportation Company provided bus transportation and, as was the case for the other routes, tourists had the option of entering or leaving via Bozeman while using another entrance for the other leg of their trip.

The first year the Northern Pacific offered service via Bozeman was reported in 1927, a year after The Milwaukee Road began offering service to the park from Three Forks and the same year the Gallatin Gateway Inn was opened. To bring attention to this new gateway and the beginning of service on this route, on June 17 the National Park Service held an opening celebration starting at Bozeman and ending at the Milwaukee's new Gallatin Gateway Inn.

In 1927 the National Park Service reported that 271 travelers arrived through Bozeman on the Northern Pacific[119], and in the following year 256 travelers used this route[120]. It increased slightly to 401 in 1929[121] and then decreased slightly to 383 in 1930[122]. In 1931 there were 331 tourists arriving through Bozeman[123], but it dropped to 33 in 1932[124], 20 in 1933[125], and only five arrived through June 30, 1934[126], when the National Park Service stopped reporting rail arrivals through each entrance. These numbers can be compared with the visitors who arrived by rail through the other entrances in Appendix B.

The Northern Pacific stopped offering service through Bozeman in the Depression years due to lack of traffic. The ride to the park was long, over gravel roads, so it was not as convenient as the other routes available to a tourist. The bus ride was also an additional 35-45 minutes beyond The Milwaukee Road's Gallatin Gateway Inn in each direction.

In 1927, the year which the Northern Pacific began offering service through Bozeman, the *Comet* stopped early in the morning at Bozeman, where the travelers transferred to the buses of the Yellowstone Park Transportation Company. The buses ran through the Gallatin Canyon, on the same road used by the buses for The Milwaukee Road passengers. They stopped at the Union Pacific's West Yellowstone facilities for lunch and to use the "comfort station."

The Northern Pacific depot at Bozeman was used for a few years to transfer train passengers to buses for a ride through the Gallatin Gateway to West Yellowstone and the park. It was never very popular due to the long ride over a dirt road required to reach the park. AUTHOR'S PHOTO

When the service was inaugurated, the Northern Pacific did not have an idea of how many passengers would use this route, but the Union Pacific doubted there would be more than 1,000 passengers[127]. As it turned out, the Union Pacific was correct, and it never posed a serious competitive threat to their service to West Yellowstone.

Northern Pacific Service to Yellowstone National Park

The Northern Pacific was responsible for establishment of Yellowstone National Park and for making it a popular tourist destination. It was the first railroad to provide convenient service to Yellowstone National Park through Gardiner, and it also provided service through Red Lodge, the last park entrance to be opened. Their route through Cody was also popular, operated in conjunction with the Chicago, Burlington & Quincy, but the Bozeman Gateway was too inconvenient to last very long. The Northern Pacific's Gardiner entrance was one of the most popular gateways to the park, second to the Union Pacific's entrance through West Yellowstone.

The Union Pacific's bear advertisements not only had bears but, if at all possible, made reference to a current event, in this case the 1948 presidential election. Old Faithful and the Old Faithful Inn can be seen in the background, and the cavalcade is entering the park through West Yellowstone. UNION PACIFIC HISTORICAL COLLECTION

54

Chapter Seven

A train arriving at West Yellowstone. The train would be turned around during the day for the return trip. BEN OSTENSON COLLECTION

"The National Park Route"
Union Pacific Railroad to West Yellowstone, Montana and Victor, Idaho

The Union Pacific Railroad advertised its line as "The National Park Route" since the railroad provided passenger service to national parks throughout the West, including Yellowstone National Park[1]. It provided service to two entrances at Yellowstone National Park, the West Entrance and the South Entrance. The railroad built a line directly to West Yellowstone and the West Entrance in 1907, beginning passenger service in the following year, and began providing service to Victor with connecting bus service to the South Entrance in 1929 following the establishment of the Grand Teton National Park. Even after train service to West Yellowstone was discontinued in 1960 the railroad maintained passenger service to Victor for travel to Jackson Hole and Yellowstone National Park for several more years.

The Union Pacific Railroad's West Entrance was the most popular rail entrance to the park, and the railroad was quick to advertise that over 50 percent of the rail visitors to the park arrived and departed through the West Entrance. This number is shown by the numbers reported by the National Park Service and listed in Appendix B. The railroad even advertised that it offered service *"to West Yellowstone, only entrance directly on the park boundary ..."*[2], which was literally true, since the depot was at the park boundary, while the Northern Pacific's station was a short distance from the park boundary.

West Entrance
Union Pacific to West Yellowstone

Tourist travel to Yellowstone National Park was the primary reason for the construction of the Yellowstone Branch of the Union Pacific Railroad to West Yellowstone, Montana. The history of the railroad to West Yellowstone and the growth of the town of West Yellowstone were closely intertwined for many years since tourism to the park was, and is to this day, the primary reason for the town's existence. Although the railroad no longer reaches West Yellowstone, there are still many reminders in the town of the time when it was the preferred means of reaching the park.

Due to the large number of the people traveling on the line and the fact that West Yellowstone was so distant from the park hotels, the railroad built extensive facilities at West Yellowstone. The other railroads avoided this expense since the Northern Pacific was only a few miles ride from the facilities at Mammoth Hot Springs and the other railroads never had enough traffic to warrant the construction of extensive facilities. The buildings at West Yellowstone included a large depot, a separate baggage building, an employee dormitory, and dining facilities to accommodate the tourists. In addition, the railroad had a train yard to handle the trains, with a water tank used to provide water for the steam locomotives and a wye which was used to turn the trains. Plans by the railroad to build a hotel to the south of the depot never materialized.

The line to West Yellowstone was also unusual because the line was always snowed shut in the winter season since there was not enough traffic in the winter months to justify the expense of keeping it open. Every year the Union Pacific had a "Spring Campaign", which was typically scheduled for March, when the railroad took several days to re-open the line from Ashton to West Yellowstone. The railroad then provided freight service to West Yellowstone and the passenger trains would start running in June. After passenger service ended in mid-September the freight trains continued running until the line was snowed shut in November. During the spring and fall months the railroad transported passengers either on an informal basis in the caboose of the freight trains or on a scheduled mixed train[3].

Before the Construction of the Yellowstone Branch

Even before the construction of the line to West Yellowstone the Union Pacific was advertising travel to Yellowstone National Park by stage from the Utah & Northern Railway, a subsidiary of the Union Pacific Railway[4]. Travelers would get off the train at Beaver, Idaho, and later at Monida, Montana, to start their trip to the park. After debarking from the train they spent the night at a hotel in town before starting their ride to the park on the stagecoaches of the Monida and Yellowstone Stage Company, which was owned by Frank Haynes. This service began in 1881, after the Utah & Northern Railway built its line through Monida. At that time this was the shortest route to the park, until the Northern Pacific built its line to Cinnabar in 1883.

The Bassett Brothers started operating their stage business in Beaver in 1881, with offices in Monida and Spencer. The trip from Monida to the park was 85 miles and required four changes of horses, and the stages initially required three days to reach the park. When the schedule was shortened tourists rode 85 miles to the Fountain Hotel in the park[5], staying the first night at Dwelle's (Grayling Inn) near the west boundary of the park. They reached the Fountain Hotel at noon on the second day. By 1882 the six Bassett brothers dominated the trade, providing tents, guides, and horses[6]. In the 1890s the Bassett Brothers moved their operations from Beaver to Monida. In 1898 a rival firm, the Monida-Yellowstone Stage, was opened by William Humphrey, providing competition for the tourist business to the West Entrance of the park[7]. Another competitor, the Gilmer - Salisbury stages, ran from Spencer to Yellowstone and used the Salisbury ranch near Henry's Lake starting in the summer of 1880[8]. The stage companies provided this service in the summer months only for the tourist traffic.

In 1884 *The Pacific Tourist* guidebook described the trip to Yellowstone Park as follows:

"*Utah and Northern Branch Union Pacific Railway, or the New Route to Montana and the Yellowstone....*

This new railroad has been lately pushing rapidly northward from Ogden, Utah, toward Montana. It is now (June, 1881) completed to Melrose, Montana, 380 miles north of Ogden, and only 35 miles south of Butte, sixty-five south of Deer Lodge, and twenty-five south of Helena, all of which points it will probably reach during 1881. Upon this road are several points of very great interest, worth the special visit of tourists for one or two days....

<u>*Dry Creek, High Bridge, China Point, Beaver Canon, Pleasant Valley, Williams, Spring Hill, Red Rock, Grayling, and Dillon*</u> *are all of little importance, except that Dillon, the present terminus, is the stage station for Yellowstone National Park.....*

ROUTES TO YELLOWSTONE NATIONAL PARK

......A second route, and one which shortens the stage ride, is to purchase an outfit at Salt Lake or Ogden, and send it ahead to Market Lake, in Snake River Valley, joining it via the railroad to Franklin and stage line to Market Lake. This saves about 230 miles of staging. It is about 100 miles by a pack train trail from Market Lake to Henry's Lake from which point the Virginia City wagon road is followed to the "Geyser Basins."

Another route from Market Lake, which is long and somewhat out of the way, but more interesting, as it gives an opportunity to visit Mount Hayden and passes some magnificent scenery, is to travel with a pack train up Pierre's River to Shoshone Lake, whence the other points of interest in the park are readily reached...."[9]

In 1885 the train arrived at Beaver Canyon at 1 A.M. where the accommodations at Beaver were reportedly *"wretched"*[10], and this may have been one of the reasons the stage companies moved north to Monida at about this time. One could also ride the stagecoach from Spencer, Montana to the park in this time period. The stagecoach riders were provided with mosquito netting and dusters[11] due to the dust from the dirt roads and the prolific mosquitoes.

At the beginning of the 20th century a guidebook titled *"Over the Range to the Golden Gate"* carried the following:

*"**Monida, Montana.** ..... At this point we leave the railway for the stage tour of the Yellowstone Park.*

The Yellowstone Park, Montana. *Monida, a station on the Oregon Short Line Railroad, on the crest of the Rocky Mountains, seven thousand feet above the tide, is the starting-point for the stage ride, and is less than one day's coaching distance from the Yellowstone Park. The Name "Monida" is a composite of the first syllables of "Montana" and "Idaho."*

The lower Geyser Basin in the park is about the same elevation as Monida, so that the stage route passes through a level country, and all the way is lined with picturesque scenes, making the coaching trip one of the most delightful in the Rocky Mountains.

Rev. T. DeWitt, who, with his party, visited Salt Lake City and other portions of the west during the summer of 1898, says: "But the most delightful part of this American continent is Yellowstone Park. My two visits there made upon me an impression that will last forever. Go in via the Monidda (sic) route, as we did this summer, and save two hundred and fifty miles of railroading, your stage coach taking you through a day of scenery as captivating and sublime as Yellowstone Park itself."

The stage road from Monida to the park threads the foothills of the Rocky Mountains, skirting beautiful Centennial Valley, the Red Rock Lakes, and after passing through Alaska Basin, crosses the Divide to Henry Lake in Idaho, whence it recrosses the range into Montana via Targhe Pass, near the Western entrance to the park. Red Rock Lakes are one of the sources of the Missouri River, and in Henry Lake originates one of the branches of the Snake. From Henry Lake are distinctly visible the famous Teton Peaks. Near the western entrance to the park prettily situated on the south fork of the Madison River, is Grayling Inn (Dwelles), the night station for tourists going in and out of the park. After passing through Grayling Inn the road enters the reservation, winding through Christmas Tree Park to Riverside Military station, following the Beautiful Madison River and cañon to the Fountain Hotel in Lower Geyser Basin."[12]

In 1899 the Monida & Yellowstone Stage Company reported it had carried 414 persons from Monida

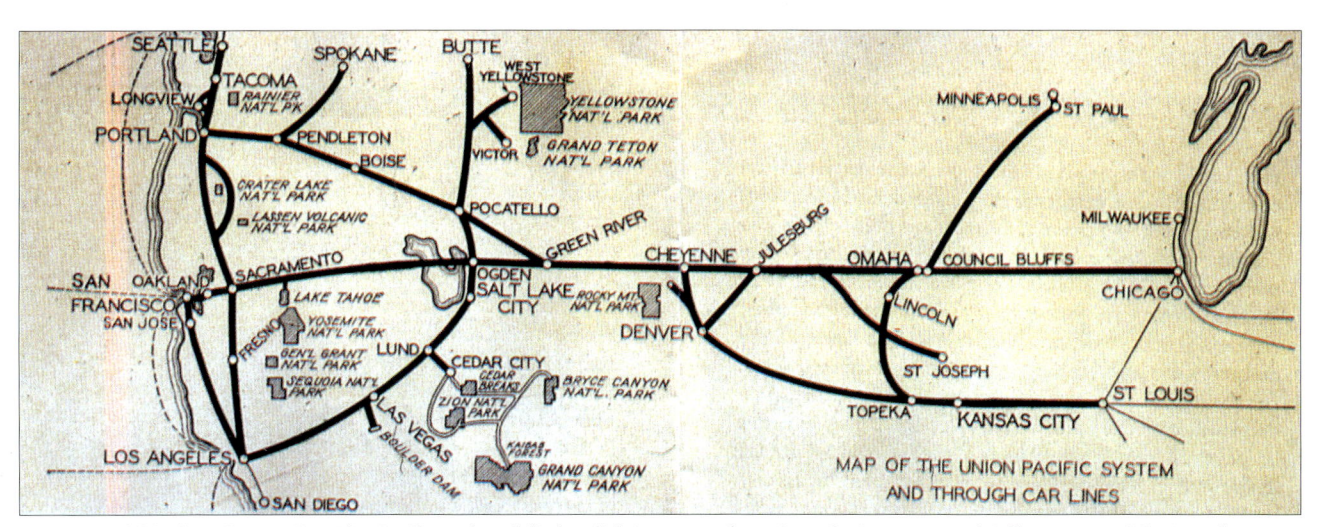

In 1933 the Union Pacific Railroad published this map showing their route to Yellowstone National Park. As was commonly the case, the railroad did not show or mention the other competing rail routes, although they did offer tickets in and out of the other entrances. UNION PACIFIC HISTORICAL COLLECTION

to Mammoth Hot Springs in the park, and brought out 157 through the West Entrance, most of whom had arrived through the north entrance at Cinnabar[13]. However, travel to the park over the Oregon Short Line was not convenient, especially when compared to travel on the Northern Pacific Railroad to the North Entrance, and the Oregon Short Line began to see the potential for passenger business to the park.

At the beginning of the 20th century Oregon Short Line Railroad officials considered building a road from Monida to the park[14] since they knew they had to improve rail service to the park to be competitive with the Northern Pacific. It was almost 10 years, however, before the railroad built what became the Yellowstone Branch from Idaho Falls, Idaho to West Yellowstone, Montana to attract the tourist traffic business to the park. Once the railroad established the railroad to West Yellowstone, the route quickly became the most popular choice of tourists, and the Union Pacific boldly advertised that over 50 percent of the park visitors arriving by rail rode on its trains to West Yellowstone[15].

History of the Yellowstone Branch

Talk of the Yellowstone Branch dated back to the construction of the Utah & Northern Railway north across the Idaho-Montana State Line to Butte in 1880. At that time the railroad considered building a branch line to Yellowstone National Park even while constructing the line north to Butte and Garrison in Montana. At that time the Utah & Northern line was the shortest route to the park, involving a transfer to a stagecoach at Beaver Canyon[16], Idaho for the final leg of the trip to the park. The proposed rail line to the park would run from Beaver Canyon, at the Idaho-Montana state line, east to Yellowstone National Park. By 1883 the railroad was running survey crews from Beaver Canyon east 75 miles to the western edge of the park. However, due to financial difficulties and other pressing needs for money by the railroad construction of this line was never started. The railroad did, however, advertise its route to the park as early as the winter of 1879-1880, when the line was being constructed to Beaver Canyon at the Idaho-Montana State Line.

Over the years there were many proposals concerning a new rail line to the west side of Yellowstone National Park. More than one map published showed a rail route from the Pocatello - Silver Bow line to the west side of the park. An 1880 map showed a line labeled the "Yellowstone Park Branch"[17] running from Beaver Canyon to the park. It is worth noting that maps of this era often had numerous errors, in many cases because they were being used for promotional purposes.

The newspapers promoted, speculated, and reported on rumors associated with a rail line to the park. In 1888 the Eagle Rock paper reported that *"Everyone can take a trip to the Park by rail this fall. A large force of surveyors pitched their tents one mile from town last Thursday....from what we consider good authority we learn that 50 miles of the Park branch will be completed this fall."*

By 1887 United States geologist Arnold Hague was urging the Union Pacific to reach the Yellowstone National Park from the south by constructing a branch line from the Utah & Northern. He was also lobbying, unsuccessfully, for a wagon road to the southwest corner of the park[18]. Jack Blickensderfer, a Dutchman who had helped survey both the Union Pacific's transcontinental line to Promontory and the Utah & Northern into Montana, was chief engineer for the Union Pacific at the time, and the railroad sent him to investigate a route to Yellowstone

The Union Pacific published this advertisement in 1889 for Yellowstone National Park in Salt Lake City.
UNION PACIFIC HISTORICAL COLLECTION, AUTHOR'S COLLECTION

National Park based on this recommendation. His report proposed a line running north and east from Eagle Rock (present-day Idaho Falls), but nothing came of this study for another 20 years. At the same time President Oakes of the Northern Pacific Railroad wrote to President Adams of the Union Pacific Railway, urging him to invest in the Yellowstone Park Association to build three hotels in the park. Oakes felt there was a high potential for tourist revenues, but at the time Adams had more pressing needs for the railroad's money[19] since the Union Pacific was having financial difficulties.

The Union Pacific Railway, predecessor to the Union Pacific Railroad, seriously considered construction of a line to the park as early as 1889. Although the railroad had evaluated building a line to the park boundary prior to that time, no work was done other than to perform surveys. The Oregon Short Line & Utah Northern Railway Company, which was controlled by the Union Pacific[20], ran through eastern Idaho between Ogden, Utah and Butte and Garrison in Montana. On December 14, 1889 the articles of the Oregon Short Line & Utah Northern were amended to allow the construction of several additional rail lines, including the following:

"... a line or lines of railway extending from a point at or near Eagle Rock station in Bingham County, Idaho Territory, on the constructed line of the Oregon Short Line & Utah Northern Railway, thence in a northeasterly direction, in and through the said County of Bingham, to and along the north fork of the Snake River, thence to the north boundary line of Idaho Territory, in Taghee (sic) Pass or Reynolds (sic) Pass, in Bingham County; thence by the most eligible route or routes, in and through the county of Madison and Gallatin, in the State of Montana, to and into the Yellowstone National Park, — the estimated length of said line of railway being 160 miles.

Also a line or lines of railway extending from a point at or near China Point in Bingham County, Idaho Territory, on the constructed line of the Oregon Short Line & Utah Northern Railway, thence in an easterly direction, in and through the said County of Bingham, to a connection with the lines last above described, near Henry Lake, in said Bingham County, — the estimated length of said line of railway being 80 miles.

Also a branch line starting from a point in the line first described, near the mouth of falls River, in Bingham County, Idaho, and running thence northeasterly in and through said County to the eastern boundary line of said territory; thence in and through Uintah County, Wyoming Territory, to the south boundary of Yellowstone National Park, near the mouth of Bechler's Fork, — a distance of about 35 miles.

Also, a branch starting from a point in the line first above described, near the mouth of Warm River; running thence up said river and Willow Creek, to and into said Yellowstone National Park, a distance of about 12 miles.

Also, such other lines or branches as may be deemed necessary or desirable in said Bingham County, Idaho, and Gallatin County, Montana."[21]

Due to the financial problems of the Union Pacific Railway, which controlled the Oregon Short Line, no construction was performed at that time, and it is possible that the railroad simply amended its charter to prevent a competing railroad from building to the west side of the park.

The need for a Union Pacific line to the park was obvious. In 1883 the Northern Pacific ran a line from its main line at Livingston south to Cin-

At the beginning of the 20th century the Union Pacific published a series of promotional brochures titled "Where Gush the Geysers" to compete with the Northern Pacific's "Wonderland" series of booklets. UNION PACIFIC HISTORICAL COLLECTION, COURTESY YELLOWSTONE HERITAGE AND RESEARCH CENTER

nabar, a short distance north of the park. It immediately began advertising the Yellowstone National Park, using a series of colored brochures titled "Wonderland", showing Alice in Wonderland at Yellowstone National Park. By 1897 the railroad was reporting a profit of $18,000 on that section of line[22]. In 1902 the Northern Pacific line was extended south from Cinnabar to Gardiner, at the north entrance to the park, making it even easier to reach the park. One of the Union Pacific general managers felt confident the Union Pacific could earn $30,000 to $50,000 in revenue if the railroad built to a point near the park[23]. The Union Pacific saw the potentials for large profits, but also knew it had to provide a more convenient means of reaching the park than currently provided. The arduous and time-consuming stage travel from Monida, on the Oregon Short Line, could not compete with the ease and convenience of the Northern Pacific's route. In addition, in 1901 the Burlington reached Cody, Wyoming, on the east side of the park, providing even more competition.

The 106.6 mile long Yellowstone Branch of the Union Pacific Railroad was an unusual line since it consisted of two distinct segments, built by two separate railroad companies incorporated with the financial backing of the Union Pacific Railroad. The first section, running north and east from Idaho Falls through the flat countryside 36.8 miles to St. Anthony, was incorporated in 1899 as the St. Anthony Railroad Company and was the first branch line constructed in eastern Idaho. The line served the farming communities in the Upper Snake River Valley and had the passenger and freight service nor-

A view of the southbound train from West Yellowstone going down the Warm River Canyon about 1920. The ride through the Island Park area was scenic, with many opportunities to see wildlife. AUTHOR'S COLLECTION

mally associated with a rural branch line.

The second section, built by the Yellowstone Railroad Company, went from St. Anthony 69.8 miles north and east through the new town of Ashton to the end of the line at West Yellowstone, Montana. This line ran through the sparsely populated and heavily forested area known as Island Park and was built specifically for the summer tourist trade to Yellowstone National Park, providing competition for the Northern Pacific line to the North Entrance at Gardiner and the Chicago, Burlington & Quincy at Cody. Since the principal purpose of the line was to provide passenger service to Yellowstone National Park for tourists, freight service was a secondary consideration, consisting largely of the transportation of forest products from the area and taking supplies to the park in the summer months. The segment of the Yellowstone Branch between Ashton and West Yellowstone was snowed shut every winter and no attempts were ever made to keep the line open due to the deep winter snows and the lack of traffic in the off-season.

The Yellowstone Branch was also noteworthy since the Island Park region which the line traversed en route to West Yellowstone was scenic, with wildlife and scenery that could be viewed from the trains. There were several station stops in Island Park which were used by sportsmen, and one of the stops was for the Harriman family's Railroad Ranch, which was also in Island Park. Members of the Harriman family, which controlled the Union Pacific, would spend their summers at the ranch, and special trains would run to the Island Park siding for the family.

St. Anthony Railroad Company

The Union Pacific was anxious to earn revenues from transporting passengers and freight and consequently promoted settlement in the Upper Snake River Valley. The St. Anthony Railroad Company was incorporated on May 11, 1899 to provide this service. It was capitalized at $500,000 with the backing of the Oregon Short Line and local businessmen. The purpose of the new line was to construct a railroad from Idaho Falls north and east to St. Anthony, providing rail service to open up the Upper Snake River Valley.

The charter of the St. Anthony Railroad Company stated:

"The purpose of which corporation is organized is to construct, own and maintain a railroad and operate the same by steam or other motive power, with such branch lines and extensions as may from time to time be deemed desirable and expedient, and as may be authorized by law.

"The said railroad is to begin at the town of Idaho Falls in Bingham County in said State of Idaho, and extend in a generally northeasterly direction, passing through or near the town of Rexburg, to St. Anthony in Fremont County... the total length of said railroad is thirty-nine miles..."

There was considerable local support for the line, and the area citizens donated land and pledged money so that the railroad would be constructed. In March 1899 William F. Rigby reported to the local church officials on his interview with the Oregon Short Line officials concerning the proposal to build a railroad from Idaho Falls starting in May of that year. The railroad officials were agreeable to the idea of the new line, providing that the citizens would give a free right-of-way for the railroad line. The leading Mormon church officials strongly supported the proposal as well and pledged to obtain the land. Rigby, an official of the Mormon church, was appointed by the railroad to procure the right-of-way and formed the Peoples Railroad Committee. The railroad agreed to acknowledge the deeds for the right-of-way and to give the property owners a silver dollar for consideration of the deeds. All but two persons, who reached private agreements with the railroad, donated their land. The persons who donated the right-of-way also agreed to help construct the line since they were all anxious to receive the benefits of the new railroad[24].

Some people in the outlying communities were hesitant to donate land or money since they doubted the railroad would benefit them. Others set down conditions, such as the one that required the railroad to construct a depot midway between Salem and Teton. The location of siding switches was also an important considerations since they indicated service would be easily available. Others made sure the railroad compensated them for any damages incurred to their crops during the construction work, while some provided their own labor in lieu of a subscription.

The proposed route was presented to the Board of Directors in Pocatello on July 7, 1899, and filed in Blackfoot on that date. Surveyors under the direction of J.C. O'Melveny were soon making the final markings for the new 37.97 mile route. Construction started on July 10, 1899[25], grading officially started on July 24, 1899, and the first rails were laid on August 23, 1899, following delivery of steel rails and ties[26]. The Oregon Short Line received a new steel crane, which was steam operated and had a capacity of 40 tons, to help in the construction of the line. The St. Anthony Lumber Company floated 25,000 ties down the Snake River[27]. Use of volunteer labor slowed the construction since the farmers had to leave to harvest their crops.

The line was completed to Rexburg on November 22, 1899, with a ceremony and special excursion being held on December 7. At this time the cost of the right-of-way was listed as being $543,196, and the construction and other costs were listed at $543,819. The line was not completed to St. Anthony until the following spring and was officially placed in service on June 1, 1900. By that time the St. Anthony Railroad was being listed as an operating subsidiary of the Oregon Short Line[28].

On July 1, 1906, the Oregon Short Line officially leased the St. Anthony Railroad for $15,500 every six months plus interest on any expenditures after the lease date for the equipment and facilities[29]. At that time the railroad was 37.472 miles long from Idaho Falls to St. Anthony, with a branch line of 2.47 miles from what is now Orvin to the new sugar factory at Lincoln, and a second branch line of 10.17 miles from Elva to Menan. There were also branch lines from Sugar City to the Snake River, 5.78 miles, and to the sugar factory at Sugar City, 0.72 miles[30].

The St. Anthony Railroad Company was sold to the Oregon Short Line on October 31, 1910 and officially dissolved on May 11, 1911[31]. The Oregon Short Line agreed to take over the railroad in return for assuming responsibility for any debts of the St. Anthony Railroad Company[32]. At this time W.H. Bancroft, who was president and general manager of the Oregon Short Line, was president of the company.

The first timetable of the railroad was published on December 11, 1899 and showed a daily train between Idaho Falls and St. Anthony. It left Idaho Falls at 8 A.M., and arrived at St. Anthony at 10:50 A.M., after stopping at Rigby and Rexburg. The return trip left St. Anthony at 2:30 P.M. and arrived at Idaho Falls at 5:00 P.M.[33] By 1908 the railroad was running a mixed train in addition to a passenger train in each direction daily. After the line to West Yellowstone was opened in 1909 the *Teton Peak-Chronicle* (St. Anthony) noted the following train schedule when commenting on the change in the train schedule due to the new "Yellowstone flyer", the first summer train running to West Yellowstone:

"Train #175 (Northbound), arrived at 11:30 a.m. and left at 12:01 p.m. Southbound, it arrived at 4:25 p.m., and left at 4:55 p.m. There was also a mixed train that left to the south at 6:30 a.m."[34]

Yellowstone Park Railroad Company

Frank Jay Haynes, who ran the stage from Monida to the park, invited E.H. Harriman of the Union Pacific to ride through the park in 1905. Not only was the ride from Monida to the park long, but the increasing traffic was taxing the capacity of the stage company. Harriman was so impressed with the potential for a line to the park that he immediately authorized the Oregon Short Line to begin surveys and to prepare estimates for the construction of a line to the park[35]. The Yellowstone Park Railroad Company was subsequently incorporated on September 12, 1905 and the articles of incorporation filed with the Secretary of State of Idaho on September 14, 1905. The purpose was to build a new rail line:

"From St. Anthony, in Fremont County, Idaho, connecting with the St. Anthony Railroad Company, and extending in a general northeasterly direction passing near the town of Marysville, and over the main divide of the Rocky Mountains by way of Rea's Pass, to a point near the western boundary of the Yellowstone National Park and three miles more or less easterly from Dwelle's Hotel, a total distance of seventy-five (75) miles, more or less.....

"A line connecting with said line first described, northeasterly of and near the said town of St. Anthony, and extending thence in a northeasterly direction a distance of twenty (20) miles more or less, thence curving to the south and extending in a southerly direction to the town of Victor..."

The railroad was thus authorized to build a line to Yellowstone National Park, which became part of the Union Pacific Railroad's Yellowstone Branch, and to Victor, which became the Union Pacific's Teton Valley Branch when it was completed. The new line had been promoted by local businessmen, including C.C. Moore and Hiram G. Fuller, who wanted the line to be extended into the Teton Basin as well as to Yellowstone National Park.

The Yellowstone Park Railroad Company had a board of directors with nine members, a president, vice president, secretary, and a treasurer, identical to the organization of the St. Anthony Railroad Company[36].

By October 7, 1905 the route for the first 16 miles was proposed by Oregon Short Line Chief Engineer William Ashton. The line was to have a 200-foot right-of-way on public lands, 100 feet on each side of the tracks. The Department of the Interior imposed several stipulations for passing through the Henry's Lake Forest Reserve in the Island Park area. The rail line was not to interfere with the occupation of the land by the government, and no timber was to be taken from outside of the right-of-way. Timber from the right-of-way could be removed, but only as necessary for the construction of the line, and the right-of-way was to be kept clear of brush to protect the land from forest fires. The trains were to use only oil or equivalent and not wood or coal, due to the hazard of the sparks starting a forest fire. In addition, the railroad was to provide, at no cost, assistance in fighting forest fires[37].

By January 5, 1906 the right-of-way to West Yellowstone had been agreed upon, and the next month the location of the station grounds at Yellowstone, in the Madison Forest Reserve, were proposed. In the following months the railroad agreed to pay the Forest Service for the timber and dead wood on the right-of-way, and to maintain, free of charge, all grade crossings. Some slight re-routing was required

A postcard showing stages leaving the West Yellowstone station for the park tour.
YELLOWSTONE HERITAGE & RESEARCH CENTER

to avoid the proposed Flat Rock Reservoir on the Henry's Fork of the Snake River in the Island Park area.

The railroad began grading of the 70-mile line from St. Anthony to Yellowstone National Park on October 1, 1905, and laid the first rails on November 6, 1905. In the October 20, 1905 issue of *Railroad Gazette*, an OSL official wrote that grading was underway from St. Anthony southeast to Marysvale[38], 18 miles. The Utah Construction Company was grading this section of the line. The first train operated north to Marysville on June 15, 1906, a short distance north of St. Anthony.

The October 30, 1906, issue of the *Railroad Gazette* noted that the Yellowstone Park line was opened from St. Anthony to Morrisville, 16 miles, in June 1906. The following March, *Railroad Gazette* noted that the Utah Construction Company, of Ogden, had the contract to extend the line from milepost 40, 23-1/2 miles north of Marysvale to the west boundary of Yellowstone National Park, a total distance of 46-1/2 miles.

In the June 14, 1907, issue of *Railroad Gazette* the OSL reported that the line from St. Anthony to the Madison River entrance to Yellowstone National Park was more than half finished and that laying of the track was intended to be completed by the end of the year. There was still a gap of 15 miles to reach the west entrance to the park. The work through the Warm River Canyon was reported to have been difficult. In October 1907, the *Idaho Falls Times* reported that the officers' car of the OSL was at milepost 55 and that the depot had been moved from milepost 49 to milepost 55, one-quarter mile from Big Springs.

The "Golden Spike" was driven on November 12, 1907[39] and service to Yellowstone, as the terminus was known at the time, started the following spring. The Monida & Yellowstone Stage Company provided the transportation services from the end of the line at Yellowstone through the park.

As each section of line was completed, it was placed in service and its control immediately taken over by the Oregon Short Line. The section from St. Anthony to Ingling was turned over to the Oregon Short Line on June 15, 1906, and on July 1 of the same year the Yellowstone Park Railroad leased its property to the Oregon Short Line. The line from Ingling to Warm River was turned over to operations on July 6, 1908, and the Warm River to Yellowstone section turned over on June 1, 1909. The line was not officially completed until June 1, 1909, although trains had been running since the spring of 1908[40]. The valuation of the new line was placed at $2,530,470[41].

The reason it took two years to build the line through the Island Park region is that the countryside was rugged and isolated, the construction season was short, and the railroad had difficulty obtaining labor[42]. Preparation of the right-of-way was performed from both ends of the line, although the ties and rails were laid from the south end only since the St. Anthony Railroad was used to deliver materials and supplies. In conjunction with the construction of the line to West Yellowstone the railroad laid heavier rail on the line to St. Anthony to conform with the weight of the rails being used on the line being built to the park boundary. The line was busy enough at that time that there was talk in a local paper in 1911 that the line between Idaho Falls and St. Anthony would soon be double-tracked.

Interestingly enough, the construction of the 200-foot-wide right-of-way through the dense forest directly helped in the construction of what became the town of West Yellowstone. As the land was cleared for the new railroad line the trees which were cut down were taken to a new sawmill built on

The Union Pacific route through the Island Park region to West Yellowstone and the loop tour are shown in this promotional brochure for the 1941 season. GADAMUS COLLECTION, YELLOWSTONE HISTORIC CENTER

the South Fork of the Madison. After being cut into lumber, much of this wood was used to construct the first buildings in West Yellowstone[43].

A brief description of the line north of Ashton is interesting, since it shows what construction of the line was like and why the train operations presented a challenge to the railroad. The Yellowstone Branch started at Idaho Falls, at an elevation of 4,708 feet, and climbed to 5,256 feet at Ashton, for a rise in elevation of 548 feet in 51.0 miles. From Ashton the line continued north and crossed the Warm River and began to climb up alongside the Warm River into the Island Park area, which has an elevation of over 6,000 feet. The Island Park region is a caldera, or collapsed volcanic cone, and the Warm River has eroded a small canyon through the wall on the south side, which provided the best route for the railroad. After passing through many relatively flat miles of pine trees and open meadows the line again climbed up to Reas Pass, at an elevation of 6,938, a climb of 1,682 feet in the 46 miles from Ashton. The line then dropped down to West Yellowstone, which is at an elevation of 6,669 feet, a loss in elevation of 269 feet in 9 miles[44]. The snow in Island Park, and at Reas Pass in particular, has always been extremely deep, and the winters severe, with the deep snows typically lasting into the late spring.

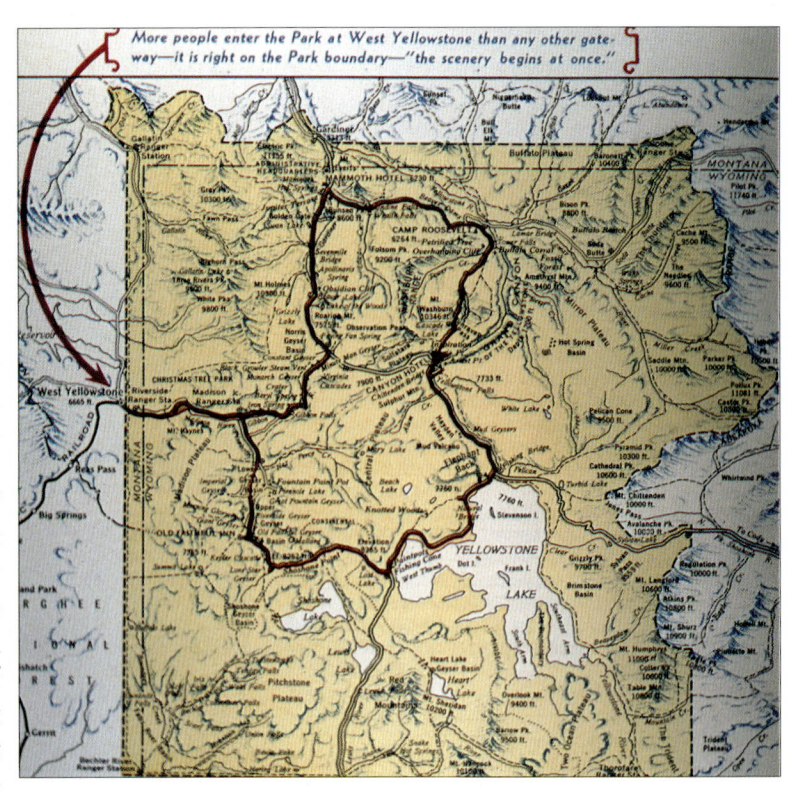

The Yellowstone Branch ended at West Yellowstone, Montana, and the terminal was a busy location in the summer months due to the numerous passenger trains arriving and departing as well as the services provided at West Yellowstone for the railroad travelers. Consequently, extensive facilities were constructed at West Yellowstone over the years.

The Town of West Yellowstone

The railroad reached the western edge of Yellowstone National Park in the fall of 1907 at what was then known as Riverside, since the location was near the Riverside Ranger Station in the park. The first post office was opened as Riverside on October 23, 1908, but the name was changed to Yellowstone by November 17, 1909. This, in turn, became too confusing for the post office, and the name was changed to West Yellowstone on January 7, 1920[45]. Apparently the railroad considered building into the park to reach the Riverside station, but decided to end the line at the park boundary instead[46].

With the arrival of the railroad, businesses were established in West Yellowstone to serve the tourists. These new businesses were built across from the depot on Yellowstone Avenue. Following the increased popularity of the automobile the business district shifted to Canyon Avenue, the main road through the town, so that the town has developed in a "T" shape. The town developed to the north and to the west of the railroad depot since it was bounded on the east by the park and by the railroad on the south.

As soon as the railroad was completed to West Yellowstone, the company began construction of a depot, eating house, and other facilities, often using local building materials, including wood and stone from the area. The railroad used a temporary depot and eating facility in the first summer, and the present depot was not completed until October 31, 1909[47]. In front of the depot there was a train yard, with one main track and several other tracks for the cars laying over during the day.

The railroad had a significant impact on the development of the town, indicated by the fact that in 1910 the railroad had a property value of $29,050, while the rest of the townsite had an assessed value of only $7,000[48]. The railroad planned to buy land for a one-million-dollar resort hotel to be built near the depot, but the plans were canceled in 1913[49]. In 1921 the railroad officially received title for land southeast of the depot for possible use for a hotel[50] but the building was never constructed. The railroad kept ownership of the land, which was south of the depot and tracks, and sold it in July 1990 to the Firehole Land Corporation to develop a grizzly bear park for tourists[51].

Train Operations to West Yellowstone

Operation of the line through Island Park required a lot of work by the railroad. The trains had to have a pusher, or helper engine, for the steep grade from Ashton up to Reas Pass, where the helper engines dropped off, turned around on a wye, and then returned to Ashton. Five cars were all that one of the steam locomotives could handle, and a sixth car would cause the locomotive to stall on the grade unless a helper engine was used. In Warm River Canyon the railroad hugged the west side of the canyon wall above the river bank, and over the years the line experienced severe problems in that area due to rockslides. On May 12, 1908, the *Idaho Falls Times* reported that a steam shovel and work crew from Ashton were being sent up onto the Park Branch, as it was then known, to clear slides from the tracks. The St. Anthony newspaper, the *Teton Peak-Chronicle* wrote the following on June 11, 1908:

> *"Men and women - hotel managers, clerks, bell hops, cooks, dishwashers, janitors, waiters/waitresses and chambermaids stalled in Pocatello on a special train of tourist sleepers. They are bound for Yellowstone park to open the string of hotels in the Wonderland of America, and came up special on the Short Line from Salt Lake last night in a train consisting of a baggage car, one day coach, a diner and 3 tourist sleepers. They are held here on account of a landslide in Warm river canyon on the Park branch which happened sometime early this morning. The Park branch construction crew is at work today clearing the track, and everything is expected to be fixed up by this evening."*

In 1916 the railroad reported that it was going to construct a tunnel to avoid the worst section of the rockslides at Warm River. This 557-foot tunnel was, in fact, built shortly after the announcement, at mile post 62.7 of the railroad in the Warm River Canyon. It was built through a solid rock outcropping and then partially lined with timbers. Wooden portals at both ends protected the tunnel openings from falling rocks[52].

Passenger service was provided on the line north of Ashton as the line was being built, with stage connections to the park. The first passenger train, called the *Yellowstone Limited*[53], arrived at Marysville, north of Ashton, Idaho on June 15, 1906, where connections were made with the Yellowstone-Western Stage Company[54]. In the following summer stage connections were made at the end-of-track at Big Springs. The first scheduled passenger train to West Yellowstone, Montana arrived on June 11, 1908[55] and continued until service was permanently discontinued at the end of the 1960 summer season[56]. During World War II there was no scheduled passenger service to West Yellowstone, with all trains on the Yellowstone Branch ending at Ashton. In addition to providing passenger service to the park, the trains also catered to fishermen who wanted to spend some time in Island Park, the area to the south. They would stop at sidings such as Trude and Big Springs to let sportsmen off for a few days of fishing. The sportsmen would stay at lodges in the area.

The railroad traffic on the two sections of the Yellowstone Branch was totally different. The southern end, from Idaho Falls north to Ashton, had the normal agricultural products and farm goods, both inbound and outbound, as did the extension of the line through the Teton Valley to Victor. In addition, the year-round passenger service was that typical of an agricultural community, with drummers, businessmen, and local people traveling on the trains.

The northern end, from Ashton to West Yellowstone, however, consisted largely of outbound loads of cattle and logs and timber to be cut at the mills in towns such as St. Anthony and Rexburg. Inbound freight consisted mostly of gasoline and other supplies for the town of West Yellowstone as well as goods and supplies for the operations run by the railroad at West Yellowstone and for the services in

The Union Pacific was quick to note that more than one-half of the park visitors who arrived by rail traveled on the Union Pacific. This advertisement, printed for travel agents at the end of the 1923 season, was typical of the cartoon bear ads they published between 1923 and 1960. These advertisements invaribly included the Union Pacific shield and the bears seen at the park. This one also showed their name train, the *Yellowstone Special*. UNION PACIFIC HISTORICAL COLLECTION

the park itself.

There was also the seasonal summer passenger traffic, with regularly scheduled and numerous special passenger trains passing over the line to and from West Yellowstone. These passenger trains were scheduled only from mid-June through early September. In the spring and fall only freight trains were operated since the population north of Ashton was too low to support a daily passenger train; a weekly mixed freight was adequate to serve the line from Ashton to West Yellowstone. As an example of this service, in early May 1922 the railroad stated that *"Train service between Ashton and West Yellowstone will begin operation Saturday May 13. This will be mixed-train service each Saturday from Ashton until the opening of the park season when this service will be continued for freight only."*[57]

At the opening of the park season the railroad would schedule its daily passenger train service to and from West Yellowstone. This mixed train service would be reinstated in the fall when the park season had ended until the line was closed by the snow. The mixed train service was again started up in the spring following the spring campaign.

The line was reopened every spring with a special "Spring Campaign". The railroad assembled two trains and a large crew. A wedge plow would clear the tracks until the snow got too deep and then a rotary plow would remove the snow from the tracks. The second train provided eating, sleeping, and maintenance facilities for the crew. It typically took up to four days to open the line and the arrival of the train was greeted by the populace in West Yellowstone since it signaled the end of winter. School was let out so the children could greet the train, and a large party was held that evening.

When the Yellowstone Branch was completed the Union Pacific Railroad immediately began advertising train service to West Yellowstone and offered tours from the West Entrance through the park. The advertising appears to have had an effect. Even before the line had been completed to West Yellowstone, travel to the park was increasing. In 1898 the Monida & Yellowstone Stage Company took 154 tourists to the park from Monida and in 1907, the last year of service, 2,270 tourists traveled on the Monida & Yellowstone Stage Companycoaches[58]. There was a total of 16,414 park visitors that year[59]. The next year 7,172 visitors arrived through the West Entrance, out of a total of 18,748 park visitors, due in large part to the arrival of the railroad and the inauguration of passenger service to the West Entrance[60].

A report issued by the park service, commenting on the new railroad, noted that " *... This will undoubtedly increase the tourist travel in the park in 1908, especially by the western entrance. The terminal station will be on the park boundary, and many people are already asking for leases on the national forest border-*

A view of the Spring Campaign at High Bridge, about the year 1909. The rotary plow required several steam locomotives to push it through the deep snows. AUTHOR'S COLLECTION

The Union Pacific staged a large Spring Campaign about March of every year to open the Yellowstone Branch, which was snowed shut every winter. A large work train and crew took several days to re-open the line north of Ashton after the winter's heavy snows. This view is from about 1920. AUTHOR'S COLLECTION

The Union Pacific operated two trains a day to West Yellowstone in the summer season in the years between World War I and World War II. The trains were known as the *Yellowstone Special* and the *Yellowstone Express*. This timetable for the 1929 summer season shows the trains scheduled trips to coincide with the train which went to Victor to reach the newly opened Grand Teton National Park. One could travel on a sleeping car between Chicago, Portland and St. Louis to and from West Yellowstone.

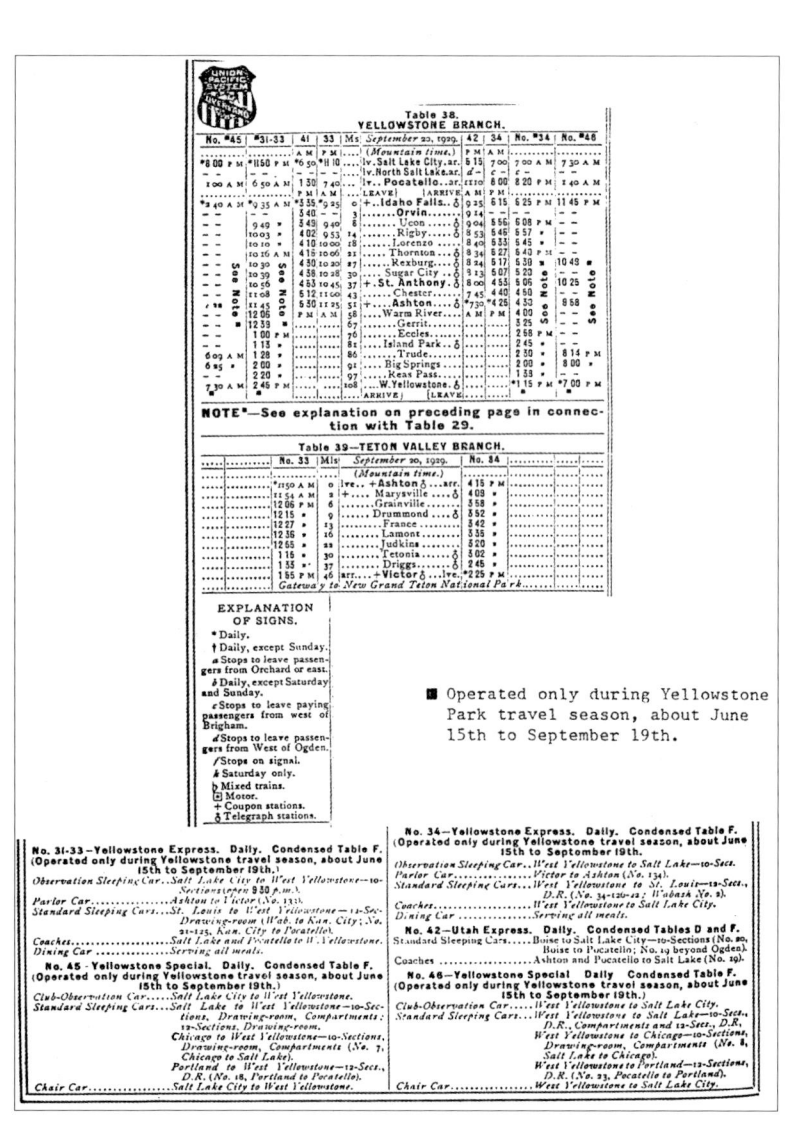

ing on the park boundary."

The number of park visitors through West Yellowstone increased to 10,783 in 1912. In 1915 it skyrocketed to 32,551, with 29,706 of them arriving by rail. The number coming through the west entrance dropped due to World War I, and didn't recover in 1919, when only 23,558 people arrived at the west entrance, 8,897 of them by train. The railroads hoped that the new autocamps were a fad, and that the travelers would return to their trains. With an autocamp the travelers could avoid the rigid schedules associated with train travel, and eat and travel when and where they pleased.

In 1923 the railroad offered through sleepers to West Yellowstone from Chicago and St. Louis on the *Yellowstone Special*. This train had an observation car and standard sleeping cars, arriving at West Yellowstone in time for breakfast in the morning and departing in the evening for Ogden and Salt Lake City. There were also through sleeping cars from the Pacific Northwest, and connections from Los Angeles and San Francisco were available at Salt Lake City and Ogden[61]. Travel to the park increased dramatically in the 1920s and was so heavy that the *Yellowstone Special* stopped providing local service to St. Anthony.

To accommodate the increasing traffic the Oregon Short Line added a daylight train, the *Yellowstone Express*, between Salt Lake City and West Yellowstone in the 1922 season. The train had a diner, observation car, Pullman, day coach, and chair car[62]. The new *Yellowstone Express* originated in Salt Lake City late at night, left Pocatello in the morning, and arrived at West Yellowstone in the early afternoon, with lunch being served in the dining car. Travelers could reach their park destination in time for dinner in the park that evening. The southbound *Yellowstone Express* left West Yellowstone in the early afternoon and arrived at Pocatello in the evening before continuing south to Salt Lake City.

There were also numerous special trains and extra sections of the scheduled trains. To accommodate the increase in traffic the railroad also upgraded the line to West Yellowstone. In 1924 the rails were replaced north of Ashton and the line was reballasted from Idaho Falls to Ashton[63].

The recommended tour was a four-and-a-half-day trip starting at West Yellowstone. Stopover privileges were available for locations such as Rocky Mountain National Park in Denver, and the tour through Yellowstone was also available as a side trip on other journeys. There was the option of longer stays for trips to locations such as the Teton Mountains in the Teton National Forest.

Train service to West Yellowstone was discontinued during World War II starting in 1943 and reinstated in 1946. However, noting the decline in train travel, the railroad chose to reinstate only the *Yellowstone Special*. Following an initial surge of traffic, the number of passengers on the Union Pacific slowly decreased, and all train service to West Yellowstone was discontinued at the end of the 1960 season.

In 1961, the first year the railroad no longer offered passenger service to West Yellowstone, a traveler could get off the *Parks Special* train at Ashton in the early morning and get on a Yellowstone Park Company bus to ride to West Yellowstone. They would have breakfast at the Stage Coach Inn in West Yellowstone since the Dining Lodge was no longer open. The *Parks Special* train continued on to Victor, where passengers had breakfast and traveled on buses operated by the Grand Teton Lodge Company. They went over Teton Pass to Jackson, Wyoming, and through the Grand Teton National Park[64] to Yellowstone National Park. They could then continue their bus ride to Ashton, where they would board the train for their return trip home. This was not a convenient schedule for the passengers, and the passenger train service was soon cut back to Idaho Falls, and finally Pocatello before the Union Pacific ended its passenger service in 1971. Probably the last passenger train to travel to West Yellowstone was a special train operated by the Idaho Falls Chamber of Commerce, run to West Yellowstone to celebrate the park's birthday. It ran on May 16, 1964, carrying several hundred passengers[65].

The West Entrance Road

Although the railroad reached the western boundary of the park, it was a 30-mile ride over the West Entrance road to Old Faithful and 47 miles to Mammoth Hot Springs. The history of the West Entrance road dates back to 1873, when Gilman Sawtell built a road from Virginia City through Madison Canyon to the Lower Geyser Basin. He owned a hotel near Henry's Lake in Idaho Territory, and called the new road The Virginia City and National Park Free Road, to contrast it with the toll road at the North Entrance. By 1877 the road was almost impassable due to fallen trees and other obstacles, and by 1880

The Union Pacific was able to offer the services of a surrey for a tour through the park in this advertisement from about 1912. UNION PACIFIC HISTORICAL COLLECTION, COURTESY BEN OSTENSON

The railroad printed this brochure for Yellowstone National Park in 1912. The railroad also promoted travel to other destinations along their line, in this case Colorado. UNION PACIFIC HISTORICAL COLLECTION, COURTESY BEN OSTENSON

the road along the Madison River was almost impassable for much of the year. Explorations led to a new route south of the Madison River to the park boundary at Riverside. Park Superintendent Norris was surprised to find this new route along the plateau, which he said was preferable since it was drier and shorter[66].

In 1896 the Army engineers improved the section of the road in the park and built a bridge across the Madison River. A few years later the engineers noted that the location of the road would have to be changed and improved due to the proposed railroad terminus and hotel at Riverside, about four miles inside the park boundary. Some work was done to improve the road in 1908, and the railroad ended outside of the park boundary at what is now West Yellowstone[67].

The road in the park was improved in 1912-13 by widening it from 12 to 18 feet and surfacing it with gravel, and in 1914 preparations were made to oil it. In the same year the president of the Yellowstone Western Stage Company, F.J. Haynes, stated that he was concerned that the road would not be able to accommodate the traffic resulting from the 1915 Panama-Pacific International Exposition in San Francisco. He also opposed construction of a hotel at the west entrance. The entire road from West Yellowstone to Madison Junction was widened again in 1916, and the first five miles from West Yellowstone were surfaced with oil macadam. A new guard gate and ranger station were built at the entrance in 1924, and in the 1930s the entire road was oiled and graveled[68].

Facilities at West Yellowstone

Even before the railroad reached Riverside on November 12, 1907 the railroad was promoting travel through West Yellowstone to the park and preparing to develop facilities at their new terminal. The local touring companies, the Wylie Permanent Camping Company and the Monida and Yellowstone Stage Company, were constructing larger tenting facilities for tourists near what became West Yellowstone as early as 1907. The Wylie Company even cut its own trail from the railroad terminal through the trees to their tent camp. Berg Clark, an early employee of the company, met the first train at West Yellowstone and transported "3 dudes" to Old Faithful and back[69].

Apparently an old boxcar served as the railroad depot in the first season, since a permanent depot had not been completed[70]. The railroad needed the rail line to be completed so that the necessary materials could be brought in to build the new facilities. The new depot was not completed until October 31, 1909[72], so that it was not used until the 1910 season. Rock from the nearby right-of-way was used to build the structure. The station, which was designed by the railroad, had the usual facilities of a railroad depot, including concrete platforms by the tracks, a waiting room and ticket office, and a door on the north side leading to the stages that transported the tourists through the park. The station also had some unusual features, including change rooms and extra baggage storage space in the west wing. The west wing of the depot also included a men's waiting room, restroom, and change room as well as a bootblack shop. The east wing had a women's waiting room, change room, and restroom. The change rooms had showers, which were a necessity since the tourists traveled over dirt and gravel roads in the park and wanted to be able to refresh themselves before boarding the train for their trip home. The central section of the depot had a ticket office and Pullman office. The west wing had a small basement which contained a small boiler to heat the building in the cooler periods of the summer, although no attempts were ever made to keep the building warm during the rest of the year.

The railroad depot building was 110 feet on the front, with two wings, 53 feet long on the west side and 72 feet long on the east side. The exterior of the building was never altered, although the interior was modified and changed over the years. Major modifications were made on the building in 1922 when the new baggage building was constructed. The east wing of the depot was converted into dressing rooms and additional toilet facilities were installed. The west wing of the depot originally housing the baggage and express room became the ladies lounge at this time. Shower baths for the men were also added. The porte cochere was extended to shelter the buses and the platforms on the north side were widened. The concrete platform by the tracks was also extended to the west to accommodate the longer trains being run.

The railroad built a 52- x 32-foot baggage building to the west of the depot in 1922 to accommodate the growing summer tourist trade. This building also had a stone veneer to blend in with the depot. Travel tended to be a more formal affair in this period, and as a result some of the travelers brought a

A view of the original "beanery" at West Yellowstone. The Union Pacific was the only railroad to provide such extensive facilities at their terminal. After arriving at West Yellowstone in the morning, the passengers would eat breakfast here before starting their park tour, and they would have dinner at the "beanery" before boarding the train for their return trip. Although the Union Pacific did expand it shortly after it was opened, the railroad built a new, larger Dining Lodge in 1925 to handle the big crowds. AUTHOR'S COLLECTION

A trackside view of the facilities at West Yellowstone about 1922. The dense lodgepole pine forests went to the edge of the tracks. The park boundary is directly behind the depot. AUTHOR'S COLLECTION

The tourists would board the stages in front of the depot for their trip through the park. AUTHOR'S COLLECTION

large number of trunks and baggage for their formal wear for the dances and dinners held at the hotels in the park.

The first dining lodge used by the railroad was a simple tarpaper building. In 1911 this was replaced by a long, low one-story yellow building, known as "the beanery"[72]. After several years this building became inadequate to handle the increasing volume of passengers, despite at least one addition to the building in 1922, when a 40 foot x 62 foot wing for a new kitchen was added[73].

A new, larger dining lodge designed by well-known architect Gilbert Stanley Underwood was constructed in 1925 and opened in the summer[74]. Underwood used native rhyolite stone for the foundation, piers, walls, chimneys, and fireplaces. Logs, both peeled and unpeeled, were used for the posts, trusses, brackets, ridgepoles, and beams. The siding was made from custom milled red fir bark slabs. Its design was intended to blend in with the surrounding wood and rock environment of the adjacent forestland.

The east end of the dining lodge was known at the Firehole Room, after a location in Yellowstone National Park, and the large dining area in the west end of the lodge was designated as the Mammoth Room for another location in the park. The Dining Lodge covered 17,000 square feet, with 7,500 square feet in the Mammoth Room, which had a 45-foot-high ceiling. The Firehole Room had a bar and both rooms had fireplaces large enough to walk in. There was another, smaller room to the north, called the Rainbow Room, along with restrooms. There was also a large kitchen 50 feet x 64 feet on the north end of the building and a 24 foot x 117 foot storeroom. In 1930 new doors were added on the north side of the lodge. The dining room had a capacity of 300 persons, and could feed 900-1,000 at a meal[75]. Passengers arriving at West Yellowstone would get off the train and have their morning meal before boarding their stages or buses to tour the park. The "Beanery Queens" would greet the guests by singing to them as they walked from their train to the Dining Lodge for breakfast.

The Union Pacific's Dining Car & Hotel Department (DC&H) operated the facilities at West Yellowstone since they were an integral part of the railroad operations. In addition to the dining services on the trains this department was also responsible for operating the dining lodges in the Utah Parks and Sun Valley when they were opened.

A view of the West Yellowstone facilities taken from the railroad water tank about 1927. The employee dormitories are on the extreme left, and the building with the large chimneys is the Dining Lodge. The baggage building is behind it and the depot can be seen in the background on the left side of the tracks. The town of West Yellowstone is to the left of the railroad facilities. The train yard had several tracks to hold the trains and a wye on the right so that they could be turned around for the return trip. AUTHOR'S COLLECTION

The second section of Train #45 has just arrived at West Yellowstone and the passengers are walking to the "beanery" for their breakfast in this view from about 1923. AUTHOR'S COLLECTION

In the first years the tour groups traveled through the park in horse-drawn stages, which were replaced by automobiles that carried small groups in 1917. The tour guides would drop off the travelers at the end of their four-and-a-half-day tour in front of the depot in the late afternoon so they could have dinner before boarding the train for their return trip. For many years the firm of Smith and Chandler would take pictures of the travelers departing the depot for their park tour in their buses, and when the tourists returned to the West Yellowstone depot at the end of their trip they could purchase the pictures to show to family and friends back home.

In 1925 the Union Pacific had a staff of 40 employees at the West Yellowstone Dining Lodge, typically local residents and college students, many of them children of Union Pacific officials from Omaha. The meals at the Dining Lodge were served by the "Beanery Queens", and they could serve 500 to 600 people at a time quickly and efficiently. When train travel to West Yellowstone was at its peak the Dining Lodge served up to 1,000 brook trout for breakfast and dinner along with 18 prime ribs of beef and more than 2,000 fresh rolls each day[76]. The railroad shipped up a refrigerator car full of food each week from Ogden, and an ice car was taken to West Yellowstone with ice to keep the food cold. In addition, local farmers supplied milk, cream, and eggs.

The train operations at West Yellowstone also required a large number of employees who worked there in the summer months only. The employees typically lived in railroad bunk cars spotted on the tracks near the depot or small cabins in the summer months. Some employees brought their families up with them for the summer. The conductors and other train employees often slept during the day in the Pullman cars, tipping the porters for the privilege. Others simply relaxed and went fishing during their layover between the morning and evening trains.

After eating breakfast the tourists would wait on the station platform to board their autobus to take them through the park. AUTHOR'S COLLECTION

After the Dining Lodge was built many summer employees used the older Eating House for lodging, but that was not adequate. To alleviate the problem of lodging the railroad built a 38 foot x 82 foot dormitory in 1927 for its employees[77]. The dormitory was designed by Underwood and constructed to the west of the dining lodge. This new building was also designed to match the other buildings and to blend in with the existing surroundings. It replaced the outfit cars which had been spotted each summer on the siding tracks.

The railroad built a 24 foot diameter, 65,000-gallon steel water tank on a steel framework in 1910, filling it with water pumped from a well[78]. Prior to this, water used by the railroad and for the construction work as well as for the horses drawing the coaches was piped in using a surface line from a spring near the South Fork of the Madison River, two-and-a-quarter miles away[79]. To the west of the Dining Lodge and dormitory there was a freight house, with corrugated metal sides and roof. No efforts were made to blend this building in with the local architecture. There was a large number of freight forwarding outfits that also used this building, and much of the construction material for the buildings at West Yellowstone and in the park itself was handled through this building. Railroad tank cars were also used to ship in the oil used to pave the park roads.

The railroad installed an electric light plant in 1918[80] and by 1946 it was used to generate electricity to power a 200 gallon-per-minute water pump which drew the water from a well up into the overhead water tank. The power plant also provided lighting for the other railroad facilities. The three-cylinder Mercedes-Benz engine also provided the power for the city when there was a local power failure. This building and the generator are also still standing.

The yard tracks ended at the park boundary. In addition to the yard tracks there was a wye where the engines and cars would be turned for the return trip in the evening. If there were numerous sections of the train, the process would be very time consuming and could take most of the day. A lumber mill on the rail end of the wye was the major source of freight revenue on the line before it was abandoned.

Gasoline came in on railroad cars in 55-gallon drums but later on it was delivered in tank cars and spotted on a siding by the local gasoline company. This was soon deemed dangerous since it was so close to the passenger cars in the yard and a bulk fuel unloading area was then developed west of the freight depot, farther away from the passenger depot.

When the passenger trains stopped running in early September only the freight service continued until the line was snowed shut. After the freight trains stopped running in the late fall the railroad would keep a man on the payroll at West Yellowstone to shovel the deep snow off the roofs of their buildings. After the Spring Campaign, when the winter snow was cleared from the line, freight service would start up again.

It is about 1911 and Train #16 is ready to leave West Yellowstone. The passengers are boarding the train for their trip south.
AUTHOR'S COLLECTION

The southbound train has stopped along the Warm River Canyon for the photographer, about 1919. AUTHOR'S COLLECTION

West Yellowstone Today

The Depression, World War II, and the family automobile all took a toll on railroad passenger travel to West Yellowstone, although rail travel did increase briefly following the Depression, just prior to World War II. The Dining Lodge was closed during World War II and reopened for the 1946 season as the tourism business began to rebound. The last of the regularly scheduled passenger train in the 1959 season ran to West Yellowstone on August 17, when the Hebgen Lake earthquake damaged sections of the line. After that, travel to the park was provided through Victor for the remainder of the 1959 season. The railroad did not feel the small number of travelers justified reopening the line for passenger traffic for what little time remained that summer. The Union Pacific offered passenger service to West Yellowstone for the last time in the 1960 season, ending over 50 years of passenger service to the park boundary.

Following the end of passenger service to West Yellowstone the future of the West Yellowstone facilities and the entire line looked bleak, and there were rumors the railroad would tear down the buildings at West Yellowstone. However, after many years of negotiations the railroad agreed to donate the buildings at West Yellowstone to the town, provided the citizens incorporated the town. This condition was met and in 1966 the first mayor of West Yellowstone was elected. On May 23, 1969 the town accepted the terminal facility buildings[81]. The town used the water tank for its water system for several years, although today it is no longer in use.

Freight service on the line to West Yellowstone was always small. With the exception of a small lumber mill at West Yellowstone, some minor wood-related sidings along the line and the seasonal livestock traffic there was no freight business on the line. The lack of a traffic base hurt the line to West Yellowstone, especially as more and more traffic turned to trucks. With the loss of the livestock business and timber traffic to trucks there was little need for the line. Finally, the only business on the section of the Yellowstone Branch north of Ashton was at West Yellowstone, where there was a small lumber mill. In the last few years of operation through the late 1970s, the railroad would run a weekly freight train up to West Yellowstone from Ashton to transport out carloads of wood chips and other wood products. Finally the lumber company, which was just south of the depot at West Yellowstone, closed. Since there was no longer any justification for keeping the line open, permission to abandon it was granted by the Interstate Commerce Commission on July 29, 1979. Proposals to maintain the line

It is August 7, 1949, and H.R. Griffiths took this view of the *Yellowstone Special* at Trude, in the Island Park area, with seven cars. The train made an impressive sight with two steam locomotives pulling it up towards Reas Pass and West Yellowstone. PHOTO H.R. GRIFFITHS, AUTHOR'S COLLECTION

August 8, 1949 had the *Yellowstone Special* leaving Big Springs for West Yellowstone. Two locomotives were needed to carry the train up Reas Pass at the Idaho-Montana border and the Continental Divide. PHOTO H.R. GRIFFITHS, AUTHOR'S COLLECTION

On July 14, 1951 the *Yellowstone Special* was photographed approaching the Warm River tunnel. The train has eight cars and is traveling at 20 mph due to the grade up through the canyon. PHOTO H.R. GRIFFITHS, AUTHOR'S COLLECTION

for a tourist railroad or to serve the small amount of business remaining never materialized. The tracks were pulled up in the summer of 1981.

In 1972 the Museum of the Yellowstone opened in the West Yellowstone depot for the summer tourist trade. The baggage building was converted into town offices, including the town jail and police station. The Dining Lodge took longer to develop. Although a few meetings were held in the lodge over the years nothing permanent was done until 1981, when the town library was moved into a corner of the building. In 1984 the town rented the dining lodge to the Federation of Fly Fishers (FFF) for use as their headquarters, and it also housed the International Fly Fishing center. The fly fishing museum moved to Livingston after several years, leaving the building vacant except for the city library and courthouse facilities. In addition to being headquarters for the FFF the town used the facilities for local events, including the local high school graduation ceremonies. The library was moved out in early 2005 and there are currently plans to stabilize the Dining Lodge so that it will not continue to deteriorate.

In 1983 the railroad facilities at West Yellowstone were accepted on the National Register of Historic Places as the Oregon Short Line Terminus Historic District[82]. Once the building was on the National Register matching funds were obtained from the Montana Historical Society for renovation work, including re-shingling the building.

By utilizing the railroad buildings for a variety of purposes, the town has been able to maintain the buildings and put them to beneficial uses at a minimal cost. It is likely that the buildings will be used for many years in the same fashion, providing a reminder of the era when passenger trains arrived and departed West Yellowstone.

There is one additional, interesting feature near the depot. There is a large stone pylon with the Union Pacific shield on two sides at the boundary between the park and the railroad lands. Although the tracks have been gone for many years, the cornerstone is a prominent reminder of the time when the Union Pacific reached West Yellowstone. It was recently restored and repainted and made part of a small city park.

There are other reminders of the railroad era at West Yellowstone. In the summer of 1995 the West Yellowstone Conference Hotel was opened, near the station. A 1903 business car, which had been converted into a summer home in West Yellowstone, was restored and incorporated into the restaurant building, and the restaurant was named the Oregon Short Line Restaurant, with a railroad theme for the decor. The Grizzly Discovery Center was also opened south of the former right-of-way, with grizzly bears exhibits on the land once owned by the Union Pacific Railroad. In 2004 the Museum of the Yellowstone had one of the cars from the 1964 Montana Centennial Train moved from the business district onto some rails laid in front of the depot. There are plans to restore the car.

The town of West Yellowstone is prospering with the tourist trade and is a major gateway to the park from the south and west. In 2000 it had a year-round population of 1,177[83]. In addition, the winter business has also helped the local economy, as snow machine owners ride the trails in the national forests. However, starting in the winter of 2003-2004 the National Park Service began putting regulations in effect which reduced the traffic in order to reduce noise and air pollution. The impact of these regulations on the town's economy is still being evaluated.

The Railroad Line to West Yellowstone Today

Although the tracks to West Yellowstone have been removed, the roadbed of the Ashton-Yellowstone section is clearly obvious, even while becoming overgrown with bushes and trees, and it is used throughout the year for recreation. Snow machines run up and down it in the winter, all-terrain vehicles use it in the spring, summer, and fall, and it is also a popular trail bike route. Instead of a railroad buckboard crossing sign where the railroad crossed the back country roads, there are now signs warning automobile drivers of the presence of ATVs on the railroad roadbed. The tunnel at Warm River, which can be seen from State Highway 47 at Bear Gulch, is still in good condition and is part of the recreational trail. The line from Idaho Falls north to Ashton is still busy with trains run by the short line Eastern Idaho Railroad, carrying agricultural products, although most of the railroad facilities have been removed.

Gilbert Stanley Underwood, Architect

Gilbert Stanley Underwood was one of the few architects hired by the Union Pacific to design its stations. He worked for the railroad in the peak years between World War I and the Depression. Among his commissions were two buildings at West Yellowstone for the Union Pacific Railroad, the Dining Lodge and the employee dormitory. He was also the architect for facilities at Bryce, Zion and Grand Canyon national parks and the Cedar Breaks National Monument. The latter were designed for the Utah Parks Company, a subsidiary of the Union Pacific Railroad. He also designed Old Faithful Lodge, located near Old Faithful Inn, in Yellowstone National Park. Many of his buildings are still standing, and some of them are on the National Register of Historic Places due to their unique and attractive designs.

A California architect, Underwood spent some of his most productive years, just prior to the Depression, designing stations for the Union Pacific and facilities in the southern Utah national parks. His last commissions for the Union Pacific were the designs of the Sun Valley Lodge and the Challenger Inn at Sun Valley during the Depression.

Underwood was born in 1890 in Oneida, New York and moved to the West Coast shortly after the turn of the century. He lived with his widowed mother in San Bernardino, California, and enrolled in San Bernardino High School. He quit school at age 18, before he graduated, and worked for a local architect. This type of on-the-job training was common at the time, since there was no formal training for architects. He continued his apprenticeship in the architectural profession by working for several other California architects. One of the architects he worked for was Arthur Benton, who was called a master of the Mission style, which had simple and honest lines. This greatly influenced Underwood's styles in later years, as evidenced by the design of several of his railroad stations for the Union Pacific.

After a year with Benton, Underwood left to work for Arthur Kelly in 1911. Kelly designed Craftsman style houses, which accentuated the use of natural materials and Indian designs. This work, too, influenced Underwood, as shown in his Rustic style designs. Following his work for Kelly, Underwood then went on to the University of Illinois in 1912 to study to become a certified architect. One of the friendships he developed at school was with Daniel Hull, who later helped him obtain commissions through the National Park Service and with the Utah Parks Company.

Underwood soon married and quit school before obtaining his degree, and spent the next several years moving around the country. After taking various classes during his moves, he eventually settled down at Yale University to obtain his B.A. degree in 1920. While he was at Yale he won a competition sponsored by a society of French architects, the "La Societe des Architectes Diplomes par le Gouvernement". Although he won the prize and the chance to study a year at the Ecole des Beaux Arts, he was not able to afford the costs of a year abroad since the prize did not include enough money to support his wife and children.

Underwood then enrolled in graduate school at Harvard University in 1921. He continued his studies and worked part-time as an architect, hiring other students to help him finish his architect work when he had to meet deadlines. He won the Avery Prize while he was at Harvard and received his master's degree from Harvard University in 1923. By this time his classmate Hull was assistant to Stephen Mather, director of the Park Service, a fact which contributed greatly to his future work.

Following his graduation in 1923 Underwood moved to Los Angeles to open his own office. California was a growing state and construction was booming, so he apparently felt there were opportunities in the state. At the same time, the National Park Service was starting on a large building program. The Park Service had been established in 1916 with a small budget, and it wasn't until after the World War I that it received funding large enough to start developing park facilities. The Park Service at that time felt the buildings should blend with the land and be nonintrusive, a new concept for the period. Prior to the National Park Service, the wilderness areas had been under the direction of the U.S. Army, so that all of the buildings looked the same in all parts of the country and were strictly utilitarian and redundant.

The Park Service was promoting the Rustic Style, which received its inspiration from the Medieval and Gothic styles of Northern Europe, as part of an effort to attract visitors to the national parks. The roofs were exaggerated and steep and utilized native materials, primarily hand-hewn wood and stone.

Massive, over-sized pieces were part of the designs.

Underwood's first attempt to design a lodge for the Park Service at Yosemite Village was not well received. He persevered, however, and his work dovetailed with the Park Service plans to develop new national parks at Zion and Bryce canyons. The Union Pacific Railroad was helping the state of Utah stimulate the demand and development of these areas, with the encouragement of the National Park Service. The railroad initially proposed that its own architect, W.P. Wellman, be used to design the lodges and other facilities in these parks. The Utah Parks Company had been established solely to develop the concessions in the parks, the formation of a subsidiary being intended to show that this work was separate from the railroad.

The Park Service review board, which included Hull, felt that Wellman's design of a single, large park lodge was not suitable for Zion, and Hull recommended Underwood to the Union Pacific. This began a relationship which lasted several years, during which Underwood designed lodges at the Zion, Bryce, and Grand Canyon national parks, the Cedar Breaks National Monument, and at West Yellowstone. Underwood also designed other facilities at other national parks as well, including the Ahwahnee Lodge at Yosemite National Park.

From 1924 through 1931 the architect also designed approximately 20 small- and moderate-sized depots for the Union Pacific, as well at the large station and home office for the Union Pacific in Omaha. Many of the depots were in the Spanish Revival style, due to the influence of his previous employer, Arthur Benton. The Gering, Nebraska, depot, however, was designed in a Classical and Tudor style, while the Omaha depot was in the Art Deco style. He used this last style on many of the other buildings he designed in later years for the federal government.

The Omaha depot was one of Underwood's last projects. His architectural business essentially ended with the advent of the Depression and he soon found himself without work and with no money. He prepared a new design for the Pullman, Washington, station, but the project was canceled due to the poor economy. The architect had some hope for additional work when the Union Pacific briefly considered him for the construction of a new, larger station in Los Angeles, but the commission went to John and Donald B. Parkinson instead.

Lacking any work, Underwood went to work for the federal government as a Consulting Architect, and moved with his family to Washington, D.C., in 1934. Most of his works during these years contained Art Deco or Spanish Revival elements. He designed a total of 20 post offices, two large federal court houses, and the San Francisco Mint. He became the Supervising Architect for the federal government between 1947 and 1949, a position which no longer exists in the federal government.

At the same time he was working for the government, Underwood performed other work on the side, creating somewhat of a strain on his work efforts for the government. Although not legal, the

In 1925 the railroad built a new Dining Lodge at West Yellowstone, designed by Gilbert Stanley Underwood. It was designed to accommodate large numbers of tourists at a single sitting.
AUTHOR'S COLLECTION

rules against moonlighting were largely ignored, but he still had some difficulty in juggling his regular work schedules with the jobs he was performing at home. He employed men in-house to do the detailed design, literally keeping them hidden from his government employer by having them work in the basement and attic. His designs included the Sun Valley Lodge and the Challenger Inn at Sun Valley, which were developed by the Union Pacific during the Depression. Underwood finally retired from his government post in 1954, at the conclusion of the construction of the Jackson Lake Lodge in the Teton National Park, going to Florida, where he died in 1960[84].

The Union Pacific Railroad commissioned Underwood to design numerous stations and facilities for the railroad, including those listed below[85]. The date listed is the date the plans were prepared, and is not necessarily the year the facility was completed.

Date	Passenger Station	Date	Passenger Station
1928	Abilene, Kansas	1927	Lund, Utah
1925	American Falls, Idaho	1930	Marysville, Kansas
1925	Black Rock, Utah1924 Parco, Wyoming	1924	Nampa, Idaho
-----	Cheyenne (alterations only), Wyoming	1924	North Bend, Nebraska
1925	Cozad, Nebraska	1930	Omaha, Nebraska
1928	East Los Angeles, California	1924	Parco, Wyoming
1924	East San Pedro, California	1929	Shoshone, Idaho
1929	Fairbury, Nebraska	1924	Sinclair (Wyoming)
1928	Gering, Nebraska	1927	South Torrington, Wyoming
1929	Greeley, Colorado	1925	Topeka, Kansas
1930	LaGrande, Oregon		

Other worked performed for the Union Pacific included the following:

Bryce Canyon:

1924	Bryce Lodge
1926	Addition to Bryce Lodge
1924	Cabin
1927/29	Deluxe Cabin
1934	Housekeeping Cabin
1928	Stable
1932	Cafeteria
1934	Laundry Cabin
1926	Addition to Pavilion

Grand Canyon:

1929	Camp Center (Store & Cafeteria)
1927	Power House
1927	North Rim Drawings, construction begins
1928	North Rim Opens (Original)
1928	Stable
1928	Comfort Station
1929	Deluxe Cabin
1930	Operator Dwelling
1927	Pump House

Zion National Park:

1924	First Version of Zion Hotel
1924	Zion Lodge
1926	Addition to Zion Lodge
1924	Pavilion
1926	Addition to Pavilion
1926	Women's dormitory
1929	Stable
1934	Comfort Station
1928	Swimming Pool & Bath House
1934	Cafeteria
1934	Laundry Cabin
1927/29	Deluxe Cabin

Cedar Breaks National Monument:

| 1924 | Dining Lodge |

Kanab, Utah:

| 1928 | Lunch Station |

West Yellowstone:

1925 Dining Lodge
1927 Men's Dormitory

Sun Valley:

1936 Sun Valley Lodge
1938 Challenger Inn

It should be noted that the facilities at Zion, Bryce, Cedar Breaks, and the Grand Canyon were built for the Utah Parks Company, a Union Pacific subsidiary. The lodges and supporting facilities were designed to improve the accommodations, which would help increase the railroad passenger traffic, so the work was encouraged and promoted by the Union Pacific.

Underwood also designed lodges at other national parks, including facilities at Jackson Lake (Grand Teton National Park), in 1954; the Timberline Lodge at Mt. Hood in 1936; and the Ahwahnee Hotel in Yosemite in 1925 (opened in 1927).

Post card view of the West Yellowstone depot and Stanley's Dining Lodge. PHPC

South Entrance

Victor, Idaho

The Union Pacific Railroad's primary entrance to Yellowstone National Park was through the West Entrance at West Yellowstone, but it also used the South Entrance for many years. After Grand Teton National Park was officially established on February 26, 1929 and dedicated on July 29, 1929 the railroad began offering service through Victor, at the end of its Teton Valley Branch, for travel through both Grand Teton and Yellowstone national parks. Although it was never a very popular route, this line was used by the railroad even after service to West Yellowstone had been discontinued. The route from Pocatello to Victor was circuitous, with the trains going from Pocatello north to Idaho Falls, northeast to Ashton, and from there back south to Victor.

Even before Grand Teton National Park was established, the railroad made some efforts to increase the awareness of the area. In the July 1924 issue of *The Union Pacific Magazine,* the railroad's employee magazine, there was an article titled "Jackson Hole and the Tetons". In a paragraph discussing travel to the park, it was stated that *Neither by motor nor train is Jackson Hole difficult to reach. It seems difficult but it isn't. If you come by train you change from the main coast-to-coast route to Ogden, or Salt Lake City, or Pocatello, and, taking the West Yellowstone express, get off at Ashton where a branch line runs to Victor, Idaho. Here you are at the very edge of the Tetons, in their western shadow. There is a mountain pass - Teton Pass - beautiful beyond description, to cross to get into Jackson Hole itself. The pass is twenty-four miles long, a stage runs each day, and at the end of the journey you come to the little town of Jackson where you will find first-class hotel accommodations, stores and an excellent center from which to see the country ...."*

When it became apparent that Grand Teton National Park was going to be established, the Union Pacific anticipated that tourists would be interested in reaching the park by railroad, and knew the line to Victor was the only practical rail route to Jackson Hole and the Tetons. In anticipation of the establishment of the park the railroad enlarged the Victor depot in 1928 for the tourist travel to the new national park and to Yellowstone[86]. An addition was built on the south side of the existing depot and included a waiting room, dressing rooms, and restrooms. A small park was built to the south of the depot.

The service through Victor did not start until Grand Teton National Park was established in the following year. The railroad scheduled through passenger car service to Victor, avoiding the inconvenience of changing cars at Ashton. The daily train in the summer was scheduled so that passengers would arrive at Victor in the morning, get off the train and have breakfast at a nearby restaurant, and then board a bus for their ride over the Teton Pass to the new national park. The tour would then go through Moran and to Yellowstone National Park through the South Entrance. The tour would end at West Yellowstone, where they would have dinner at the Dining Lodge before boarding the train for their trip home.

In 1931 the Park Service broke down the number of visitors arriving at Yellowstone National Park through the South Entrance by railroad and noted that 40 out of 161 rail travelers through the South Entrance came through Victor, the balance arriving from Lander[87]. In the following year 33 of the 60 rail visitors arriving through the South Entrance came over the Union Pacific through Victor[88]. In 1933 travel to the park continued to drop due to the effects of theDepression, and 11 of the 19 visitors who arrived through the South Entrance by rail came through Victor[89]. In the government fiscal year October 1, 1933 through June 30, 1934, three of the seven people arriving through the South Entrance by rail came through Victor[90]. The Park Service stopped maintaining records of rail visitors after this date, but it is apparent that the number of travelers arriving through Victor was never very great.

After World War II the railroad continued to advertise the service through Victor. The cars were taken off the *Yellowstone Special* at Ashton and taken to Victor on the *Northwest Special*. There was a slight increase in business immediately following the war and the Union Pacific noted that the only gateways showing increased business in 1948 over the previous years were the ones through West Yellowstone and Victor. The railroad had 238 tourists pass through Victor in 1947, and 390 in the following year[91]. When train service to West Yellowstone was discontinued at the end of the 1960 season service to Victor became a more popular route because passengers did not have to get off the train at Ashton to ride a bus to West Yellowstone at an early hour. The train operated only in the summer season, which by now had been abbreviated to June 18 through August 23 and was designated the *Park Special*. The train operated out of Pocatello with connecting service to and from Salt Lake City. It had through coaches, 10 roomette/6 double bedroom sleeping cars, and a lounge car to Victor. The 1963 summer schedule showed the train leaving Salt Lake City 7:30 P.M., arriving at Ashton at 5:45 A.M. and reaching Victor at 7:30 A.M. the following morning. Returning the train left Victor at 8:15 P.M., arriving at Ashton at 9:55 P.M., and got into Salt Lake City at 8:00 the next morning. The railroad also ran a mixed train between Idaho Falls and Victor for local traffic[92].

The Union Pacific continued to promote and advertise tour packages through Victor, but by 1966 service had been cut back to Idaho Falls, with bus service provided from there to both Yellowstone and Grand Teton national parks. The service through Victor was never very popular or successful, although the schedule in the latter years of operation made it a preferred route for tours to the park, but by this time the private automobile was becoming the preferred means of travel to the park.

In 1929 the Union Pacific released this flyer promoting travel to both Yellowstone National Park and the newly established Grand Teton National Park. UNION PACIFIC HISTORICAL COLLECTION

The Union Pacific from Wyoming

There was consideration of extending a road from the park south to a connection with the Union Pacific Railroad in Wyoming as early as 1891. In the Annual Report of the Park Superintendent dated August 15, 1891, the superintendent noted that a road could be extended south from the park to Jackson Lake. From there he felt a road would undoubtedly be extended south to a connection with the Union Pacific. This had the potential to become a popular route and increase the number of visitors to the park since the World's Columbian Exposition in Chicago was to be held the following year[93]. This road was not built for many years, and travelers to the World's Fair had to go through Livingston on the Northern Pacific or Monida on the Union Pacific to reach the park. Interestingly enough, the stage and freight route to Lander and the Wind River Indian Reservation had originally been from the Union Pacific main line at Green River, a 150-mile trip.

At the same time the Chicago and North Western was beginning to offer service from Lander to the park in 1923 there were reports that the Union Pacific was planning to provide service to the park through Rock Springs, but it is not clear if the service ever took place. A road was apparently opened through Hoback Junction and the Jackson Hole country from Rock Springs in 1922, but it was a rough 200-mile trip and similar to the route from Lander, which was only 189 miles. Businessmen from towns such as Rock Springs and Pindedale unsuccessfully tried to promote the route in the 1920s. Following the dedication of the road from Lander they wrote the Union Pacific and the National Park Service in an effort to gain their support. The Commissioner of Immigration in Wyoming wrote that the road from Jackson through Hoback Canyon was *"in splendid condition"* and that this road *"will be maintained henceforth"*. He went on to say that *"I went over this road and found it one of the best highways in the State of Wyoming"*.

The National Park Service, however, felt that the route did not have potential as far as rail traffic was concerned, and referred the Wyoming businessmen to the Union Pacific for additional support and promotional efforts. However, the long distance, poor accommodations, and inferior roads made the route a poor choice, and it was not only not promoted but it was not offered for a long time period. The Union Pacific apparently considered the potential of the route, but concluded the road was too long, and that the only potential for service out of Rock Springs was for the dude ranch business[94].

However, as late as 1966 the Union Pacific offered a bi-weekly bus service from Rock Springs to Jackson during the ski season[95]. This was apparently not very successful due to the long bus ride.

The Union Pacific Service to Yellowstone National Park

The Union Pacific line to West Yellowstone was the most popular route to Yellowstone National Park since it reached the park boundary and because convenient train service was available from so many cities both on the West Coast and in the Midwest. It was also the last railroad to provide passenger train service to the park boundary. The line to Victor was not as popular, but remained in use for several years after the train service to West Yellowstone had been discontinued.

The railroad built several buildings at West Yellowstone which remain in use today, even though the tracks were removed many years ago. The Union Pacific also prepared numerous advertisements over the years, notably the cartoon bear advertisements, which provide a vivid reminder of what visiting the park was like at the time.

THE BUFFALO BILL

Burlington Route

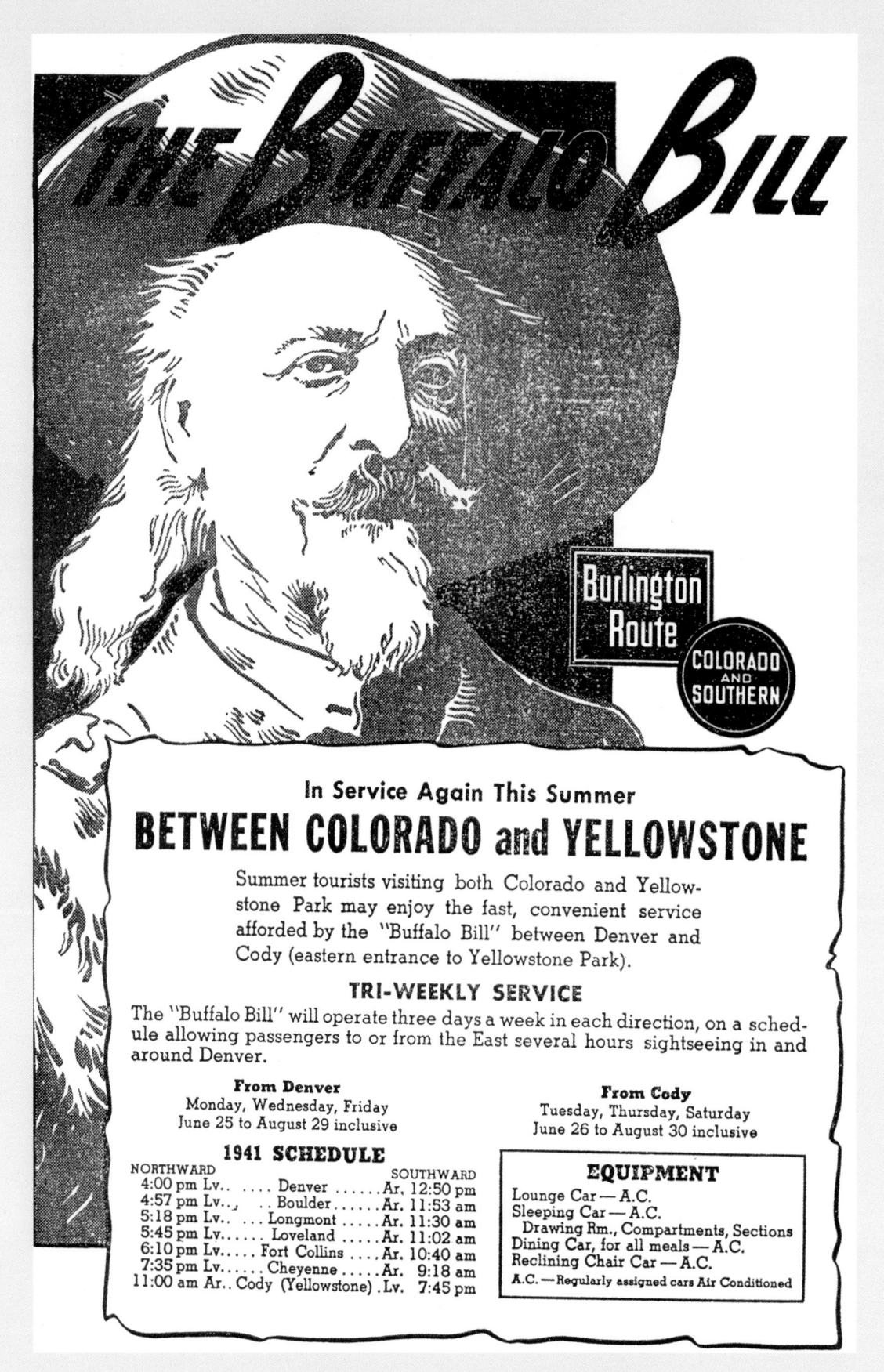

COLORADO AND SOUTHERN

In Service Again This Summer
BETWEEN COLORADO and YELLOWSTONE

Summer tourists visiting both Colorado and Yellowstone Park may enjoy the fast, convenient service afforded by the "Buffalo Bill" between Denver and Cody (eastern entrance to Yellowstone Park).

TRI-WEEKLY SERVICE

The "Buffalo Bill" will operate three days a week in each direction, on a schedule allowing passengers to or from the East several hours sightseeing in and around Denver.

From Denver
Monday, Wednesday, Friday
June 25 to August 29 inclusive

From Cody
Tuesday, Thursday, Saturday
June 26 to August 30 inclusive

1941 SCHEDULE

NORTHWARD		SOUTHWARD
4:00 pm Lv.	Denver	Ar. 12:50 pm
4:57 pm Lv.	Boulder	Ar. 11:53 am
5:18 pm Lv.	Longmont	Ar. 11:30 am
5:45 pm Lv.	Loveland	Ar. 11:02 am
6:10 pm Lv.	Fort Collins	Ar. 10:40 am
7:35 pm Lv.	Cheyenne	Ar. 9:18 am
11:00 am Ar.	Cody (Yellowstone)	Lv. 7:45 pm

EQUIPMENT

Lounge Car — A.C.
Sleeping Car — A.C.
    Drawing Rm., Compartments, Sections
Dining Car, for all meals — A.C.
Reclining Chair Car — A.C.

A.C. — Regularly assigned cars Air Conditioned

The Chicago, Burlington & Quincy inaugurated *The Buffalo Bill* in 1937, offering through service between Denver and Cody. It ran three days a week in the summer months and was popular until it was discontinued due to World War II.

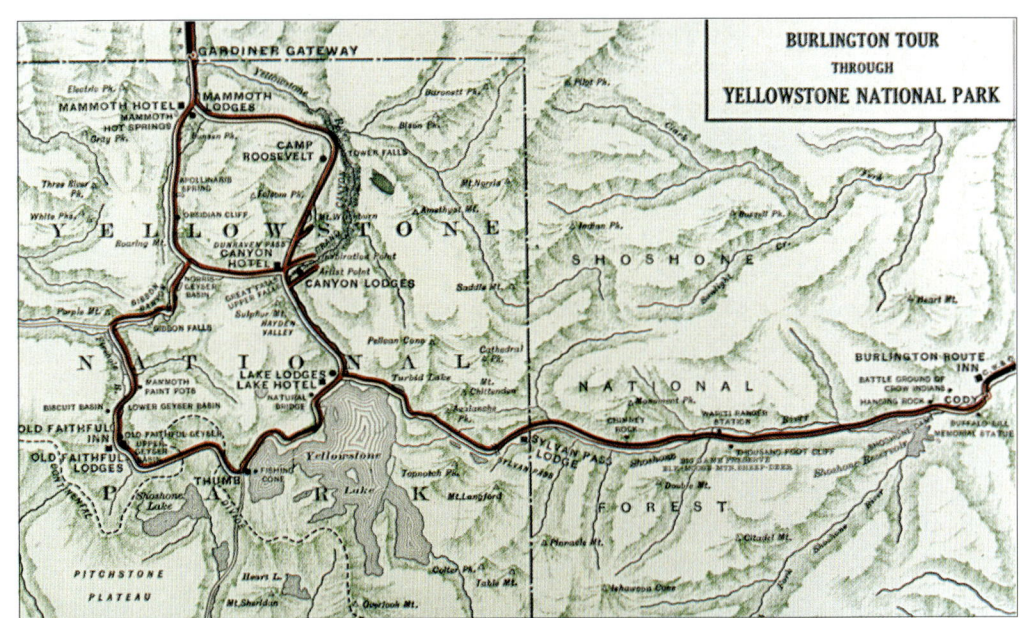

Chapter Eight

The Burlington route through Cody included a long ride to reach the East Entrance of the park. This is from a 1926 booklet promoting travel through Cody.
YELLOWSTONE HERITAGE & RESEARCH CENTER

"The National Park Road"
Chicago, Burlington & Quincy Railroad
to
Cody, Wyoming

"If You Don't See the Cody Road - You Don't See Yellowstone Park"
The Cody gateway of Yellowstone park was thrown open to the public in 1916 and ever since has been ranked as one of the **most spectacular features of the Yellowstone tour**. The Cody Road is fast becoming the most popular of all Yellowstone gateways.

One goes to Cody on **The Burlington** and **The Northern Pacific Railroads**, and, breakfast over, boards a twelve-passenger touring car, whirls down the double hairpin turn, crosses the bridge over the Shoshone River, and spirals up the opposite slope to the old frontier town which was Buffalo Bill's home.....

On and on runs the Cody Road...for forty miles through the vast Shoshone National Forest to the edge of the park. Luncheon at Sylvan Pass Lodge and we whirl away again ...up the seven-mile hill to the snow on Sylvan Pass where the Cody Road crosses the Absaroka Range...."[1]

Service to the East Entrance of Yellowstone National Park through Cody, Wyoming was provided by both the Chicago, Burlington & Pacific Railroad and the Northern Pacific Railway, although the Burlington owned and operated the line to Cody. Since it was a 53-mile drive from Cody to the park entrance, the route did not become popular until the road was improved. The principal market for travel to the park through Cody was for tourists from Denver, although through train service was available from Chicago over the Northern Pacific, with connections at Billings to Cody. Today the entrance through Cody is one of the most popular routes to the park, and, Cody is a popular tourist destination, home of the world-famous Buffalo Bill Historical Center.

The Town of Cody

John Colter was the first white man known to have passed through what is now Cody. He went through the area while following the Shoshone River in the fall of 1807. The area became known as "Colter's Hell", the river originally being known as "Stinking Water River" for the springs on the river, but the name was changed to the Shoshone River in 1902 to make the area sound more agreeable and appealing[2].

Cody is in the Big Horn Basin, an area of 12-15,000 square miles and one of the last areas in the West to be settled. By the late 1870s there were cattle ranches and some small settlements in the basin. In 1885 the Cody area was known as DeMaris Springs, for homesteader Charles DeMaris. The Big Horn area was authorized as a county by the state legislature in 1890, but it needed a population base before it could be established.[3]

The first significant settlements came in 1894, when settlers started a townsite one mile downstream of the present-day Cody. Initially known as Shoshone, its name was changed first to Richland, and finally Cody[4]. In the year it was settled George T. Beck of Sheridan sent a survey party into the Big Horn Basin to explore the area and to see if it had any potential for development. The survey party included Horton Boal, son-in-law of Buffalo Bill Cody. Beck was hoping the area could be developed using irrigation water from the Shoshone River. Although there was some mining in the area, irrigation was needed for farming since it was a dry, treeless land.

Following a successful report, Beck formed the Shoshone Land and Irrigation Company[5]. At this time Buffalo Bill had family in the Sheridan area and was managing the Buffalo Bill Inn in Sheridan. Becoming interested, he became a partner in the proposed company and was welcomed due to his fame. He also knew the area well and felt that someday it would be a gateway to Yellowstone National Park[6].

In 1895 Cody traveled west from Cody over Sylvan Pass and felt that the route could be a popular entrance to Yellowstone[7]. A townsite was platted in that year by the three partners, Beck, Cody, and banker Horace Alger, and it was settled by the following year. A post office named Richland was opened at the new townsite, located near the De Maris Spring[8]. When Beck wanted to move the townsite downstream Cody agreed, but Beck thought the new town should be named "Cody" because it would please Buffalo Bill and because the name recognition would help develop the town[9], Cody's name being well known at this time due to his colorful and varied experiences. He had gained fame as a western frontiersman, killing 4,280 buffalo in 18 months for the construction crews of the Kansas Pacific Railroad, later part of the Union Pacific. He had also been a frontier scout and had ridden for the Pony Express. Cody was a true showman and in 1882 he started his "Wild West Show," traveling throughout the United States and Europe for many years[10].

Completion of the Chicago, Burlington and Quincy line to Cody in 1901 made it easier to bring in supplies and the area became more accessible. Promotional advertisements in 1896 showed Buffalo Bill proclaiming "Fine Land Waits the Plow" and "Unlimited Water Waits the Cultivator[11]." He went so far as to relinquish claims for land so that Mormon farmers could settle and grow crops on it. He also encouraged European immigrants to settle in the area. When Cody published the town's first newspaper in 1896, it was not to inform the county residents, but to promote the location[12].

The town of Cody was incorporated in 1901, when it had a population of 550. This was the same year the railroad reached the townsite. In the new town the north-south streets were numbered and the east-west streets named after associates of the land company and Union and Confederate generals. The streets were 100 feet wide so that a team of horses with a wagon could turn around in them[13]. The Lincoln Land Company, a subsidiary of the railroad, claimed ownership of half of the town lots when the railroad reached the town[14]. The town of Cody did not, however, become the Big Horn County seat, despite attempts to move it there. It was not until 1911, when Park County was created, that Cody became a county seat[15].

Buffalo Bill also realized the importance of transportation, and promoted better roads and opened a livery stable. He used his influence to encourage the Chicago, Burlington and Quincy to build a line to Cody and entertained officials of the railroad company. The railroad line was apparently built following a commitment by the president of the railroad to Buffalo Bill.

The area grew and prospered following completion of the rail line. The 1902 Shoshone Reclamation Project expanded irrigation and led to the construction of the Shoshone Dam and the Buffalo Bill Reservoir on the Shoshone River, which were completed in 1910[16]. They provided electricity, water, and flood protection for the Big Horn Basin. The Elk Basin Oil Field, once one of the most productive oil fields in the country, was discovered in 1915 north of Cody. The oil in the Oregon Basin south of Cody was also developed.

The famous Irma Hotel, which is still open today and listed on the National Register of Historic Places, was built by Buffalo Bill in downtown Cody. Erected in 1902, the two-story stone hotel was the largest single investment by a single person in the town to that time[17]. There were originally 40 guest rooms on the second floor with the lobby and dining facilities on the first floor. Cody felt a first class hotel was needed to encourage visitors to the park and that stables and associated facilities would help this business. Unfortunately, it had to be sold a month after he died on January 10, 1917 since he had no money and had left large debts. Buffalo Bill Cody also opened the Pahaska Tepee in 1901 ("Longhair's Lodge")[18], a dude ranch just outside the park which remained in operation until 2005.

The Railroad to Cody

In the late 19th century traffic on the CB&Q was increasing and the railroad was expanding in the northwest corner of its railroad empire. In 1892 the railroad built a line to Sheridan, Wyoming, on the route to Billings, Montana, which was reached in 1894[19]. This provided a through line from Omaha, Nebraska.

In the spring of 1901 the railroad began construction of a line from Toluca, Montana, on the line to Billings, 151 miles west to Cody[20]. The grading was performed by Mormon farmers who had settled in the area[21]. This was a difficult line to construct and operate due to the rugged terrain, and the line had steep grades, sharp curves, and a 300-yard-long tunnel at Pryor Gap.

The first train arrived at Cody on November 11, 1901. The train, which had left Billings the previous evening, consisted of Superintendent Gillette's private car, carrying Senator William Clark and other officials, two other passenger cars, and an express car. It was met by a large party, including Buffalo Bill Cody in his private stagecoach. There was the usual celebration, with a parade led by the Billings Brass Band starting at the Buffalo Bill Barn, and, in the afternoon a large roasted ox was served to the crowd of more than 1,000. There were fireworks in the evening followed by dancing and a midnight banquet at the Cody Club. All costs for the festivities were paid by Buffalo Bill[22].

The line to Cody was intended not only to access Yellowstone National Park but also to serve the productive Big Horn Basin area. A route was apparently surveyed to the park, but no work was performed west of Cody[23]. The trains had an average speed of only 20 mph, taking seven-and-a-half hours to make the run. The train was called the "Squaw Train" or the "Toluca-Cody" run[24] by the locals. It was also known as the CF&BM, or "Cody to Frannie & Back Maybe"[25]. The trains were run in a leisurely fashion, and reportedly the train would stop so the passengers and train crew could shoot coyotes or game, to chase cattle off the tracks, and to pick up Indians or other travelers along the way[26].

The railroad facilities at Cody were across the Shoshone River from the townsite since the railroad felt building a bridge across the Shoshone River was too expensive. The first station was a two-story wooden building with an adjacent water tank for the steam locomotives, along with other facilities needed for the railroad terminal[27]. A footbridge was originally used to cross the river along what is now 12th Street, and each side of the canyon had a long stairway down to the river. The wagons had to ford the river. It was over a mile into town from the depot, but the train crews, bus drivers, and some of the arriving and departing tourists all walked between the two locations. The pathway was covered with red gravel, and soon became known as "The Red Path".

In 1905 the railroad began construction south from Frannie towards Kirby, 100 miles to the south.

The "Dude Train" has arrived at Cody, Wyoming and is being greeted by a group of horsemen. The first depot at Cody was a simple, two-story wooden structure, located a mile from the business district.
PARK COUNTY ARCHIVES, CODY, WYOMING

Kirby was reached on September 3, 1907 and on April 24, 1911 the railroad completed construction of the line from Frannie north towards Billings. Trackage rights were used over the Northern Pacific from Fromberg to Billings, and on April 11, 1911 the Toluca Branch was abruptly abandoned between Toluca and Warren, Montana, just north of Frannie, Wyoming. On December 15, 1915 a through line between Frannie and Denver was completed, using Colorado & Southern tracks south of Wendover, Wyoming[28].

The transportation of oil from the Oregon Basin was a profitable source of revenue for the railroad for many years. The Oregon Basin was shut down in 1929 and not reopened until 1936. Some of the rail traffic was lost to the Illinois Pipeline Company which completed a pipeline to Cody in 1927[29].

In the summer of 1930 the Chicago, Burlington & Quincy offered three trains a day to Cody. One of them, train #11, operated only in the summer, and the other two were motor cars, providing service along the route.

Railroad Service to Cody

The first train service to Cody was rudimentary. Passengers on the main line trains had to get off their train at Toluca and board a three-times-a-week mixed train to Cody. The mixed train consisted of an old wood coach and a few freight cars pulled by a small coal-burning steam locomotive and took eight hours to travel the 165-mile route. Meals were taken at boxcars on a siding along the route. Transfers from the depot at Cody to the hotels across the river were made using a Concord coach, going down from the high bench across the river and into town[30].

Train service improved over the years as the number of passengers increased. A 1920 timetable shows Cody as being the "Eastern Entrance, Yellowstone Park". In January 1920, a time of year when the park was closed, the railroad ran two trains a day to Cody from Billings, a daily except Sunday mixed train and a daily train with connections to and from Denver. In the summer months the railroad ran two trains a day to Cody in addition to a local train. These trains arrived at 6:00 A.M. and 12:50 P.M. and departed Cody at 9:00 A.M. and 8:00 P.M., with passengers changing trains at Billings. Through sleeping and chair car service was provided between Omaha and Cody[31]. In 1921 three trains a day were scheduled to arrive and depart Cody during the summer months[32]. In the summer of 1930 the railroad had twice daily motor car service between Frannie and Cody in addition to another summer-only train which ran from Billings. The motor car train connected with the main line trains. The through train arrived at 7:15 in the morning and left at 7:30 in the evening[33].

In 1903 the railroad started construction of the Burlington-Cody Inn near the depot. The inn was expanded in 1924 and had 99 rooms and a dining room which could seat from 400 to 500 people. It was located near the depot, a mile from the downtown area. Previous to this time tourists had their meals at the Burlington Cody Café, and the Burlington ticket offices were in the Irma Hotel[34]. When the hotel was expanded the depot had to be moved to make room for the brick walkway between the tracks and the hotel[35]. To help publicize the Cody name the Old Cody House was moved to the station grounds. This was the original house where Cody was born on February 26, 1846 in Eau Claire, Iowa. Up to 50

It is 1918 and a large group is waiting for the arrival of the train to Cody. The Burlington Inn can be seen behind the depot. The countryside surrounding Cody is barren and needed irrigation so the area could raise crops. PARK COUNTY ARCHIVES, CODY, WYOMING

This train is arriving at the Burlington Inn at Cody. A band is about to play for the arriving travelers, and the redcap on the left is ready to unload the baggage. PARK COUNTY ARCHIVES, CODY, WYOMING

buses would be parked in front of the inn each day to take tourists to the park in the summer months. Meals at the inn were often included in the tour packages[36]. During the 1920s and 1930s the inn was a favorite dining location for local residents.

On June 23, 1937 the CB&Q introduced its new "Buffalo Bill" train to improve service from Denver to Cody. The train was #29 from Denver to Cody and #30 from Cody to Denver and ran in the summer months only. There were large celebrations for the first train[37], with parades in both Denver and Cody. The train was so popular that on some days it had a helper locomotive[38] in the front to handle the large number of cars. The train included Pullman sleeping cars, coaches, and a diner/lounge car. In 1939 the train ran three times a week, leaving Denver on Monday, Wednesday, and Friday at 4:00 P.M., arriving at Cody at 11:00 the following morning. Returning it departed Cody at 7:45 P.M. on Tuesday, Thursday

This brochure for the 1935 season included the tours to Yellowstone National Park. Travel to the park dropped dramatically during the Depression years, and the railroads did all they could to promote travel on their line. Air conditioned equipment was just being introduced on the railroads at this time. GADAMUS COLLECTION, YELLOWSTONE HISTORIC CENTER

The Chicago, Burlington & Quincy operated the Burlington Cody Inn for travelers to Yellowstone National Park. The tourists could get off the train, eat their meal and then board their motor buses for the tour of the park. BOTH PHOTOS AUTHOR'S COLLECTION

and Saturday, reaching Denver at 1:00 P.M. the following day[39]. On arrival and before departure passengers would eat their meals at the Burlington Inn in Cody.

The line to Cody was unique since the Northern Pacific also offered passenger service to Cody over its line, making connections with the Burlington trains at Billings. In 1921, for example, the Northern Pacific timetable showed a standard sleeping car from St. Paul to Billings, which was forwarded to the Burlington for the final leg to Cody. The 1922 train, the *Yellowstone Special*, operated by the Northern Pacific, also had cars to Cody, as did the *Yellowstone Park Comet* in later years. This service continued through the Depression years, ending with the advent of World War II. In the 1920s tourists could travel overnight from Cody to other tourist destinations including Edgemont, South Dakota, in the Black Hills, and to Glacier National Park in conjunction with the Great Northern. Over the years the Burlington also offered Pullman sleeping car service to and from Casper, Omaha, and Chicago[40].

In 1937 travelers could ride on a through Pullman via Billings to Cody from Seattle, Tacoma, Portland, and Chicago as well as Denver. There was one train a day to Cody plus three buses operated by the CB&Q's subsidiary Burlington Trailways Bus Line[41]. Service from Chicago and Seattle was shown in the 1942 timetable but was discontinued the following summer due to World War II. Following the end of the war the railroad re-instituted through Pullmans from Chicago to Cody. The service was shown as late as 1949, running on the Northern Pacific's *North Coast Limited*. In 1950 the railroad still offered a through car to Cody, after the Northern Pacific service to Gardiner had been discontinued[42]. In 1953 the Northern Pacific ran a sleeper between Chicago and Cody in the summer months only, interchanging it with the Burlington at Billings. The through Pullman sleeping car ran on the *North Coast Limited* between Chicago and Billings[43].

The last through service from Denver to Cody shown was listed in the 1953 timetable. After that one had to transfer to a bus at Billings or at Deaver, Wyoming for the trip to Cody[44]. Transfer was made to the Yellowstone Park Transportation Company buses at Cody. The Chicago, Burlington and Quincy continued to offer tour packages with the other railroads, however, in an effort to retain some passenger traffic. As late as 1970, only a year before the railroad exited the passenger business, the railroad was distributing a pamphlet titled "Burlington Northern Tours to the Western Wonderland", but the tourist traffic had just about ended.

In addition to promoting travel to the park, the railroad also advertised dude ranches in the area in the 1920s. These were popular at the time and another source of revenue. Their popularity waned during the Depression and never recovered after World War II.

Travel to Yellowstone National Park Via Cody

The road from Cody into the park was essentially divided into two distinct sections - the road in the park and the road from Cody to the East Entrance at the park boundary. Two routes were considered in the park, through either Sylvan Pass or Jones Pass, both of which were difficult. Captain Hiram Chittenden chose the route through Sylvan Pass due, in part, to its scenery and the fact that it had an elevation of 8,577 feet, 1,000 feet lower than Jones Pass. The route went from the mouth of Yellowstone Lake east to a point on the eastern park boundary where it crossed the Shoshone River. The road was opened on July 3, 1903 despite a steep slope on the east side of Sylvan Pass and even though the road was not officially completed for another two years. Three hundred people traveled the road that first year despite the rough road. It was well-known for its "corkscrew" bridge below Sylvan Pass.

At the same time the road in the park was being constructed the Cody Road to the East Entrance from Cody was built starting in 1901, coinciding with the arrival of the Chicago, Burlington and Quincy into Cody. The road was built using federal funds and was a popular route to the park. Funding for the East Entrance road from Cody was approved on June 6, 1900 and construction began on July 1, 1901.

The Cody Road was opened by 1903 and followed an old Indian path along the Shoshone River, traveling through an area of virgin timber. It was narrow, with occasional signs saying "Slow-down-to-six-miles-per-hour-blow-your-horn"[45], and Interior Secretary John Barton Payne was told that there were times when *"women came in (to Cody) in automobiles from the park weeping because of the very great danger..."*[46]. It was maintained for 18 miles from the park boundary using park service funds[47], an unusual occurrence, especially considering the limited funding available. This was not, however, the only instance of the park service maintaining a road outside of the park boundary, they also maintained the

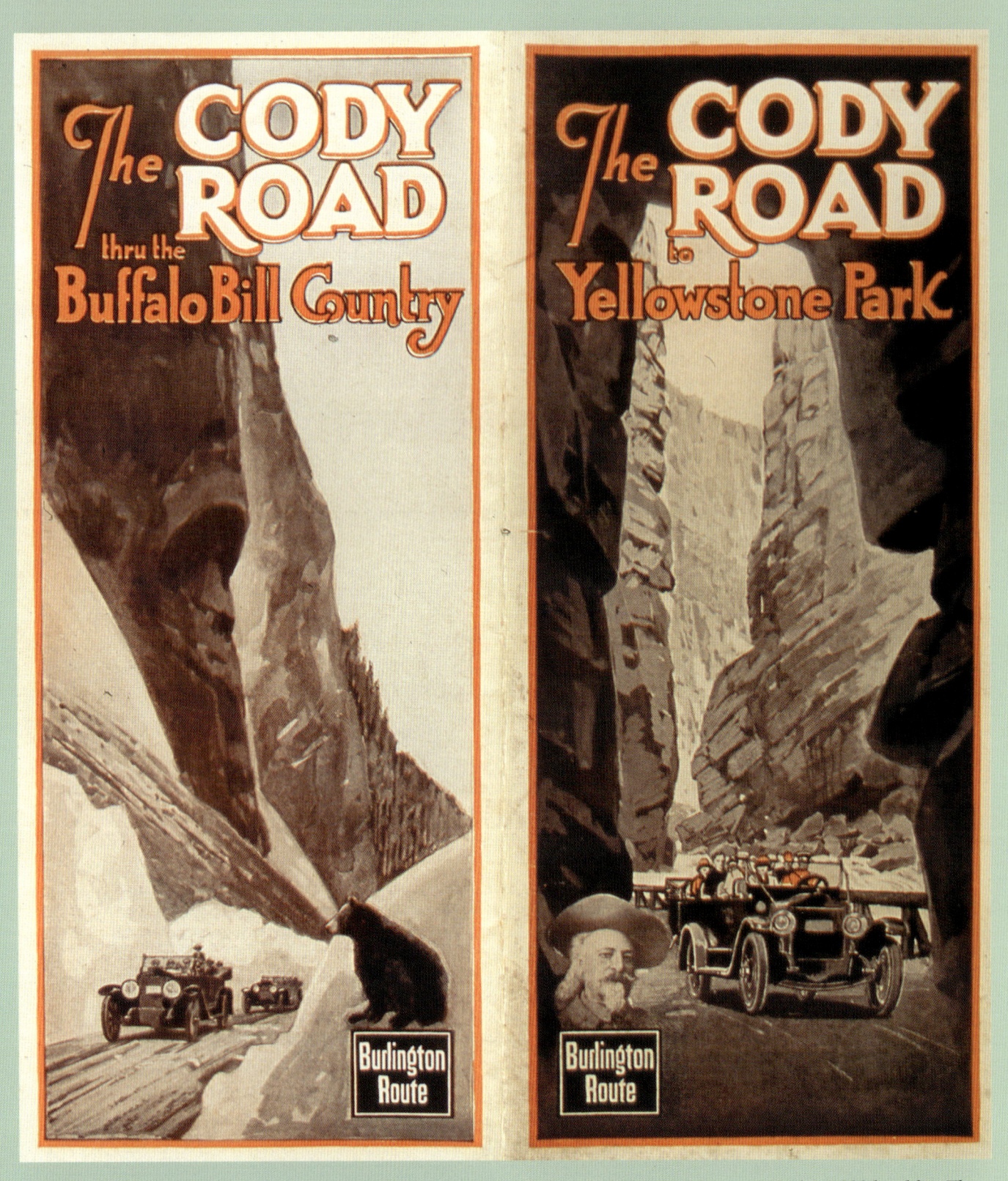

The Burlington advertised the scenic trip through the canyon to reach the park, as seen in this 1929 booklet. The road traveled on the route of an old Indian path along the Shoshone River, providing a scary ride for the timid tourist. They rode in open top motor buses on gravel roads to reach the park. YELLOWSTONE HERITAGE & RESEARCH CENTER

The trip in the open 12-passenger touring cars over Sylvan Pass to the park could be an exciting ride. The cars have stopped here so the tourists can view the Shoshone Dam, located on the Shoshone River between Cody and the park. PARK COUNTY ARCHIVES, CODY, WYOMING

The road over Sylvan Pass included this corkscrew section with the road passing over itself. The road opened in 1903, although it was not officially completed for another two years. AUTHOR'S COLLECTION

The road along the Shoshone River was frightening to many of the tourists as it wound along the canyon wall and through the tunnels. GADAMUS COLLECTION, YELLOWSTONE HISTORIC CENTER

road to Moose, south of Yellowstone National Park.

With the opening of the road, various transportation and camping companies began operating out of Cody. Travel through Cody was helped by Dr. Frank Powell, also known as White Beaver. He was the overseer of the construction of the Pahaska Tepee and Wapiti Inn on the North Fork[48]. The roads were opened in time for the completion of the wagon road to the East Entrance and helped draw sightseers to the area and into the park. In 1904 there were 584 travelers through the East Gate.

Tourists who arrived at Cody by train traveled to the park on the Cody-Sylvan Motor Company vehicles. Originally these were horse-drawn stages but after 1911 motor buses were used to the East Entrance, where visitors transferred to horse-drawn coaches. The buses were originally open-top automobiles with three rows of seats. Cody residents petitioned the National Park Service to be allowed to drive private automobiles into the park as early as 1908. When automobiles were finally allowed in 1915, travel through the East Gate doubled.

The Cody-Sylvan Motor Company was incorporated on April 4, 1916 in West Virginia to avoid Wyoming taxes and fees[49]. It was backed by the Chicago, Burlington and Quincy, and the president was Frank Haynes, who represented the Yellowstone-Western Stage Company, and other directors were also associated with other park businesses[50]. The bus company was taken over by the Yellowstone Park Transportation Company the following year. The first buses ran from Cody to the Lake Hotel on July 1, 1916[51]. The average speed was 10 mph, so that Lake Junction was not reached until the late afternoon[52]. Since the automobiles had to stop to let horse-drawn vehicles pass them, the schedules were seldom met. Tourists left Cody at 8 A.M. and had lunch at Pahaksa, and in later years lunch was provided at Sylvan Pass Lodge.

Other minor improvements were made over the years, although no work was performed during World War I. The Park-to-Park Road which linked three national parks[53], was completed in 1920 and the Black and White Trail was completed in the same year. Three miles of the road were surfaced in 1923. A 1925 estimate indicated $400,000 would be needed to upgrade the road to the East Entrance. The Bureau of Public Roads and the National Park Service reached an agreement concerning the construction of a new road. It was rebuilt in segments over the following years and in 1937 surfacing was completed. At this time it was the most popular road in the park. Additional work was done through World War II.

The Railroad Today in Cody

The Chicago, Burlington and Quincy ended its operations of the Burlington Inn in 1956[54]. The inn was leased, ironically, to the Husky Oil Company[55] and was torn down in 1980, although some sections were retained and are still being used by the oil company[56]. An addition to the Irma Hotel was built in 1930 and it was sold several times over the years. It fell into disrepair but has recently been renovated and is listed on the National Register of Historic Places[57]. The Burlington Northern Santa Fe, successor to the Chicago, Burlington and Quincy, still uses the stucco depot at Cody for its freight operations.

Chicago, Burlington & Quincy Service to Yellowstone National Park

Cody continues to be a popular entrance to Yellowstone National Park. It has grown and prospered with the tourist services and with the growth of the Buffalo Bill Historical Center. The population of has grown slowly in recent years, and in 2000 was officially 8,835[58].

The Chicago, Burlington and Quincy route through Cody was one of the first routes established to the park, but it could not compete with the Northern Pacific and Union Pacific lines, both of which reached the park boundary. However, the railroad built an inn and provided convenient bus service, so the gateway was the preferred route for tourists from Denver. The railroad even ran a tri-weekly name train, the "Buffalo Bill," to Cody, in the summer months to better serve the tourists, and service to Cody lasted longer than it did to Gardiner, but not to West Yellowstone. Today Cody is a popular gateway for tourists.

Chapter Nine

It is 1922 and two of the Lander-Yellowstone Transportation Company buses have stopped in front of the new Two-Gwo-Tee Inn at Brooks Lake. One of the buses is headed for the park and the other is returning to Lander. It was a long, dusty ride to reach the South Entrance to the park. PIONEER MUSEUM, LANDER, WYOMING

"Where Rails End and Trails Begin"

Chicago & North Western Railway
Lander, Wyoming and West Yellowstone, Montana

"From Lander, the western terminus of the Chicago and North Western Railway, across the historic Indian reservation; along the picturesque Wind River with its criss-cross mountain streams; through two great National Forests, and over the Rocky Mountain Continental Divide (at Two-Gwo-Tee Pass), The Lander-Yellowstone Park Transportation Company takes you comfortably in high-powered motor stages through most attractive scenery (including that of the far-famed Teton Mountains) to the new Southern entrance to Yellowstone National Park."[1]

Although the Chicago & North Western Railway is probably best known for operating trains between Milwaukee and Chicago, to Minneapolis and St. Paul, and to the Wisconsin resort areas, the railroad also ran trains to Yellowstone National Park. Despite the fact the Chicago & North Western never reached the park boundary, starting in 1922 and continuing into the early years of the Depression, the railroad offered a route through Lander, Wyoming to the South Entrance of the park. The railroad also offered service to the West Entrance at West Yellowstone in conjunction with the Union Pacific Railroad until the Union Pacific began using The Milwaukee Road for the connecting train between Chicago and Omaha in 1955.

The history of the Chicago & North Western Railway route to Lander and the autobus ride from Lander to the South Entrance of the park is an overlooked part of the history of railroad travel to Yellowstone National Park since it did not operate for many years and since so few tourists used the service. The route was not successful due to the long drive required to reach the park from Lander, where tourists transferred from the train to special autobuses for the drive to the park. In an unusual variation of travel to the park and in order to promote travel through Lander, the Chicago & North Western offered packages by which the tourists would travel to Lander by rail and would then reach the park on horseback.

The joint operations of the trains to West Yellowstone with the Union Pacific are an interesting aspect of the Chicago & North Western service to the park, since the railroad provided connecting passenger train service at Omaha for many years. Tourists could travel over the Chicago & North Western from Chicago to Omaha, and then from Omaha they went over the Union Pacific line to the West Entrance of the park at West Yellowstone, Montana.

It was a long train ride to Lander followed by a dusty bus trip to the South Entrance of the park. Because of this, the route through Lander was not successful. AUTHOR'S COLLECTION

The South Entrance

Lander, Wyoming

Lander, Wyoming lies on the east side of the Wind River Range, at an elevation of 5,357 feet, and was the westernmost point reached by the Chicago & North Western Railway. Lander has always been a western town, with the first commercial rodeo being held there in 1863. The town is also known for the fact that the man who designed the cowboy silhouette which is on the Wyoming state license plate came from Lander[2]. Lander is in Fremont County, which was named for Lt. John Fremont, who passed through the area in 1842[3]. Explorer and trapper John Colter is believed to have passed through the area in 1807, and the first trappers are thought to have traveled through what is now Lander in 1811[4].

The settlement was originally known as "Push Root" because the warm spring winds seemed to push plants up by their roots, and was the site of Fort Augur, later named Camp Brown[5]. In 1875 the town was named for Gen. Frederick West Lander, who surveyed along the Oregon Trail in 1857 at the request of the government. At that time he surveyed the Lander Cutoff from the east side of South Pass to Fort Hall in what became Idaho Territory. Construction of the wagon road was started by Lander in the following year[6], and when it was opened in 1859 over 13,000 travelers passed over it in the first year alone[7].

In June 1869 Fort Augur was built on the bank of the Popo Agie River at the site of present-day Lander to protect the Shoshone Indians on the Wind River Indian Reservation. In 1871 the fort was moved 16 miles to the northwest, and a small settlement and post office were established at the site of the former fort[8]. The settlers in the area raised crops and cattle for the gold miners in the nearby South Pass area. One of the first settlers at Lander was a friend of General Lander named B.F. Lowe, who named the town for his friend[9]. Two of the first businessmen were Eugene Amoretti and Noyes Baldwin[10].

In the 1870s the first stage and freight route to Lander and the Wind River Indian Reservation ran from the Union Pacific main line at Green River, a 150-mile trip through South Pass that took 24 to 30 hours of continuous travel. The stage line was discontinued on June 30, 1906 when the railroad approached Lander from the east[11], replacing the stage service from Green River.

The town of Lander hoped to be the site of the state agricultural school, and residents were disappointed when that did not occur. The town did become the site of the weather bureau and the government land office, helping it become the area business and trading center[12]. An Indian school was built at nearby Fort Washakie in the 1890s. South Pass mining activities were never very successful, but oil was found in the area starting in the 1880s. This activity increased in the second decade of the twentieth century[13] and provided an economic base for the area, supplementing the ranching industry.

Although it is the county seat Lander is isolated and has never been a very large town. The population in the Depression years was approximately 1,826[14] and in 2000 it was 6,867, with a county population of 35,804[15].

There were several proposals for a railroad through Lander before the Chicago & North Western Railway reached the town in 1906. The Portland, Dalles and Salt Lake Railroad Company was chartered by W.W. Chapman in 1871 to build a line from Portland east to connect with the new Union Pacific/Central Pacific transcontinental line[16]. Chapman was not able to raise any money to build the line and in 1876 he renamed his railroad the Portland, Salt Lake and South Pass Railroad, which would have passed through South Pass if the railroad had been built. The line was planned along John Fremont's proposed path to the Columbia River, believing it was preferable to Isaac Stevens' proposed transcontinental route which had been surveyed to the north in 1853[17]. The line would have provided competition to the Northern Pacific Railroad, which was being constructed along Stevens' survey. Chapman was again not able to raise money, and construction was stopped after only four miles of roadbed had been graded[18]. Within a few years the Northern Pacific line was built to the north of Lander and the Union Pacific had been built to the south, isolating the area.

In 1906 a railroad known as the Denver, Laramie and Northwestern Railway Company was incorporated in Wyoming to build a line from Denver to Seattle to provide competition to the Union Pacific. Initial plans were to have the line go from Denver north to Lander and then west to Seattle[19]. By the time construction started in 1908 the route had been revised so that the line would go north to Laramie and then west[20]. Operations between Denver and Greeley began in 1910, when the railroad reorganized as the Denver, Laramie and Northwestern Railroad Company[21]. The proposed extensions, including the line through Lander, were never built.

Over the years there was talk of extending the Chicago & North Western line to the gold mines in the South Pass area near Lander, but again no line was built. The Chicago & North Western first entered Wyoming through the acquisition of the Wyoming Central Railway Company, which had built a line from the east boundary of the Wyoming Territory to Douglas in 1886[22]. At the Nebraska-Wyoming line the Wyoming Central connected with the Fremont, Elkhorn & Missouri Valley Rail Road Company. The Wyoming Central was extended from Douglas to Casper in 1888, and on June 1, 1891 the Fremont, Elkhorn Valley and Missouri Valley Rail Road Company and the Wyoming Central Railroad were consolidated into the Fremont, Elkhorn & Missouri Valley Railroad Company. The Fremont, Elkhorn & Missouri Valley Railroad was then absorbed into the Chicago & North Western on March 1, 1903[23].

On January 9, 1897 the Chicago & North Western incorporated The Wyoming and North Western Railway Company to build a line west from Casper through Natrona, Fremont, and Uinta counties to the western border of Wyoming. The company was capitalized at $6 million[24]. Amended articles of incorporation were filed with the State of Wyoming on November 10, 1904 and the company was renamed the Wyoming & Northwestern Railway Company. The company was authorized to build west from Casper through Natrona, Fremont and Big Horn counties and any Indian reservations in those counties to Thermopolis, with a branch line to Lander. The railroad company was capitalized at $5 million and was backed by the Chicago & North Western. The articles were again amended on July 20, 1905 and the capitalization was increased to $13 million. At this time the estimated overall length of the line was 500 miles[25]. Marvin Hughitt, president of the Chicago & North Western, was also president of the Wyoming and Northwestern Railway Company. The company headquarters were in the Chicago & North Western depot at Casper. The Wyoming and Northwestern Railway Company was sold to the Chicago & North Western on April 30, 1920[26] and the articles of incorporation of the Wyoming and Northwestern Railway were officially revoked on July 19, 1927[27].

The line between Casper and Lander was completed on October 1, 1906[28]. Completion of the line coincided with the relinquishment of land in the Riverton area by the Shoshone and Arapaho Indians, so that the area was opened for settlement. Construction west through Idaho to Coos Bay, Oregon, and Eureka, California was discussed and some surveys were made, but no further actions were taken by the Chicago & North Western after company president Marvin Hughitt put the rumors to rest in that year, stating that the railroad was not going to build to the West Coast.

Rumors of an extension continued, however, and in 1909 *Railway Age* reported that the Chicago & North Western was surveying a line from Lander to the west and then north, paralleling the Butte-Salt Lake City branch of the Oregon Short Line in eastern Idaho. The line would pass along the border of Yellowstone Park and then go through a pass to Armstead, Montana. A month later an officer of the Chicago & North Western firmly denied this rumor in *Railway Age*[29]. In 1915 there was a rumor that the Chicago & North Western was going to build a line from Lander to the west down the Hoback River to the south fork of the Snake River and to the mouth of the Grand Canyon (in Yellowstone Park) where they would build a power plant[30]. This line was never constructed.

In 1910 the railroad ran a daily passenger train from Casper to Lander on the Wyoming and North Western line to Lander. Connections were made at Casper with the train from Chicago. The daily passenger train left Casper at 4 P.M., arriving at Lander at 9:30 P.M., taking 5 and a half hours to travel the 148 miles. The return train left Lander at 6 A.M. and arrived at Casper at 10:50 A.M. Connections with stages were made at Lander to Fort Washakie, Shoshone, Dubois, and other points[31].

It was during this time that the affectionate name for Lander, "Where the Rails End and Trails Begin" came into use, but the area businessmen wanted to change that image. H.O. Barber was a local businessman who sold coal to the railroads from his mines at Hudson and had interests in some of the large buildings in Casper and Riverton. He collaborated with his partners, one of whom was Fred. F. Noble, to build the Noble Hotel in Lander. The men were anxious to develop Lander as an entrance to Yellowstone National Park, following the opening of the road over Togwotee Pass to automobiles in July 1917, although one had to be truly adventurous to drive the highway. The Noble Hotel in Lander was to be part of this development and the $200,000 building was completed in August, 1918. The local newspaper proclaimed it one of the finest small luxury hotels west of the Mississippi. When it was opened the hotel was under the management of J.R. Chambers, who had been assistant superintendent of the Chicago & North Western dining car department for nine years[32].

The arrival of the railroad was beneficial to the town. In 1890 the population of Lander was 525, in 1900 the population was 737, and in 1905, a year before the arrival of the railroad, it was 956. The 1910 census showed that the population had doubled in five years to 1,812. Growth began in earnest with the discovery of the oil fields in Fremont County in 1910. The buildings of this period are now part of the Lander Downtown Historic District, which is listed on the National Register of Historic Places[33].

The Road from Lander into Yellowstone National Park

Even after the railroad reached Lander a tourist still had to travel over 130 miles to reach the park boundary, a long and time-consuming drive on the unimproved roads. It was obvious to everyone that the development of the road to the park was the critical factor in the development of Lander as a gateway.

The route from Lander into Yellowstone National Park can be divided into two distinct segments. The first segment consists of the road from Lander to Moran and the South Entrance of the park, approximately 120 miles. The road passes over Togwotee Pass, at an elevation of 9,658 feet[34]. The second segment consists of the road to the park from Moran to the South Entrance and in the park from the South Entrance to the "Grand Loop" at West Thumb, a distance of approximately 40 miles.

Lander to the South Entrance

The first white man believed to have gone over the Continental Divide at the head of the Wind River using what is today known as Togwotee Pass is believed to have been John Colter, who passed that way in December 1807[35]. Other mountain men may have crossed in 1811[36], and Captain William Raynolds of the U.S. Topographic Corps tried to cross it in June 1860 but was turned back by deep snow. In May 1874 Capt. Robert A. Torrey commander of Camp Bown (Fort Washakie) had orders to build a wagon road through the pass. He got within eight miles of the pass but then turned back, saying it was impossible to build a road

The route through Lander, Wyoming, was long and arduous–not only to reach the park by road, but to reach Lander by train. This schedule from a 1930 timetable shows the long trip required to reach Lander from Chicago. For many years the Chicago & North Western scheduled a through Pullman sleeping car to Lander from Chicago, operating in the summer months only. AUTHOR'S COLLECTION

on that route. Wyoming Gov. John Hoyt (1878-1882) tried to get the federal government to build a road from the Wind River to Yellowstone Lake, with no success. During the First Session of the 47th Congress in January 1882, Senator Post of Wyoming introduced a bill to construct a road from Fort Washakie to Yellowstone Park, but it was adversely reported out of the Military Affairs Committee and no action was taken[37].

In the fall of 1883 some California businessmen explored the area to see if they could build a railroad from Rawlins through the pass at the head of the Wind River, but nothing came of that proposal. In April 1891 Wyoming Sen. Francis Warren tried to obtain a $75,000 appropriation for a road from Fort Washakie to Yellowstone, and it, too, was denied. When he tried again in the following year his request was also denied because the federal government apparently saw no need to improve the roads in the area[38].

However, in 1895 the Bannack and Western Shoshone Indians went to Jackson Hole to hunt elk and several Indians were killed in skirmishes. In response to this Indian scare the Army subsequently pushed for funds to build a road across Togwotee Pass, and they received the money in June 1897. Surveys were performed that summer and construction began on the Yellowstone side the following June. In October 1898 the crude wagon road was finished between Fort Washakie and Fort Yellowstone, at Mammoth Hot Springs in the park. Some work on the road from Fort Washakie side had previously been performed in 1895 by men from the Ninth Calvary. The new road was originally designated as the "Military Road" on maps and joined the trail along the east shore of Jackson Lake to go into Yellowstone Park[39].

Eventually known as the Rocky Mountain Highway and State Highway 287, the road ran from Lander through the Wind River Indian Reservation past Fort Washakie to Dubois, and then through Togwotee Pass to Moran Junction, near the south boundary of the park. The distance from Lander to Dubois was 75 miles, and from Dubois to Moran another 55 miles. From Moran tourists could go north through the South Entrance into Yellowstone National Park or south to Jackson Hole, the location of the future Grand Teton National Park. Although the road from Lander to the park was opened for automobiles in 1917, it was a rugged highway. The first automobiles into Brooks Lake, on this route, were not able to run over the road until November 1917, on a trip which required many repairs to automobiles' tires. The Burlingham Hill was so difficult that in 1919 teams of horses were stationed at the bottom of the hill to help autos get over it, at no cost to the traveler[40].

In 1919 some major road improvements were started and were completed in 1921. Dedication ceremonies for the road were held on August 21 of that year, with Wyoming Gov. Robert Carey, Sen. John Kendrick, and other dignitaries in attendance. Stephen Mathers, Director of the National Park Service, was present, as was Horace Albright, superintendent of Yellowstone National Park. Shoshone Chief Dick Washakie also attended, and a man thought to be the son or grandson of To-go-tee, a member of the Sheep Easter Indian Tribe for whom the pass was named, is believed to have been at the ceremonies[41].

With some assistance from the National Park Service the road was graveled in 1922, and in that year bus service between Lander and the park was offered for the first time[42]. The main road work for the summer was to improve the road from Brooks Lake to Togwotee Pass and to add gravel onto the road to Brooks Lake[43]. In later years the road was gradually improved, but it was a long time before it was oiled and some of the steep grades eliminated. It was not until the end of World War II that the highway was kept open in the winter months.

South Entrance to West Thumb

The road into the park from the South Entrance has its own history and development. It was first used by tourists starting about 1890, but even at the turn of the century the road from the South Entrance of the park to Geyser Basin was not much more than a cleared pathway. Army engineer Hiram Chittenden described it as being "merely grubbed and clear, with trees and stumps left in middle of roadway most of the distance. The whole road is in a wretched condition and a disgrace to the Government." The road was slowly improved using a $20,000 appropriation. Ten bridges and 14 culverts were built in 1902, but the road was used largely by military personnel going to and from the Snake River Soldier Station on the South Entrance Road[44]. The North Entrance to the park continued to be the most popular gateway since the Northern Pacific Railway reached the park boundary, and Mammoth Hot Springs was only a short stage ride from the depot.

However, with the potential of allowing automobiles into the park, more improvements were made to the South Entrance road starting in 1915, and by 1917 all but two miles were considered as being improved. Although in 1915 the park roads had been opened to automobiles in 1915[45], in the first years that the road was not heavily used by tourists since it was still a rough gravel road.

Anxious to promote automobile travel through their town, the Lander Chamber of Commerce advertised the route as being the shortest and most scenic route from Denver to the park. Although this was true, it was not necessarily the most convenient and fastest due to the long drive over the road from Lander to the park. Nor was it the cheapest route for rail travelers, because the route through Lander cost tourists traveling by rail $42 more in each direction in 1922 than alternate routes to the park due to the long drive required to reach the park[46].

Travel Through Lander to Yellowstone National Park

Railroad Service to Lander Prior to 1922

Prior to offering service for tourists to Yellowstone National Park through Lander the Chicago & North Western provided the conventional passenger service of the time to Lander. Although this service varied over the years, it essentially consisted of one or two trains a day in each direction. A timetable for December 1916 showed that the railroad offered daily service from Sioux City, Iowa through Chadron and Casper to Lander, with the train arriving at 7:30 P.M. in the evening and departing Lander at 6:30 A.M. in the morning. The train included a drawing room/sleeping car and coach and chair cars[47]. The service did not change much over the years. In August 1920 the railroad advertised service

A view of the first scheduled passenger train to arrive at Lander, many years before a road connected the town to the park. The local residents are eagerly awaiting the new form of transportation. According to legend, when the train arrived, the engineer leaned out of the locomotive and told the residents he was going to turn the train around. The engineer meant he was going to the wye at the end of the tracks, but the residents, afraid he was going to turn the train around in the same manner as they turned a wagon, ran behind the buildings so they wouldn't be run over. PIONEER MUSEUM, LANDER, WYOMING

from Chicago to Lander through Omaha, leaving Chicago at 12:15 A.M. and arriving at Lander at 9:30 P.M. the following day, traveling a distance of almost 1,300 miles. The returning train left Lander at 8:45 A.M. and arrived at Chicago at 7:35 A.M. two days later. The train took approximately 5 and a half hours to run the 148 miles between Casper and Lander. There was also a daily-except-Sunday mixed train between Casper and Lander, which ran on a more relaxed schedule, taking approximately 10 hours to run the 148 hours between Casper and Lander[48].

In 1922 the Chicago & North Western began offering passenger service to Yellowstone National Park through Lander in conjunction with the Lander-Yellowstone Transportation Company. Called the "Southern Gateway Tour" by the Chicago & North Western, passengers arrived in the evening at Lander on the train from Casper, which connected with the train from Chicago. After spending the night at Lander the tourists departed for Yellowstone National Park on standard park tour buses the next morning. This bus service was initially provided by the Lander-Yellowstone Transportation Company and later by the Yellowstone Park Transportation Company.

The Lander-Yellowstone Transportation Company

The Lander-Yellowstone Transportation Company was an essential link in travel to the park from Lander. The bus company was established in March 1922 to run buses between Lander and Moran, Wyoming. After it was formed the company signed a contract with the White Motor Truck Company to buy its buses and made an agreement with the Chicago & North Western to provide passenger service. The buses were the same as those used in the park. Prior to inaugurating the bus service the bus company had a meeting in Chicago with the National Park Service to make sure the park bulletins and advertisements included information on the Lander gateway[49].

One interesting detail of the five-year agreement with the Chicago & North Western, which was renewable for another five years, was that Lander was to be the *"exclusive destination for the railroad company for transportation on its line for all tourist travel to and from Yellowstone Park; that about $10,000 shall be expended in advertising this route by folders, personal solicitations, etc.; that tickets for the bus line routing will be placed in over 5,000 ticket offices in the United States..."* The agreement committed the bus company to provide 10 passenger buses for daily service from Lander, with a lunch stop at Dubois and a night at Brooks Lake. The accommodations there were to be typical of those provided at Yellowstone Park. The morning after the stop at Brooks Lake the guests would continue to Moran for lunch at noon, and connections were made there with the park's bus line, where the tourists would continue on into the park, arriving at the Lake Hotel for the night[50].

Businessman H.O. Barber was the major backer of the bus company, using the Finance Corporation of Wyoming. The officers of the bus company were all from Lander and included Frank Arnold, who was manager of the Noble Hotel. The Lander newspaper supported the new bus company, stating that Lander would become the "Indian Gateway" to the park. Support for the new venture was also provided by Roe Emery, who was president of the Denver Cab and Omnibus Company in Denver, which operated buses through Estes Park (present-day Rocky Mountain National Park) and Glacier National Park[51].

The hotel at Brooks Lake, which became known as the Two-Gwo-Tee Inn, was to be built that summer, and the Jackson Hole accommodations were to be at the Amoretti Inn, which had both cabins and a lodge. The Amoretti Inn was near the present-day Jackson Lake Lodge. The lunch stop at Dubois was at the Welty Inn, which was a converted log home[52].

Train/Bus Operations

By May 1922 the Chicago & North Western had folders advertising the Lander route ready for distribution. Titled "Teton Mountain Route to Yellowstone Park", the schedule showed that a person could leave Chicago just after midnight (12:15 A.M.) and arrive at Omaha at 3:21 P.M. that afternoon. An hour later he would be on board the Lander train, leaving at 4:45 P.M., and the next evening the train would arrive at Lander at 7:15 P.M.[53] At the same time the folders were printed, a road crew was preparing to go to Brooks Lake and finish working on the road to the park, while work was also starting on the new hotel at Brooks Lake. Unfortunately, the winter weather had kept the men from doing much more than getting the logs to the jobsite. The crew actually building the hotel at Brooks Lake did not arrive at Lander until mid-June, arriving by train[54]. The railroad set up a ticket office in the Noble Hotel on June 14 while work on the highway to the park was continuing. Rain cleared the snow in mid-June and the new buses to be used on the road left Denver on June 25 for Lander, with an expected arrival three days later[55].

The Chicago & North Western apparently began to think more positively about the idea of travel through Lander that spring, agreeing to run a through train to Lander using steel cars instead of the older wood ones. The railroad also promised that the new train would include baggage, mail and day coaches, Pullman sleepers, and a dining car that would run through to Lander from Omaha. The train was scheduled to arrive at 7:15 A.M. in the morning, an hour earlier than the previous schedule, and leave at 9:45 P.M., with an arrival in Omaha several hours earlier than the previous train schedule[56]. When the first train arrived on June 25, it was greeted enthusiastically by the Lander citizens. The local newspaper noted that effective July 1 the train would include a dining car from Omaha to Casper, but at that time it was not known if the car would continue on to Lander[57].

The bus company managers inspected the route to Brooks Lake and the lodge on June 17. The new buses arrived as scheduled on June 28, 1922. The body of the yellow buses had a portrait of Chief Washakie painted on the side. The bus drivers were specially trained and wore a uniform which consisted of a full cowboy outfit. By then 200 men were working on the lodge, and hundreds of other men were working on the highway. Barber made another trip of the route on June 29, and when he returned he indicated he was satisfied with everything[58].

Bus service began on Saturday, July 1, 1922. The day before a bus had left Lander for Dubois so that it would be ready for the return trip, and to everyone's surprise it carried nine passengers. The first official bus for the park left Lander on July 1 at 8 A.M., with two paying passengers from Chicago. Two additional passengers were picked up en route at Crowheart, since the buses also provided local service along the route. On the first two days the service was slow in part because the rains had washed out bridges on the tracks east of Casper, and there was a railroad strike which started on July 1. Due to this strike the daily passenger load on the bus line was only 4-5 passengers a day instead of the 10-12 hoped for.

The bus left Lander at 8 in the morning and arrived at Dubois at 1 in the afternoon. After a one-hour lunch stop the bus left at 2 o'clock and arrived at the Two-Gwo-Tee Inn on Brooks Lake at 5 that afternoon, and the guests spent the night there. The bus left the lodge the next morning at 9, went over Two-

Bus enroute to the Two-Gwo-Tee Inn on Brooks Lake. AUTHOR'S COLLECTION

Gwo-Tee Pass, at an elevation of 9,545 feet, and arrived at the Amoretti Inn at noon. After lunch the passengers left on a Yellowstone Park Company bus at 1:30 P.M. to pass through the South Entrance into the park. The buses did not carry trunks, and passengers were limited to 25 pounds of luggage. In addition to scenery and wildlife along the route, passengers could see the tie drives down the Wind River. In the summer of 1922 over 400,000 railroad ties were floated down the river[59].

The Amoretti Inn was built in 1922 by Eugene Amoretti of Lander under the auspices of the Amoretti Hotel and Camp Company. It was at the approximate location of today's Jackson Lake Lodge and included cabins and tent cabins. Some cabins had running hot and cold water and toilets, and the lodge could accommodate 125 guests. By 1924 Amoretti had plans for a series of lodges and camps, combining resorts and dude ranches[60].

Bus service ended on September 15 in the first year of operations with the only interruption being a blizzard which closed the road on July 17 and 18. In the first season 99 tourists took this route, although the National Park Service was optimistic that more would take the route when it became better known[61]. Although the bus company did not make money the first year, it hoped to become profitable the following summer[62]. In addition to providing bus service to the park, the company also transported passengers to the towns along the route. A trip from Lander to Fort Washakie cost $2 and to Dubois was $10. The fare from Lander to Moran was $25. Other costs reported in the Lander newspaper were as follows[63]:

- Lander to Moran, including lunch at Dubois, dinner, lodging and breakfast at Brooks Lake, and lunch at Moran, for $32.
- A tour of the park, which included 14 meals and four night's lodging (4-1/2 days) for $32.
- Bus fare in the park for $35.
- Total costs for a tour of Yellowstone Park from Lander was $128.
- Bus fare in the park and to Cody was $30.
- Going in by Lander and leaving via Cody was $91.
- If one stayed at the camps in the park instead of the hotels there was a savings of $9.

In the following year the Lander-Yellowstone Transportation Company began operations between Lander and Moran on June 25, 1923, when the snows had melted and the roads had been repaired. The Chicago & North Western sent out a movie camera crew to take pictures of the park and the Lander route. The route through Lander was becoming more popular, so hotel accommodations were expanded. Many of the people traveling by automobile were camping in the Lander city park[64].

Travel was discouraged somewhat when the Union Pacific put some restrictions on the use of Pullman cars to Lander, apparently fearing the competition with their entrance through West Yellowstone. The Union Pacific announced that it would provide competition with bus service to the park from Rock Springs starting June 20, with a stopover scheduled at Pinedale. The businessmen along the route through Pinedale were anxious to promote the route through Pinedale[65]. However, the Union Pacific's bus service from Rock Springs was not very successful and the railroad discontinued it a short time after it was inaugurated[66].

Barber's finances started to crumble in 1922 when the market for coal from his mines declined. In late 1924 or early 1925 the bondholders took over the Lander-Yellowstone Transportation Company and formed the Amoretti Hotel Company, which included the bus company, the Two-Gwo-Tee Inn, and the Lewis Lake Camp in Yellowstone Park. The company sold off the various entities, and Jim Gratiot bought the Lewis Lake Camp and the Two-Gwo-Tee Inn. He also took over the Two Ocean Pass packing outfit, which had been formed to transport guests by horseback from the lodge to Lewis Lake. He turned the Two-Gwo-Tee Inn into the Diamond G Ranch and operated it as a dude ranch. He was so busy in the summer of 1925 that he could not accommodate bus passengers at the lodge, so the tourists had to continue on to Moran[67], which improved the bus service to the park.

In 1925 bus service from Lander started at 7:30 on the morning of June 25, taking nine hours to reach Moran. When the mountain slid into the Gros Ventre River in August 1925, flooding the road, the road closure caused travel to decline that summer, but it was a good summer overall, and the prospects for the following summer looked good. Other bus lines also began working out of Lander to locations including Casper, Thermopolis, and Rock Springs[68].

On June 21, 1930 W.F. Smith, president of the bus company, sold the Lander-Yellowstone Transportation Company to J.T. Gratiot. The sale included three White 10-passenger buses which had been used between Lander and Moran and the remains of a fourth bus which had been in a wreck. The sale included other bus parts and the franchise to operate the service. The sale amount was $5,000, payable in installments over two years. Gratiot was to operate the service daily during the summer season, and in the first summer the Lander-Yellowstone Transportation Company name could be used. The bus service was quickly absorbed into the Yellowstone Park Transportation Company and the buses were all painted the standard yellow color[69].

Promotion and Travel on the Lander Route

The Chicago & North Western initially did not actively promote the route through Lander because there was no passable road from Lander to the park until 1922, but the railroad apparently considered the possibilities of advertising the route as early as 1912. In that year Chicago & North Western's stationery had a letterhead which showed the Chicago & North Western routes. The map showed the line to Lander with a connecting road to Yellowstone Park[70].

The National Park Service established a radio advertising campaign in the spring of 1925 to inform visitors of the route through Lander[71]. A 1925 brochure distributed by the Chicago & North Western called it the "Lander Gateway - The Southern Entrance", but had to state that it "Costs a little more but worth it" due to the scenic drive[72]. In addition to offering service to and from Lander, the Chicago & North Western worked with the other railroads and offered packages so travelers going through Lander could use any of the other entrances to enter or leave the park at no extra fare, as was common for all of the railroads reaching the park.

In 1929 the Department of the Interior published a "Manual for Railroad Visitors" with schedules for the tour routes through the park. That year tours ran from June 20 through September 19, and they give an indication of the possibilities available when travel to the park was at an all-time high. The tour route through Lander was as follows[73]:

> Day 0 - Chicago & North Western passengers left Lander on the Lander-Yellowstone Transportation Company buses at 8 A.M.– They arrived at Jackson Lake Lodge (Moran) late that afternoon, spending the night there.
> Day 1– Jackson Lake Lodge to Yellowstone Lake
> Day 2–Yellowstone Lake to the Grand Canyon
> Day 3– Grand Canyon to Mammoth Hot Springs
> Day 4–Mammoth Hot Springs to Old Faithful
> Day 5–Old Faithful to the Jackson Lake Lodge (Moran) for the night. A bus then returned the travelers to Lander, where they boarded the evening train for the trip back home.

The Chicago & North Western transported 167 passengers for Lander to the park in 1923, compared to 23,116 over the Union Pacific to West Yellowstone, 14,117 over the Northern Pacific to Gardiner, and 7,407 over the Chicago, Burlington and Quincy in the same year[74]. When the joint Union Pacific/Chicago & North Western Department of Tours advertised travel to Yellowstone National Park, their brochures were careful not to mention the Lander route, since the Union Pacific was concerned that travel through Lander would take away from its business. This meant the Chicago & North Western had to advertise the Lander route by itself.

The bus trip from Lander to the park was the longest and most arduous of all of the bus routes to the park, and initially the route also involved the cost of an additional night's lodging at Lander. In 1924 there were 207 passengers through Lander[75], and in 1925 there were 225[76]. In the following year 271 tourists arrived over the Chicago and North Western[77], and 109 came in 1927[78]. Only 108 arrived in the following year[79], and 261 in 1929[80]. The number of rail travelers arriving through the South Entrance decreased to 90 in the first year of the Depression[81] (some of whom arrived through Victor), and was 121 in 1931[82]. Only 27 arrived in 1932[83] and eight in the following summer[84]. Only four passengers arrived from Lander through June 30, 1934[85], and after that date the Park Service no longer reported arrivals by rail for the different gateways since the automobile had become the predominant form of

TETON MOUNTAIN ROUTE TO YELLOWSTONE PARK

Lander Gateway
The Southern Entrance

PICTURESQUE WIND RIVER
HISTORIC INDIAN COUNTRY
AND
JACKSON HOLE
TETON MOUNTAIN REGION

CHICAGO AND NORTH WESTERN LINE

In 1930 the Chigaco & North Western Railway printed this brochure for travel through Lander which they called the Indian Gateway! They tried to cover all aspects of the trip–from the Teton Mountains to the scenic trip to reach the park.
UNION PACIFIC HISTORICAL COLLECTION, GADAMUS COLLECTION, YELLOWSTONE HISTORIC CENTER

108

transportation to and in the park.

However, the Chicago & North Western did advertise the Lander entrance in 1934, despite the fact it was obvious that it was neither profitable nor popular. The route was handicapped by the long distance to the park, which detracted from its appeal. By this time the railroad offered only motor coach service in the summer between Casper and Lander due to the decline in passenger traffic[86]. Even in 1932, however, in the depths of the Depression, the company stated that it would run four special Pullman trains that summer to Lander from Chicago[87].

Roads and automobiles were improving, syphoning traffic from the Chicago & North Western and the other railroads serving the park. By this time Lander was no longer being considered a gateway. A 1941 brochure put out by the Department of the Interior made no mention of the Lander Gateway, nor did it show the town on its map[88].

An interesting variation to the tour offered by the railroad in 1927 involved traveling over several railroads to and from Lander. One could go over the Chicago & North Western from Chicago to Council Bluffs, over the Union Pacific to Denver, and then on the Colorado & Southern to Wendover. From there one could travel over the Chicago, Burlington and Quincy to Casper, and then on the Chicago & North Western to Lander[89]. Presumably this was not a popular route due to the numerous transfers between trains.

The Chicago & North Western operated a Department of Tours in conjunction with the Union Pacific and offered packages to Yellowstone National Park and other national parks. It advertised the route from the Chicago & North Western Union Station in Chicago over the line to Omaha, and from there over the Union Pacific to West Yellowstone and other western national parks. Separate brochures advertised the "Teton Mountain Route to Yellowstone Park" through Lander and the South Entrance. These brochures promoted the scenic Wind River country, the Indian territories, and the Jackson Hole and Teton Mountain region.

In addition to promoting travel to the park, the Chicago & North Western promoted travel to dude ranches in the Lander area. The 1920s were a time when dude ranches were popular, with the number increasing from one dude ranch in the area in 1909 to 20 in the summer of 1928. In the summer of 1927 the railroad advertised an interesting variation to its standard park tour. Instead of riding motor coaches from Lander to Yellowstone, the visitors could go to the park on horseback. Tourists could take the train to Lander and after spending the night there would ride a motor coach to the Diamond G Ranch in Dubois. They could then ride a horse to Yellowstone Lake, camping out along the way for six nights and seven days. The price for a trip from Chicago to Lander, the horse trip, a tour of the park, and return through any of the other gateways was $238.50[90], expensive for the time.

In 1928 the railroad published a book titled *Wyoming Wild West Ranches*, giving descriptions on the various dude ranches in the Lander area[91]. In addition to dude ranches, other hotels were promoted along with the route between Lander and the park. The hotels included the Stringer Hotel in Dubois and the Yellowstone Highway Lodge, built in 1921, 20 miles west of Dubois at Tie Camp[92].

The Union Pacific, of course, followed the development of the Lander route with great interest, since it could potentially compete with its established route to West Yellowstone. The Union Pacific offered no advertising or support for the route, and noted that the park personnel they talked to felt that the route had no possibility of succeeding[93].

Brooks Lake Lodge

An integral part of the route from Lander to Yellowstone Park was what is now called Brooks Lake Lodge. In the first years of bus operations travelers had to spend their first night at the lodge, which was originally known as the Two-Gwo-Tee Inn. The Two-Gwo-Tee Inn was barely finished in time for the opening of the gateway in the first year. As would be expected at a western lodge, the furnishings included bedframes made from native lodgepole pines.

It was located on the western edge of Shoshone National Forest, two miles east of the Continental Divide and on the shore of Brooks Lake. The original Lander-Yellowstone Road went past the lodge complex, which took up 22-1/2 acres north of present-day U.S. Highway 26/287. It was practically inaccessible in the winter months due to the heavy snowfalls. There were originally 15 cabins, of which seven remain. The original lodge, gas station, bunkhouse and other buildings also remain standing and are in use today.

A bus unloading passengers at the Two-Gwo-Tee Inn (later named the Brooks Lake Lodge) on Brooks Lake. AUTHOR'S COLLECTION

When the proposed route from Lander to the park was being discussed, Lander businessman Eugene Amoretti stated that his newly formed Amoretti Hotel and Camp Company would operate the lodges along the route to the park. The company was organized in April 1922 and by July of that year he had built lodges at Brooks Lake and at Moran in Jackson Hole. Due to poor weather workmen began construction on the Brooks Lake Hotel in April, but by May 23 the walls had not yet been started, and by June 14 the walls were still not up. Shortly after this a group of carpenters arrived by train from Casper and the hotel was completed byJuly 1[94], just in time for the new service to the park.

The first year, 1922, was a good one for the hotels. They charged $6 a day per person, or $35 a week. Tourists initially spent their first night out of Lander at the ranch. When Jim Gratiot took over the ranch he operated it as a dude ranch; it was not a working ranch[95]. Business dropped during the Depression and World War II, but recovered in the following years. In the 1950s the popularity of dude ranches waned, and the Diamond G was sold to the Morton Salt Company, which used it as a recreational ranch for its employees. It was soon traded for another ranch and then went through a series of owners before being renamed the Brooks Lake Lodge. After being closed for several years it was purchased once again and has been restored as a ranch for tourists. The Brooks Lake Lodge is now on the National Register of Historic Places[96].

The End of Service from Lander to Yellowstone

Establishment of Grand Teton National Park at Jackson, Wyoming on February 26, 1929[97] did not help travel through Lander, and promotion of the Lander Gateway by the Chicago & North Western appears to have ended at the conclusion of the 1934 season. With the ending of the unsuccessful service through Lander, the Chicago & North Western continued to promote travel to West Yellowstone over the Union Pacific. However, even when the Chicago & North Western no longer offered service to the park its timetables showed the schedule to Lander, and the Lander station name was followed by the words "Yellowstone National Park". Even an advertisement for freight business from 1951 for the Chicago & North Western which showed the line to Lander depicted the highway from Lander to Yellowstone National Park[98].

Service to Lander varied according to the season and changed over the years. The January 1938 timetable showed a daily train with coaches[99], but by June 1939 the Chicago & North Western was offering a daily-except-Sunday service from Chadron in a motorcar[100]. In September 1940 the off-season service between Chadron and Lander was daily except Sunday, with through coaches between Chadron and Lander. By this time the railroad had cut back sleeping car service to Chadron.

The Chicago & North Western to Lander – Abandonment

In 1943 the line between Casper and Shoshone was abandoned and trackage rights received from the Chicago, Burlington and Quincy[101]. The tracks were pulled up and used for scrap during World War II. However, the line to Riverton and Lander remained. Oil and products were taken out of Riverton for many years, and the town was the site of a tie plant. Many carloads of wood were also taken from this area. By the end of World War II through passenger service from Chicago to Lander had ended, and connections were made with the mixed train at Casper[102].

In 1972 the 22.20 mile segment of the line from Riverton (Milepost 725.60) to Lander (Milepost 747.80) was abandoned[103]. For many years the railroad had a tie treatment plant at Riverton and used the mines at Hudman to supply coal to the railroad, but the coal was poor with a low BTU value. The Chicago & North Western closed the tie plant and the railroad no longer needed coal, so in 1989 the railroad abandoned the line from Casper west to Riverton, with the segment from Bonneville to Riverton being sold to the Bad Water Line[104] and subsequently abandoned.

Today the Lander depot is used by the local Chamber of Commerce. A former Union Pacific caboose is at the Jaycee Park. Caboose #25574 was donated in 1989 to the local Junior Chamber of Commerce[105].

View of the Lander depot in 1971, with the local switcher spotted in front of it. This line was abandoned the following year. AUTHOR'S COLLECTION

The depot at Lander was a simple, one-story wooden-framed building adequate for the small volume of traffic. It has been restored and is used by the local Chamber of Commerce, and a Union Pacific caboose is on display in a nearby park. ART PETERSON COLLECTION

The West Entrance

Travel to West Yellowstone Over the Chicago & North Western/Union Pacific

The route operated to West Yellowstone in conjunction with the Union Pacific developed in a different manner than the Lander Route. The Chicago & North Western reached Council Bluffs, Iowa on January 17, 1867 under the auspices of the Cedar Rapids and Missouri River Railroad[106]. Here the railroad made connections with the Union Pacific Railway to provide transcontinental train service between Chicago and the West Coast, as well as to West Yellowstone when that line was completed. When the Union Pacific completed its line to West Yellowstone in 1908 the Chicago & North Western began offering through car service from Chicago to the park in conjunction with the Union Pacific.

Over the years the Chicago & North Western and the Union Pacific Railroad jointly operated a Department of Tours to promote travel to the park and to other scenic destinations in the West. The Union Pacific route to West Yellowstone was the most popular route, a fact the Union Pacific was quick to advertise. The two lines worked together to promote travel for many years.

All Chicago & North Western service to Yellowstone National Park, directly and indirectly, ended on October 31, 1955, when the Union Pacific terminated joint operations of passenger trains to Chicago with the Chicago & North Western. The Union Pacific shifted all of its train operations to the Chicago, Milwaukee, St. Paul & Pacific Railroad (The Milwaukee Road) effective that day, ending all connections of the Chicago & North Western with service to Yellowstone National Park[107].

Chicago & North Western Service to Yellowstone National Park

The Lander Gateway through Lander to the South Entrance was never popular, despite efforts by both the Chicago & North Western and the local businesses to promote it. The line to Lander had been built previous to the thought of using Lander as a gateway. Only when the road from Lander to the park began to be passable to automobiles did the possibility of promoting it as a route become apparent. Improved train service and a bus line were provided with the hope that the tourist traffic through Lander would grow. The route was inaugurated in 1922 and operated through the early years of the Depression, when bus service was quietly discontinued. The distance from Lander over unimproved roads was a detriment to the popularity of the route. Not only was it inconvenient, it was never widely advertised since the Union Pacific would not include it in its advertising brochures. The Lander Gateway was the shortest-lived and least used of all of the gateways.

The Chicago & North Western was more successful in its promotion of the route through West Yellowstone in conjunction with the Union Pacific, but that connection was lost when the Union Pacific discontinued its agreement with the Chicago & North Western to operate passenger trains to and from Chicago.

Chapter Ten

A postcard view, published by The Milwaukee Road, showing the railroad's buses in front of the Galatin Gateway Inn. The railroad operated its own buses from Three Forks after World War II.
AUTHOR'S COLLECTION

The Historic – Scenic Route

The Milwaukee Road
Gallatin Gateway and West Yellowstone, Montana

"....*It is the <u>only</u> one operating regular Park Tours in regular Park motor coaches from a main line point of any transcontinental railroad – no branch travel.*

It traverses a virgin country rivaling the Park itself in scenery.

It includes a portion of the park not heretofore included in any of the regular Park Tours.

It traverses a country of unusual historic interest closely identified with the early explorer and pioneer.

It gives a longer tour than any of the other Park Tours at no greater expense.

It enables the traveler, for the first time, to include Yellowstone Park as a side trip on a Pacific Coast tour over the only transcontinental railroad....."[1]

The last railroad to build a line to reach Yellowstone National Park was The Milwaukee Road, officially known as the Chicago, Milwaukee & St. Paul Railway at the time the railroad company built its line to Gallatin Gateway, Montana[2]. The route was never very popular both because it was established after rail travel to Yellowstone National Park had peaked and because it was not as convenient as the Union Pacific and Northern Pacific routes, which reached the park boundary. Not only did passengers have to take a side trip from the railroad's main line to get to Gallatin Gateway, but it was then a long road trip from that gateway to the West Entrance of the park at West Yellowstone. The railroad did, however, offer package tours to the park in conjunction with the other railroads.

When The Milwaukee Road constructed its line across southern Montana in 1907-1908 its route went to the north of Yellowstone National Park. In the early 1920s the Chicago, Milwaukee & St. Paul Railway saw the potential profit in offering service to the park. Despite a drop in overall rail traffic to the park, the railway initially began promoting travel to the park from the main line at Three Forks, Montana in 1926, but the service was never competitive with the Northern Pacific and Union Pacific lines because the trip was a long 100-mile bus ride over gravel roads from Three Forks to the west entrance of the park.

In an attempt to compete for the tourist business to Yellowstone the railroad built the Gallatin Gateway Inn in 1927. This was the first large hotel in Montana outside of a national park and was

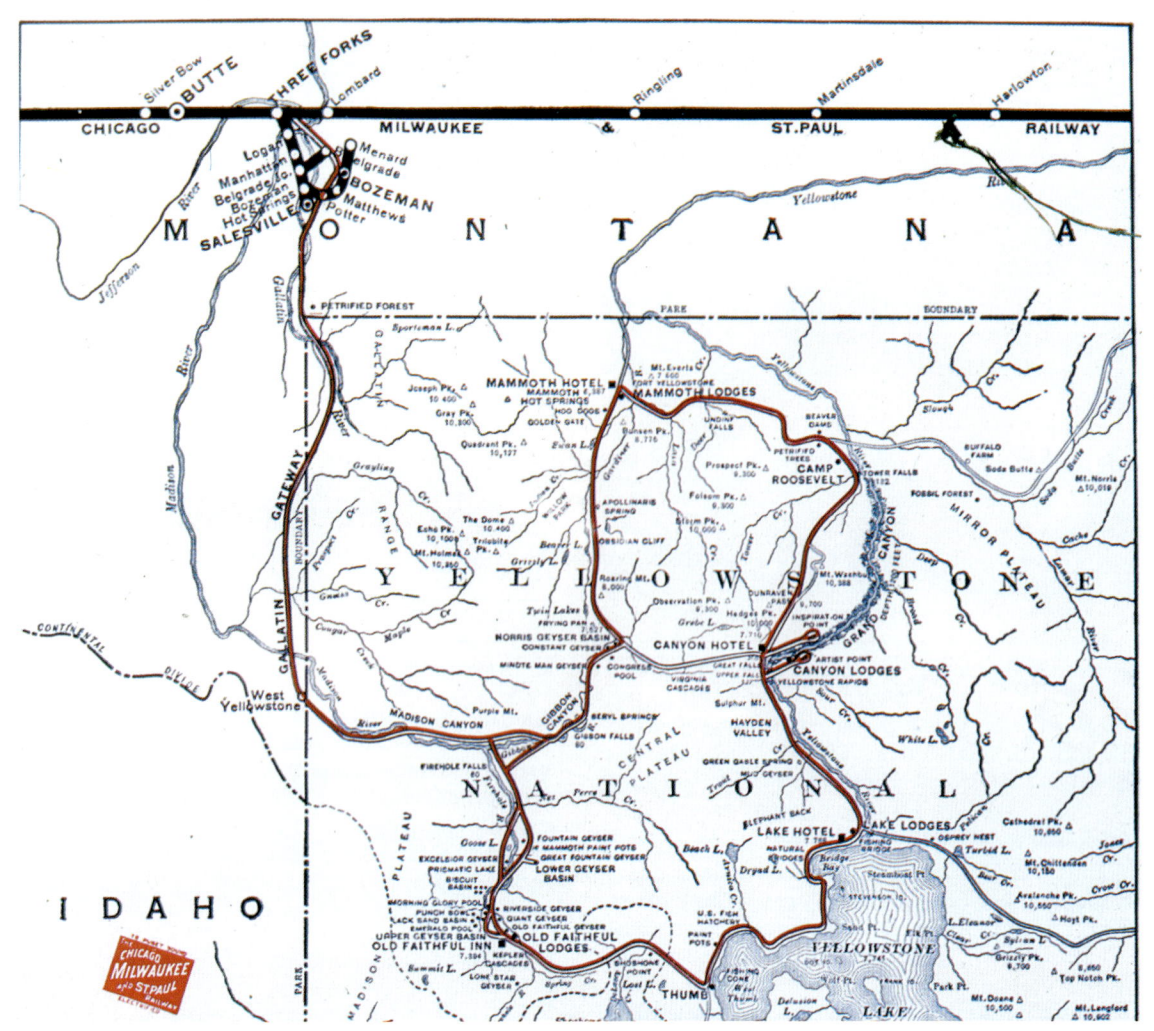

The Milwaukee Road advertised their new route to Yellowstone National Park from Three Forks through Salesville, which became Gallatin Gateway, in this 1926 map. The route through Gallatin Gateway was opened for the following season. AUTHOR'S COLLECTION

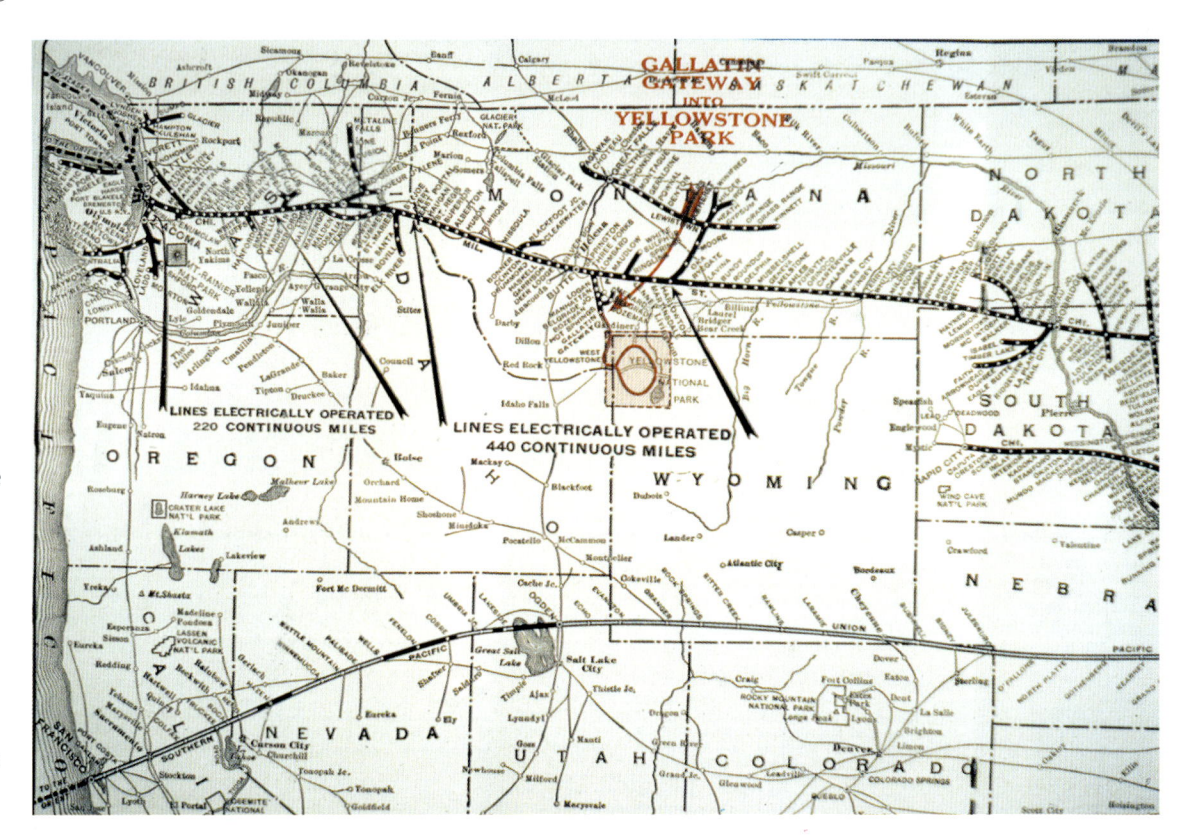

A map published by The Milwaukee Railroad in 1927 shows the new route to Yellowstone National Park through Gallatin Gateway. GADAMUS COLLECTION, YELLOWSTONE HISTORIC CENTER

located at the newly named town of Gallatin Gateway, formerly known as Salesville. As soon as the hotel opened the Chicago, Milwaukee & St. Paul Railway Company began running passenger trains to the inn over its newly constructed branch line from Three Forks. The Gallatin Gateway Inn never reached the popularity envisioned by the railroad and fell a victim to the Depression, World War II, and the increased popularity of the private automobile and improved highways. The railroad discontinued passenger service to the inn, sold the inn and removed the tracks. Fortunately, new owners restored the inn to its former grandeur, a reminder of the time when one could travel over The Milwaukee Road to reach Yellowstone National Park. The inn is still in operation today. The history of the inn and the Milwaukee Road's line to Gallatin Gateway is an interesting part of the history of rail travel to Yellowstone National Park.

The Railroad to Gallatin Gateway

The rail line to Gallatin Gateway, which was originally known as Salesville, dates back to April 5, 1892 with the incorporation of the Gallatin Light, Power & Railway Company. Formed to build and operate a trolley line to Bozeman, Montana the GLP&R Company built a line from the Northern Pacific depot on the north side of town to the south side of Bozeman[3]. In a spurt of optimism the local newspaper went so far as to say that the line would soon be extended to Yellowstone Park[4]. The Bozeman Street Railway Company was incorporated on December 1, 1897 and took over the Gallatin, Light, Power & Railway Company on December 18, 1897[5]. The initial success of the trolley line led to the construction of the interurban line to Salesville several years later.

The Gallatin Valley Railroad initially operated an electric interurban car between Bozeman and Salesville. Following the completion of the line between Three Forks and Salesville, The Milwaukee Road renamed the town Gallatin Gateway.
GALLATIN COUNTY HISTORICAL SOCIETY

The settlers in the Gallatin Valley[6] had seen the need for a rail line when the Northern Pacific completed its line across southern Montana in 1883. It was a long, time-consuming trip to reach the nearest railhead at Bozeman. Although the Gallatin Valley was a prosperous agricultural area, there were not enough people to support a rail line, nor was there enough money to build one. The Northern Pacific considered building a line from Bozeman up the West Gallatin River to the park, but chose instead to build its line from Livingston to Cinnabar. Although the route through the Gallatin Valley would have been more scenic than the Gardiner line, it would have been longer and more expensive to build due to the narrow Gallatin Canyon[7].

Discussions in 1907 by Bozeman businessmen led to the promise of the construction of a rail line into the Gallatin Valley, and their plan was greeted with the enthusiastic support of the valley residents. Outside backers of the line apparently envisioned that this line was going to connect Bozeman with the new Milwaukee line being built across southern Montana. The local investors wanted the line built from Bozeman to Salesville, and so this was the first section of the line to be built. An interurban line was selected in lieu of a steam railroad due to the popularity and success of other interurban lines throughout the country at that time. It was felt that trains powered by electricity would be more profitable and faster than steam trains[8].

Local farmers subscribed $50,000 to the new interurban company by the end of October, 1907 with another $100,000 being sought at that time in Bozeman. In mid-November Bozeman residents promised an additional $20,000 and the city was asked to donate a right-of-way and land valued at $30,000. Spokane businessmen promised to build the line if $107,000 was raised by March 1908[9].

The Gallatin Valley Electric Railway (GVER) was subsequently organized on March 18, 1908 and the articles of incorporation were filed with the state on March 23, 1908. Capitalized at $800,000 in common stock and $200,000 in preferred stock, the GVER was to build a line from Bozeman west to what is now Bozeman Hot Springs with a branch line south to Salesville[10]. The railroad announced plans to resurrect the bathhouses at Bozeman Hot Springs[11], although the railroad never did anything to improve them after the line was completed.

Probably because there was difficulty raising the money, construction did not start for another year. The contract for the construction of the GVER was not awarded until March 1909, and the groundbreaking ceremonies were performed in Bozeman on April 21, 1909[12]. The new line was opened to Bozeman Hot Springs, 11.7 miles west of Bozeman, on September 16, 1909, and operations to Salesville, 4.9 miles south of Bozeman Hot Springs and 16.6 miles from Bozeman, began on September 26, 1909[13]. The first revenue car of freight, containing barley, was shipped over the new line to the Bozeman Brewing Company[14]. The line had been completed using only stock subscriptions and had no debt. The GVER had taken over the Bozeman trolley line in order to make it easier to interchange cars with the Northern Pacific and was operating the trolley line in Bozeman on May 1, 1909. However, it was not until November 27, 1909 that the Bozeman trolley line was officially transferred to the GVER. The operations of the trolley and interurban lines were always kept separate[15].

The Chicago, Milwaukee & St. Paul Railway Company of Montana had reached Three Forks in 1908, and the Gold Spike ceremony to complete the nation's last transcontinental railroad was driven on May 14, 1909[16]. Freight service on the newly completed railroad began in less than a year, with local passenger service starting by August 15, 1909 and transcontinental passenger service on May 28, 1911[17]. Although the Northern Pacific Railway never expressed interest in the GVER, the Chicago, Milwaukee

In the summer of 1926 The Milwaukee Road advertised their new service to Yellowstone National Park from Three Forks.
MARIAN SCHENCK COLLECTION

& Puget Sound Railway Company, successor to the Chicago, Milwaukee & St. Paul Railway Company of Montana, thought the line would be a valuable source of desperately needed revenue[18]. On October 28, 1909 the GVER was officially taken over by Spokane businessmen, who had purchased 7,994 of the 8,000 shares of the company. They represented The Milwaukee Road, which wanted to reach Bozeman using the GVER. These businessmen had incorporated the Gallatin Valley Railway Company (GVR) on September 8, 1910 with the backing of The Milwaukee Road. The purpose of the GVR was to take over the GVER and build a connection with the Milwaukee line at Three Forks. The GVER was officially renamed the GVR at this time. The president of the GVR was C.A. Goodnow, assistant to the president of the Chicago, Milwaukee & Puget Sound Railway Company[19].

The articles of incorporation for the line were officially amended on April 15, 1910 for a 27.2 mile line between Bozeman Hot Springs and Three Forks, and surveys and construction began soon thereafter. The first steam powered train ran over the new line from Bozeman to Three Forks, a distance of 38.9 miles, on October 31, 1910[20].

The articles of incorporation were soon amended again for a 5.5-mile line from Belgrade Junction, located on the new line between Three Forks and Bozeman Hot Springs, to Belgrade. This branch line was built in 1911[21], and in 1913 the railroad built the Menard Branch, approximately 25 miles long, north and west from Bozeman to Menard[22]. By 1914 the GVR was operating 16.4 miles of electric track and another 34.3 miles of steam railroad, for a total of 50.7 miles. This did not include the 24.7-mile long Menard Branch. The headquarters for the line was in Bozeman[23].

On December 1, 1918 the GVR was officially absorbed into the Chicago, Milwaukee & St. Paul Railway Company[24]. Prior to that date the line had owned its own motive power and equipment lettered for the GVR, but the railroad used Milwaukee locomotives and cars when it was absorbed into the Milwaukee line[25]. The initial passenger service using steam powered locomotives between Three Forks and Bozeman could never compete with the parallel Northern Pacific trains, and there was never enough traffic on the interurban line to Salesville to make it financially successful.

Although the operation of the line was not profitable, it did serve as a valuable feeder line to The Milwaukee Road, more for freight business than its passenger business. The GVR had the dubious distinction of being the longest interurban railway in the country which required only a single car to accommodate the passengers. In its peak years the rail line had four scheduled passenger trains a day in addition to a single freight train, a far cry from the traffic projected by its promoters[26].

Ridership declined with the increasing use of the private automobile and improved roads, and the trolley line in Bozeman was the first service to be discontinued. When the trolley line began to lose money after World War I the railroad offered it to the city of Bozeman with no success, and operations ceased in 1921[27]. The interurban operation had decreased to one train a day when it, too, was discontinued on January 1, 1931, although freight service continued[28].

The Road to Yellowstone National Park

Following World War I all of the railroads which had a rail line anywhere near Yellowstone National Park wanted to benefit from the increasingly popular tourist business. The majority of the tourist business arrived on the Northern Pacific Railway and Union Pacific Railroad trains since these two railroads reached the park boundary. The Milwaukee Road was not able to offer service to the park until there was a good road from Bozeman to West Yellowstone.

In 1904 citizens from Bozeman had petitioned their United States senator to construct a road from the West Fork of the Gallatin River over Bighorn Pass into Yellowstone National Park, and a survey was performed in 1907[29]. The conclusion of the survey was that a road could be built but that it would not benefit the public, so the proposal was not acted on. The county commissioners continued to press for a road through the canyon and in 1910 permission was received to survey and build a road between Bozeman and West Yellowstone, some of which would pass through the western edge of the park. The wagon road from Bozeman south to the West Entrance of the park at West Yellowstone, first completed in 1911[30], was not very good when it was first opened, but over the years improvements were made. In 1913 automobiles were allowed over the new wagon road for the first time[31].

In 1923 the Chicago, Milwaukee & St. Paul Railroad requested permission to survey a road from the Gallatin Canyon over Bighorn Pass to connect with the existing road between Norris and Mammoth in the park. It was believed the railroad was willing to spend $300,000-$400,000 on this road so that it could bus tourists from Bozeman. The Secretary of the Interior denied this proposal, but the request indicated the railroad was beginning to become interested in reaching Yellowstone National Park[32]. Following World War I the Milwaukee had started transporting tourists to Ashford, Oregon, where connections were made with buses to Mount Rainier National Park[33], and the railroad wanted to repeat this profitable business at Yellowstone National Park.

In 1924 Pete Karst began offering bus service to the park from Salesville, at the terminus of the Gallatin Valley interurban line from Bozeman[34]. For many years he operated his Karst Stage Line in the Gallatin Valley as well as the Karst's Cold Springs Resort, a popular dude ranch in the Gallatin Valley for many years[35]. A resolute traveler could get off the Northern Pacific train at Bozeman, ride the interurban to Salesville, and then take a tour bus to Yellowstone. This was not a convenient or quick means of reaching the park, but it was a scenic ride through the Gallatin Canyon over the dirt roads. The county didn't gravel the road until 1925, and it was a vast improvement over the original dirt road[36].

Seeing the potential profit of offering passenger service to Yellowstone National Park, The Milwaukee Road began promoting travel from Three Forks in 1926, where connections could be made between its transcontinental trains and the tour buses to the park. The first buses were operated by the Yellowstone Park Transportation Company and ran from Three Forks into the park on August 1, 1926. In an effort to make the most of a bad situation, the Milwaukee Road tried to show the advantages of this route in its brochure published in that year, before the Gallatin Gateway Inn was opened. The Milwaukee boasted that the route from Three Forks included areas in the park not on regular park tours and that the buses went directly from the main line trains. The bus tour left Three Forks at 8 A.M. and arrived at the "Lunch Station", north of the park boundary, at noon, before continuing to West Yellowstone and into the park. The railroad advertised various tour routes through the park, giving travelers the option of entering through Three Forks and leaving through a different entrance on one of the other railroads.

In that year passengers to the park got off at the Three Forks station, which had been upgraded and improved. The roadway to the station and the ballast in front of the depot had been covered with white crushed stone, and the pavilion and platform floor laid with red tile to improve the depot facilities. Travelers passed under a large log arch with the words "Gallatin Gateway to Yellowstone National Park" flanked by the Milwaukee Road's insignia on both sides. Built by the railroad, the arch acted as an "official" gateway to the park and was located a few miles south of the inn on the road to the park.

A view of the Three Forks station, with the Sacajawea Inn across the street.
THE MILWAUKEE ROAD COLLECTION, MILWAUKEE PUBLIC LIBRARY

In the summer of 1930 The Milwaukee Road's premier train, *The Columbian*, carried through cars between Seattle/Tacoma and Chicago and Gallatin Gateway.

In the 1932 summer season The Milwaukee Road operated *The Gallagater* two times a day to connect with the main line trains, in addition to a daily-except-Sunday mixed train between Three Forks and Gallatin Gateway.

The motor buses waited at the Three Forks station for the tourists arriving on the train. They would soon be on their way through the Gallatin Canyon over the gravel road.
YELLOWSTONE HISTORIC CENTER

The Three Forks station in a view probably taken in the 1960s, after service to the park had ended. The wooden depot is on the left, and the archway on the right was for the arriving passengers.
AUTHOR'S COLLECTION

The arch was featured in many advertisements and was even on the railroad's 1930 company calendar. It was probably based on the popularity of the log arch over the road at the Nisqually entrance to Mount Rainier National Park. That arch, built in 1911, greeted travelers who had come from The Milwaukee Road's connection at Ashford, Oregon[37].

A view of the arch over the gravel road through the Gallatin Canyon. The arch was modeled after a similar arch at Rainier National Park, which was also served by The Milwaukee Road. GADAMUS COLLECTION, YELLOWSTONE HISTORIC CENTER

The highway to the park, by now designated as State Highway 191, had been improved in previous years, and interest in the route had exceeded the railroad's expectations. State, federal and county governments had collaborated to improve the road, but in 1926, when Yellowstone Park Transportation Company's bus service to the park was started, sections in the park were described by park engineers as "...little better than a trail: it is narrow, and is a one-track road with many sharp, blind curves and crosses Grayling twelve times on log bridges...". It was not until 1928 that the park service spent any significant money to improve the road, in contrast with the connecting state highways which had been improved in 1927[38]. Despite drawbacks of the long bus ride, however, these promotional efforts had some success. The National Park Service noted that in 1926 there were 813 visitors who arrived through the new entrance at Three Forks on the Chicago, Milwaukee & St. Paul Railway Company trains, traveling on the buses of the Yellowstone Park Transportation Company to the park[39].

The Gallatin Gateway Inn

Even as it advertised this route The Milwaukee Road was planning a more convenient means of reaching the park. The railroad decided to build the Gallatin Gateway Inn at the mouth of the Gallatin Canyon and to provide train service directly to the new hotel in an effort to capture some of the profitable tourist traffic. Tourists would be able to ride their train directly to the new luxury hotel and could either stay at the inn or immediately board a bus for their tour of the park.

Construction of the new Gallatin Gateway Inn was performed on a tight schedule. Work started on February 18, 1927 and the building was dedicated on June 17, 1927. In late May workmen were shoveling snow from the roofs so that construction wouldn't be delayed, and workers even used large bonfires in the rooms to speed up drying the plaster. While workmen were plastering the north wing, other men were framing the south wing. The 42,000-square-foot Spanish-style building took a crew of up to 500 workers four months to complete[40].

The railroad advertised the inn as having a semi-Spanish design, patterned after a country club, and boasted that it had cost $260,000 to build, in addition to the cost of improving the rail line between Three Forks and Gallatin Gateway[41]. Schack, Young and Meyers of Seattle designed the inn, and although it was the largest building in the county the architecture had no particular ties to the area. At the same time the inn was being built the railroad was improving the line between Three Forks and Gallatin Gateway, ballasting and installing heavier rail on the line with a crew of up to 200 men. The rail was 65-pound rail in 33-foot lengths[42].

The inn was situated so that the guests would have a view of the surrounding mountain ranges. In addition to providing lodging to railroad passengers, the inn was easily accessible to the public from the adjacent State Highway 191 and was located across the road from the Flying D cattle ranch. It was reported to be one of the most luxurious railroad-owned hotels when it was opened.

The building had a textured, buff-colored stucco exterior, red tile roof, and plastered interior walls. It was 250 x 40 feet with a kitchen/residential wing on the south end. A dining room and ballroom were located in the center, and the rooms were in the north wing. The dining room could seat up to 186. The main entrance, on the east side, had a canopy using patterned copper and decorative glass panels, with a second entrance on the track, or west, side.

Travelers entered through a high vaulted hallway in the center of the building, which was approximately 60 feet x 40 feet x 35 feet high. The main entrances on the east and west sides were 13 feet wide and approximately 25 feet high, each with four entrance doors. The front desk looked like a ticket window while the hallway held a newsstand, curio shop, telegraph office, desks for arranging bus and rail transportation, and a confectionary stand along the walls. The ballroom, to the south of the entrance, was approximately 70 feet x 40 feet x 35 feet high, with a series of French doors leading to an exterior colonnade on both the east and west sides. This room had narrow oak flooring and a fireplace made with decorated cast stone and was furnished with expensive furniture and carpeting in the lounge area. The beamed ceiling had stenciled Greek patterns. The dining room was also 70 feet x 40 feet with a 15-foot ceiling with stencils on the beams, and one could look out at the Gallatin Range while dining[43]. In the event of a large crowd, the dining room could be rearranged to seat 350.

The kitchen had an electric dishwasher, refrigerators, ice-maker, bakery, and an ice cream machine. The basement contained areas for food preparation, including storage refrigerators, another ice making machine, and an automatic vegetable peeler. There was even a special, separate refrigerator for fish. The railroad was so proud of the new electric equipment in the kitchen that women guests were encouraged to tour the facilities[44].

A press release from the railroad stated that the hotel had the following floor areas[45]:

Basement:	3,000 sq. ft.
First floor:	15,540 sq. ft.
Second floor:	8,650 sq. ft.
Total:	27,190 sq. ft.

On the first floor the hotel had the following:

Dining Room:	2,652 sq. ft.
Lounge:	2,660 sq. ft.
Foyer:	1,972 sq. ft.
Baggage and Parcel room:	1,530 sq. ft.
Kitchen:	819 sq. ft.
Veranda:	840 sq. ft.
Lobby:	510 sq. ft.
Women's rest room:	240 sq. ft.

The interior of the building used Philippine mahogany which was stenciled and a plaster finish with a stucco appearance. There were decorative beams and high-arched windows. The light fixtures were wrought iron and the floor was a heavy linoleum tile in a checkered black and tan color. There were fire extinguishers throughout the building, a fire water system, and numerous fire alarm pull boxes. The building was heated with steam using an oil furnace.

The guest rooms were in the north wing. The hotel included only 26 bedrooms since it was assumed most travelers would arrive in sleeping cars in the morning and leave immediately for their tour of the park. The bedrooms had baths and the rooms were finished in mahogany and had large windows to view the Gallatin Range. The linen was embroidered with the initials "GGI" and there were special curtains, tapestries, and carpeting in each room. The rooms even had their own telephones.

A large baggage check room was available for travelers who wished to leave some bags at the inn

An artist's rendering of what travel through the Gallatin Gateway would look like.
GADAMUS COLLECTION, YELLOWSTONE HISTORIC CENTER

The Gallatin Gateway Inn was elegant and comfortable so that travelers would be encouraged to spend time there before or after their tour through the park. YELLOWSTONE HERITAGE & RESEARCH CENTER

The exterior of the Gallatin Gateway Inn has not changed over the years since this photograph was taken, although it is safe to say that archery is not being performed on the front lawn today. This was part of a 1956 brochure advertising both the stay at the Gallatin Gateway Inn and travel to Yellowstone National Park, after The Milwaukee Road no longer owned the inn. YELLOWSTONE HERITAGE & RESEARCH CENTER

during their visit through the park. There were shower baths and restrooms with individual change rooms designed for those travelers who were not spending the night but who wanted to refresh themselves after their trip through the park and before boarding the train for their trip home. The restrooms and wash rooms were located in the north wing, next to the baggage room. The railroad welcomed both extended stays at the inn and those who only wanted to "pass through" between the trains and buses[46].

The garden and landscaping were still being finished on the 12 acres of grounds when the opening ceremonies were being held. There were large flowerbeds and a large lawn area watered using a sprinkler system supplied from the railroad's water tank. The centerpiece of the lawn was a 125-foot flagpole, brought from the Pacific Coast on four flat cars[47]. Although the railroad had originally allowed $3,000 for landscaping, the budget was increased to $17,000 so that a golf course could be built and concrete walkways and hedge fences could be added[48]. The buses arrived and departed on a circular driveway on the east side of the inn.

The first staff were women from Montana State College in Bozeman[49], and they lived in the adjacent employee quarters, which had its own lounge area. Only one of the bungalows for employee housing out of the planned four was completed when the inn was opened. Designed to blend in with the surroundings, this 10-room bungalow was located north of the inn, while the other bungalows were to be built on the west side of the inn, across the tracks. The lounge area in the bungalow even had an $1,100 phonograph, identical to the one in the lounge area in the inn. The manager of the Gallatin Gateway Inn was Arthur R. Naething, who had come from Chicago where he had lived while working for six years as the chief dining car steward on the Milwaukee's *Pioneer Limited*[50].

Although the inn originally had 26 bedrooms and suites on the second floor of the north wing, there were plans to expand the hotel with another 127 rooms[51]. Until the additional rooms were built the railroad planned to spot Pullman cars on the tracks by the inn to act as overflow sleeping quarters. These expansion plans were never carried out when the anticipated growth in business did not occur, although additional living quarters, a wood framed building with 12 apartments, were built for the staff on the west side of the tracks. Only one of the planned units to the north of the inn was built.

The inn had a long concrete platform along the tracks on the west side of the inn. Travelers arrived by rail on the west side of the inn, and after getting off the train walked up a concrete sidewalk and then climbed the stairs to the lobby to eat in the dining room or to register for a stay at the inn. The tour buses left from the entrance on the east side of the hotel. Since it was intended for summer use only the inn was not insulated, but it did have heat.

The terminus at Gallatin Gateway also had a stockyard, ice house, coal and oil house with an elevator, water tank and pump house, car department office, battery charging building, and coal dock. The original 20 feet x 60 feet wood-framed depot, built in 1910 at Salesville[52], was apparently retained for other purposes[53].

As part of the promotional effort for the location, the town, originally known as Salesville for Zacariah Sales, who had built a sawmill on the Gallatin River in the 1860s, was renamed Gallatin Gateway in 1927[54]. The location is near the mouth of the canyon formed by the Gallatin River, which flows north to Three Forks on the west side of Yellowstone National Park.

The inn officially opened on June 17, 1927 and numerous congressmen and other officials were invited to the event. A free lunch was provided to the general public. The *Bozeman Daily Chronicle* claimed that the number of visitors on opening day was 20,000, although this may have been an optimistic number. The opening of the hotel even overshadowed reports in the local papers of Lindbergh's flight across the Atlantic Ocean. A large group assembled at the Northern Pacific depot in Bozeman, 10 miles away, where festivities were held that morning. There was then a parade, complete with a marching band, to the Gallatin Gateway Inn, for afternoon and evening festivities. The celebration at Bozeman was held to mark the opening of the Northern Pacific's route to the park through Bozeman.

The rest of the festivities were held at the new Gallatin Gateway Inn. Many Milwaukee Road officials were reported to be at the opening events. Harry Byram, former president of The Milwaukee Road and one of the road's receivers at that time, was one of those present. Approximately 10,000 guests had lunch at the inn that day, eating two tons of beef, two tons of potatoes, 500 cases of hens, and 500 pounds of bacon. The Montana governor was the speaker and guest of honor, and that night 2,000 people danced in the ballroom[55].

Travel Through the Gallatin Gateway

The Gallatin Gateway Inn was a popular destination both locally and nationwide for several years, with parties and dancing in the ballroom. The Milwaukee Road, which had projected up to 10,000 visitors a year passing through Gallatin Gateway[56], claimed the inn was *"the handsomest and finest hotel in the State of Montana."*[57] Describing the inn in 1928 in its employee magazine, the railroad noted that guests could *"experience the pleasure of a sight of agricultural magnificence unrivaled in the West, as they glimpse through the car windows, the rolling Valley and broad acres of growing crops..."* and that the hotel was *"built at a cost of a half million dollars by the Milwaukee Road ... (and) is the handsomest and finest hotel in the State of Montana."*[58] The railroad also boasted that it was *"(t)he only electrified transcontinental railroad serving Yellowstone National Park."* [59] The bus ride was provided by the Yellowstone Park Transportation Company, which would *"take you smoothly, with hardly a change of gears, directly to Old Faithful and the geyser, through gloriously fresh, untouched country of startling beauty ... The fine new road upward through Gallatin gorge is not overcrowded with traffic ... The cost is quite reasonable."*[60] Travelers to the Gallatin Gateway Inn had the option of getting directly on a bus of the Yellowstone Transportation Company in front of the hotel, staying at the inn for one or more nights before beginning their tour of the park, or taking side tours while staying at the inn.

When The Milwaukee Road began service through Three Forks in 1926 it had 813 tourists pass through the station to the park in the first year[61]. When the Gallatin Gateway Inn was opened the following year, The Milwaukee Road immediately began offering service to the Gallatin Gateway Inn and through West Yellowstone. Travel through the Gallatin Gateway in the first year was promising. In 1927 the National Park Service reported that 2,788 visitors arrived by way of the Milwaukee Road's Gallatin Gateway route[62], showing the success of the road's promotional efforts. Another 271 tourists arrived through the west entrance from the Northern Pacific's Bozeman station, a route which was not competitive for travel to the park and which also went through Gallatin Canyon. In contrast, during the 1927 season the Union Pacific brought in 17,157 tourists directly to West Yellowstone[63]. In the following year, 1928, there were 3,337 visitors over The Milwaukee Road through Gallatin Gateway, while 17,408 came in on the Union Pacific to West Yellowstone, and 256 on the Northern Pacific through Bozeman[64]. Although most of these tourists arrived through Gallatin Gateway, many apparently left through other park entrances on other railroads, taking advantage of tour packages.

The motor coach trip was long, approximately 68 miles from the inn over a scenic, winding road. In contrast with the Union Pacific, whose trains reached West Yellowstone, one had to travel four hours

This colorful cover of a travel brochure showed the arch in the Gallatin Gateway Canyon, using some artistic license. The arch was a trademark for The Milwaukee Road's Yellowstone advertisements. GADAMUS COLLECTION, YELLOWSTONE HISTORIC CENTER

and 15 minutes by motor coach from Gallatin Gateway to reach West Yellowstone before the park tour could even begin. This was a decided inconvenience, made worse by the fact that the roads were not very good.

Motor coaches were scheduled to stop at the Union Pacific's West Yellowstone station for a rest stop. Due to the large number who arrived on the tour buses, The Milwaukee Road travelers had to use the facilities at both the depot and dining lodge. Since the Union Pacific was already using the dining lodge to serve lunches on its noon train, The Milwaukee Road and Northern Pacific travelers from Bozeman were allowed to eat there as well, at a cost of $1.25 each. The use of restrooms was an important consideration, and the Union Pacific was anxious to let travelers know they were using its facilities. The railroad put up signs and notices to let Milwaukee passengers know they were using Union Pacific facilities. The Milwaukee Road travelers were allowed to buy lunch and use the restrooms, even though the Dining Lodge did not have adequate facilities for such a large number of travelers[65].

One of the more momentous events at the Gallatin Gateway Inn took place at the official opening of Yellowstone National Park for the 1929 season. In the 1920s the National Park Service held a special opening ceremony at different gateways each year. In 1927 official ceremonies were held at Bozeman and Gallatin Gateway Inn to celebrate the opening of the Bozeman and Gallatin Gateway routes, two days prior to official park opening ceremonies at Cody. On June 20, 1929 they were again held at "...*the Chicago, Milwaukee St. Paul and Pacific's entrance to Yellowstone. The address of welcome was made by the Superintendent of the Yellowstone and Hon. Horace M. Albright, President of the Milwaukee Road, H.A. Scandritt (sic)....*". Other congressmen and dignitaries were also invited.[66]

Representatives for major movie studios made motion pictures for newsreels. The "boisterous" Terry Montana Cowboy Band was part of the opening ceremonies, making sure the audience was awake after long, tedious speeches. About 50 Indians from the Flathead Indian Reservation in Montana participated by offering traditional war dances. Following the dances, they initiated three white men into their tribe in the Mammoth Tepee in front of the inn. Horace Albright, Park Superintendent, and H.A. Scandrett and W.B. Dixon, President and General Manager, respectively, of The Milwaukee Road, were initiated as brothers in the tribe. Following the ceremonies the Indians and tourists headed for the park[67].

According to the National Park Service there were 3,126 visitors over The Milwaukee Road route through the Gallatin Gateway in 1929[68], decreasing to 1,637 visitors in 1930[69], reflecting the impact of the Depression. In that year the Milwaukee Road maintained full passenger service for travelers to Yellowstone National Park. These trains ran in the summer months only, and in the summer of 1930 there were three *"Gallagater"* trains in each direction, making connections with the main line trains *"The Columbian"* and *"The Olympian"*. *The Columbian* had through standard sleeping cars between Chicago and Gallatin Gateway and between Gallatin Gateway and Seattle/Tacoma. Not only were individuals welcome, but the railroad also encouraged tour groups to use its facilities. The trains between Three Forks and Gallatin Gateway, designated as the *"Gallagater"* in the timetable, took one hour and 20 minutes for the 32.1-mile run, with no intermediate stops. In addition, the railroad also ran a mixed train between Bozeman and Three Forks and between Bozeman and Gallatin Gateway, daily except Sunday[70].

In 1931 the number of rail visitors through Gallatin Gateway decreased to 1,261[71]. Due to this decline, through connections to Gallatin Gateway were changed to *The Olympian* the same year, following the discontinuance of *The Columbian*. With this new, revised schedule tourists arrived at West Yellowstone in the late afternoon, so they did not need to use the Union Pacific's dining facilities. They were, however, allowed to use restroom facilities, and the Union Pacific received $10-$20 a month for providing this service. Departing tourists however, continued to stop at West Yellowstone for lunch[72].

In 1932 the railroad returned to busing passengers from Three Forks. Train service to Gallatin Gateway was used only when the passenger count exceeded the bus capacity. The timetable stated *"Steam service is provided in either direction between Three Forks and Gallatin Gateway in connection with the OLYMPIAN trains whenever required for the handling of special equipment or for a number of passengers exceeding the seating capacity of the busses."*[73]

The number of visitors through Gallatin Gateway decreased to only 590 in 1932[74], and in 1933 only 538 visitors were recorded[75], followed by 58 through June 30, 1934[76]. The National Park Service changed

A travel brochure from 1927 when the Gallatin Gateway route was being promoted as a new route to the park. The trademark arch was prominently featured on the cover.
GADAMUS COLLECTION, YELLOWSTONE HISTORIC CENTER

A 1928 brochure published by The Milwaukee Road showing sights of the park.
YELLOWSTONE HERITAGE & RESEARCH CENTER

its reporting methods that year, so the number of visitors through Gallatin Gateway was no longer recorded separately and is not known.

The railroad continued to offer tours in conjunction with the other roads. A brochure from 1938 was vague on the form of transportation between Three Forks and Gallatin Gateway Inn, while making it clear that travelers would be on the Milwaukee train to Three Forks and on buses from Gallatin Gateway Inn, but it only stated *"From Three Forks we travel to Gallatin Gateway for lunch ..."* They called the bus the *"Gallagater"*, however, to maintain the name[77]. An advertisement in 1941 promoted both the Gallatin Gateway Inn and Yellowstone National Park[78].

The park was essentially closed during World War II and all bus service from Three Forks was discontinued on August 29, 1943 through the end of the war[79]. Following World War II the private automobile became the predominant form of transportation to the park, but The Milwaukee Road continued to offer service to the park, with connections at Three Forks. It ran trains to Gallatin Gateway only as required. In 1946 there were 500 arrivals on the Milwaukee Road, despite optimistic projections of up to 30,000 guests[80]. By 1947 the railroad had its own fleet of three buses to connect with the new *Olympian Hiawatha* and *Columbian* passenger trains at Three Forks[81].

When the *Columbian* was cut back in 1955 so that it no longer ran to Three Forks the Milwaukee ran only two buses to connect with the *Olympian*[82]. A Milwaukee Road brochure from 1956 advertised service to Yellowstone and Grand Teton national parks, noting that the Gallatin Gateway Inn was privately owned, but suggested spending a few extra days at the inn. At this time passengers on the *Olympian Hiawatha* arrived at the inn in the mid-afternoon, so their park tour did not start until the following morning[83]. An advertisement for the 1957 season showed travelers getting off the train at Three Forks and did not mention the Gallatin Gateway Inn[84].

The 1958 Milwaukee timetable was the last one to list bus service to Gallatin Gateway. In 1959 the railroad offered connecting bus service at Three Forks through Bozeman to the park, bypassing Gallatin Gateway and using a single bus. The 1960 timetable was the last one to list any service to the park, but through Bozeman. In 1961 the *Olympian Hiawatha* was cut back and ended at Deer Lodge and the Milwaukee's timetable promoted travel to Yellowstone on the Union Pacific's *Cities* trains, using the West Entrance to the park, on a totally different route[85]. Passengers now rode on The Milwaukee Road's trains from Chicago to Omaha, and from Omaha they rode Union Pacific trains to West Yellowstone. When the Union Pacific discontinued passenger service to West Yellowstone at the conclusion of the 1960 season, all Milwaukee connections to the park ended.

The Gallatin Gateway Inn After World War II

After World War II the inn was allowed to deteriorate, although the railroad claimed it had accommodated approximately 25,000 guests a year in the summer seasons prior to World War II. After closing the inn during the war the railroad opened it again on June 20, 1946 when the park was also reopened. The railroad purchased new buses to run from Three Forks, brought in the best dining car chefs, and hired 17 Montana State College home economics students to staff concessions and clean rooms. The railroad hoped to have 36,000 guests that year. This apparently did not materialize, and soon rumors began to surface that the inn would be sold. The head of the Montana Society of Natural Earth Sciences approached the railroad to see if the society could obtain the inn for a museum, but the railroad instead sold it to Paul L. Holenstein of Helena in 1951 for $125,000[86]. He continued to operate the inn, including the dining facilities and lounge, but eventually sold it to Mohawk, Inc., of Illinois. It went through several owners and in 1980 the owner went so far as to spray the ballroom with acoustical foam to accommodate bands playing there[87].

The inn was purchased in 1985 by Bill Keshishian, who had once tended bar there, along with his mother and some other investors, under the name of the Gateway Inn Corporation[88]. By that time the rooms had been converted into apartments, although the dining facilities were still being used. They slowly restored the inn and renovated the kitchen so that it could be used to prepare gourmet meals at the restaurant. The bar in the baggage room remained open and the rooms were renovated into apartments and overnight rooms.

The restored dining room was reopened in 1986, followed by the opening of the hotel in the next year. It is once again a luxurious inn with 35 rooms and suites, all of which are decorated differently.

The inn is used for banquets, meetings, weddings and other special events. When it was restored the features of the inn, including The Milwaukee Road herald, much of the original kitchen equipment, and other fixtures, including the restroom facilities and clock in the main lobby, were all retained. The building was also insulated so that it can be used year-round. There is a fly-casting pond, since fly fishing is a popular area attraction, as well as an outdoor hot tub. A swimming pool was also opened and some of the employee housing is available to guests. The inn actively promotes nearby recreational activities. The Baggage Room Pub and Fireplace Lounge are also still popular meeting places[89].

The depot was added to the National Register of Historic Places in 1979[90], at the same time as the Sacajawea Inn in Three Forks[91]. The Gallatin Gateway Inn was recently sold and the new owner intends to maintain the high quality and service.

The Gallatin Gateway Line Following World War II

Although The Milwaukee Road no longer ran passenger trains to Gallatin Gateway it continued to provide freight service on the line until it was no longer economical. Authorization to abandon the line was received from the ICC on February 24, 1978 and the last train ran on April 17, 1978. The tracks were pulled up shortly afterwards[92].

The depot and freight house at Three Forks were saved and have been converted into other uses. The depot is available for office space and the creamery is used for apartments. The archway and trackside shelter were torn down, but at least one of the pillars was reportedly saved and is stored in a nearby city park. The Sacajawea Inn, across the road from the depot and once used by travelers on The Milwaukee Road and by Milwaukee employees, has been restored into a very nice inn. The Headwaters Heritage Museum, located in an old bank building, has an extensive collection of Milwaukee Road memorabilia.

The Gallatin Valley Railway's substation at Bozeman Hot Springs was sold and the two story brick building is now an office building on the east side of the highway. The Gallagator Park Trail, a segment of the original interurban line in Bozeman on the south side of town, is used as a recreational trail. The Milwaukee Road's depot in Bozeman was used for a creamery for many years but was closed and allowed to deteriorate. A fire destroyed part of the building and the site is being used for a new Bozeman Public Library. The Bozeman freight house was converted into an antique mall and is now an office building.

The line between Belgrade Junction and Belgrade, known as the Menard Branch, was abandoned in 1962. A short section out of Belgrade was retained to service the Plum Creek sawmill west of Jackrabbit Lane. It is now owned and switched by Montana Rail Link. Some tool sheds were left on the south side of the tracks and west of Weaver Street in Belgrade, but the depot, which was west of the Broadway Street crossing, is gone.

Although it was never very busy, the Menard Branch remained until the last days of The Milwaukee Road and the final train ran in April 1978. When the line was opened in 1913 the railroad had offered daily passenger service, running what was known locally as the "Turkey Red Special", after a type of wheat grown in the area. Few people rode the train and service was quickly cut back to bi-weekly, and then weekly, before being discontinued in 1915[93].

The Milwaukee Road's Service to Yellowstone National Park

The Milwaukee Road's Gallatin Gateway route to the park was built too late and was too distant from the park to be successful. By the time the rail line and inn had been built tourists were deserting the railroads for their own automobiles. The Depression, World War II, and the family car all made it so that The Milwaukee Road route was not successful. The railroad built a large, luxurious hotel at its railhead at Gallatin Gateway, but it could not compete with the convenience of the other railroads which reached the park. Fortunately, the inn is still open, and has been restored to its original grandeur, even if the rail line has been removed.

Yellowstone—Pacific Northwest

From steaming geysers to glaciers of blue ice... timbered mountains to Pacific Ocean sands... bustling waterfronts to wilderness chalets, the Pacific Northwest is a bountifully endowed vacationland.

What could be better than going there on The Milwaukee Road's Olympian HIAWATHA? The scenery is glorious, the service superb and accommodations may be chosen to suit your travel budget. Private-room cars with Skytop Lounge, unique and thrifty Touralux sleepers, Luxurest coaches, diner and Tip Top Grill.

OLYMPIAN Hiawatha

H. Sengstacken,
The Milwaukee Road
702 Union Station, Chicago 6, Ill.
Please send me illustrated booklets:
☐ Yellowstone ☐ Pacific Northwest
☐ Yellowstone-Salt Lake City
☐ Yellowstone-Colorado ☐ Pacific Northwest-California ☐ Pacific Northwest-Canadian Rockies.

Name_____
Address_____
City_____ Zone____ State____

THE MILWAUKEE ROAD

Mention the National Geographic—It identifies you

Following World War II, The Milwaukee Road continued to advertise their route to the park but travelers had to get off the train at Three Forks.
AUTHOR'S COLLECTION

The Milwaukee Road's diamond insignia is still above the entrance to the Gallatin Gateway Inn.
AUTHOR'S PHOTO

129

Chapter Eleven

Proposed Railroads to Yellowstone National Park

In addition to the Union Pacific and Northern Pacific lines which were built directly to the West Entrance and North Entrance of the park respectively, and the Chicago & North Western, The Milwaukee Road, Northern Pacific, and Chicago, Burlington & Quincy lines which were built to access the West, South, East and Northeast entrances, there were numerous additional proposals over the years for the construction of other railroads to the park boundary. Some proposed lines were so preliminary that they weren't even named, while other lines were authorized to build to reach Yellowstone National Park when they were incorporated. Some railroads weren't even planned to go near the park, but used the aura of the national park name to help raise interest and money for the line.

Some of these proposed railroads included the following:

The Billings & Cooke City Railway Company: The Billings & Cooke City Railway was incorporated in August 1908 to connect Billings and Cooke City. It was capitalized at $2 million and the 110-mile line would have gone from Billings through Laurel and Nye to Cooke City. The option of using electric power was noted in the articles of incorporation, and the power would have been provided by overhead catenary using electricity from The Madison Power Company. The company also proposed to build an amusement park near Billings, a popular side business for trolley lines at that time. Surveys were made and some of the right-of-way was reportedly purchased[1]. Directors for the line were Edward Horsky of Helena; M.E. Estep of Chicago, George E. Savage of Butte; and B.G. Shorey and A.L. Babcock of Billings[2].

Bozeman: In August, 1914 there were reports of an electric line 150 miles long which was to go from Bozeman across the Gallatin Valley and along Elk Creek to the Madison Valley. It would then go south to the West Entrance. This railroad was being considered by Eugene W. Dawes of Bozeman, Charles L. Loomis of Kansas City, and associates[3].

Central Pacific Railroad/Southern Pacific Railroad: Apparently the Central Pacific Railroad and Southern Pacific Railroad considered constructing a line to the western boundary of the park as early as 1882. They released a map that year showing a "proposed" line from Kelton, Utah, a short distance west of Promontory, north and east through Pocatello to the western boundary of the park. The line would continue north to Fort Ellis[4] in Montana, where it would connect with the Northern Pacific line across Montana[5].

Columbus & Cooke City: In July 1908 it was reported that work had started on a line known as the Columbus & Cooke City. Work had reportedly been started at the mouth of the Stillwater River and was being hurried to completion. The railroad may have been tied into the Billings & Cooke City Electric Railway Company[6].

Cooke City: In September 1915 an electric line from Nye south to Cooke City was proposed. Mayor E.A. Gerhart of Billings was involved in this venture[7].

Denver, Laramie & Northwestern Railroad: This line, which was incorporated in Colorado in 1909, had hopes of reaching the West Coast, and in 1910 the company stated it was going to reach Yellowstone Park by 1913[8]. The railroad ended up operating between Denver and Greeley in Colorado.

Denver, Yellowstone and Pacific Railway Company: In 1906 *The Railway Age* reported that the Denver, Yellowstone & Pacific was being proposed to run from Denver through Atlantic City and Pinedale to Jackson and the south edge of the park. From there it would continue on to Seattle. It was incorporated in Wyoming on November 11, 1905 and in Idaho on June 20, 1905. Previously the company was known as The Colorado, Wyoming and Idaho Railway Company. After the initial enthusiasm there were no further reports on the line[9].

Grand Island Wyoming Central Railroad: In 1894 there was a proposal for a railroad to be known as the Grand Island Wyoming Central Railroad. It was to be built to encourage travel to the park, but there was enough opposition so that no work was performed.[10]

Idaho and Wyoming Railroad Company: The Union Pacific Railroad proposed building to the south edge of the park under the auspices of Idaho and Wyoming Railroad Company. The company went so far as to perform extensive surveys for proposed routes through the Jackson Hole region.

The Idaho & Wyoming Railroad was incorporated on December 21, 1905 to build a line from Elva (present-day Ucon) in Idaho on the Oregon Short Line to the head of the Hoback River in Wyoming, a distance of approximately 139.5 miles. A branch line of the railroad was to go up along the Snake River through Jackson Hole to the south edge of Yellowstone National Park. There was also to be a branch line from the Hoback River 48 miles southeast to connect with the Oregon Short Line near Cokeville. The total length of the rail line was to be approximately 273 miles.

In February 1906 William Ashton, chief engineer of the Oregon Short Line, announced that surveys would be performed in the summer but that construction plans were indefinite. In 1912 there was another proposal to have the railroad build other branch lines of the Idaho and Wyoming to connect with the Oregon Short Line to the south and east. The total length of the railroad with these branch lines was to be 365 miles. At this time E.E. Calvin was president of the Idaho & Wyoming Railroad, and the directors were W.H. Bancroft, William Ashton, E. Buckingham, T.J. Duddleston, P.L. Williams, and G.K. Smith, officials associated with the Union Pacific.

As it turned out, no construction was performed by this railroad company. After the Yellowstone Park Railroad built a line to the western edge of Yellowstone National Park the Union Pacific felt it did not need to construct the Idaho & Wyoming. Consequently the company was officially dissolved at the company's 1923 annual meeting[11].

Longmont and Great Western Railroad Company: In 1881 the citizens of Longmont, Colorado formed the Longmont and Great Western Railroad Company. The railroad was capitalized at $10 million and was authorized to build a line from the Longmont headquarters to San Francisco with branches to San Diego; Leadville, the Colorado anthracite region; another point on the Pacific Coast; Denver; a point near Nebraska City on the Missouri, and Yellowstone National Park. The line was never built.[12]

Midland Pacific Railway Company: This railroad was proposed in the late 1880s to build a line from Sioux Falls, South Dakota to the West Coast. It was to have gone through northern Wyoming and around the south side of Yellowstone Park and then down the Salmon River, reaching Lewiston, Idaho. From there it would continue west to Seattle. The line was capitalized at $80 million. Some surveys were made, but further work was stopped by the Panic of 1893[13].

Ogden, Logan & Idaho Railway: At the same time the Yellowstone Park Railroad Company was being constructed Dave Eccles envisioned building an electric line from Salt Lake City to Yellowstone National Park. The line was to start with the Ogden, Logan & Utah, which later became the Utah Central[14]. The Ogden, Logan & Idaho did build into southern Idaho, reaching Preston, but construction ended at that town.

The Saint Anthony and National Park Railway Company, Limited: This railroad was incorporated in eastern Idaho on August 11, 1898 by local businessmen from Saint Anthony. They knew the Upper Snake River Valley residents needed a rail line to be able to prosper, and supported the construction of a rail line to Saint Anthony. They apparently incorporated the words "National Park" into the company's name to encourage investors. The articles of incorporation for this proposed railroad were filed by Saint Anthony businessmen. The line was to be built from Sand Holes (sic), (present-day Hamer) on the Oregon Short Line to Saint Anthony, through Edmunds, Egin and Parker. The estimated length of the proposed line was 30 miles, and $30,000 had been subscribed by these men when the articles of incorporation were filed[15]. The company did not perform any construction.

The St. Anthony Railroad was organized less than a year later, on May 18, 1899 with the backing of the Oregon Short Line, to build through the Upper Snake River Valley from Idaho Falls. This line was completed to St. Anthony in the following spring, and the operations immediately taken over by the Oregon Short Line. The Yellowstone Park Railroad Company was then incorporated a few years later to extend the line north and east to West Yellowstone.

The Snake River National Park and Pacific Railway Company: The Snake River National Park and Pacific Railway Company was incorporated in Idaho on July 22, 1891 to build a line from Idaho

Falls to the coal fields in Uintah County in Wyoming, on the Grosventre[16] River, about 35 miles from where the river empties into the Snake River. This was an area known at the time as the Snake River Coal Fields. There was to be a branch from Idaho Falls to the south end of Jackson's[17] Lake and the overall length of the line was to be approximately 160 miles. It is interesting to note that the line included the words "National Park", due to the popularity and fame of the relatively new Yellowstone National Park, and "Pacific", although the line was never envisioned to do more than connect Idaho Falls with the coal fields in Wyoming. There was, apparently, hope that the name would generate interest in the outside business community for additional financing.

Despite the enthusiasm and interest in the line no construction was performed. Within a few years the Oregon Short Line built a large network of branch lines throughout southern Idaho and had total control of the area. It was not possible for another rail line to compete with them, and the coal fields never materialized to any extent, another common occurrence at the time.

Three Forks, Helena and Madison Valley Railroad: In 1911 this railroad proposed in to build a line from Helena 150 miles to Yellowstone National Park. The line was initially capitalized at $50,000 and the capitalization was soon increased to $4.5 million. The company was authorized to build a line from Three Forks to Radersburg, to the north of Three Forks and then to Helena and from Three Forks to the Town of Yellowstone (present-day West Yellowstone). The company planned to build only the line from Three Forks to Radersburg immediately, and the extensions would be built at a future date[19]. Another report indicated the line to the park was to be an interurban railroad going from Three Forks through the Madison Valley to the park. Little work was reportedly performed in 1912-13, and a contract was reported to have been let in 1915 to Clifton, Applegate and Company of Spokane to build from Three Forks to Radersburg. Following this there were no further reports on the line[20].

Western Pacific Railway: The Western Pacific briefly considered the construction of a line to the park but nothing came of this idea. In 1914 it reportedly evaluated the possibility of a line from Nevada through Twin Falls to Idaho Falls and continuing to Yellowstone National Park. They were particularly interested in the tourist traffic to the park[21].

White Sulphur Springs and Yellowstone Park Railroad: This railroad was incorporated in Montana on June 18, 1910, to build a line from White Sulphur Springs south to Yellowstone National Park, a distance of 125 miles. Provisions were also made to extend it northwest to Great Falls. Construction was performed from June through November 1910 between White Sulphur Springs and Dorsey, Montana. Financing of the line was aided by The Milwaukee Road, which owned 51% of the stock. The new railroad connected with The Milwaukee Road at Dorsey, and later at a town known as Ringling, named for the circus businessman John Ringling. The line never had a lot of business, and abandonment was first proposed in 1944. With the abandonment of The Milwaukee Road in 1980 the White Sulphur Springs and Yellowstone Park Railroad was finally shut down[22].

Yellowstone Park Rail Road Company: This company was incorporated in 1905 in Maine to build a line from Bridger, Montana southwest 125 miles to Cooke City. The company was capitalized at $3 million[23] and backed by the Bear Creek Coal Company. Only 22 miles of the line were built, from Bridger to Bear Creek. The line was officially completed in 1907 and conveyed to the Montana, Wyoming and Southern Railroad in 1909. The extension to Cooke City was never built and the line was abandoned in 1953[24].

Yellowstone Park Railway: This company was incorporated in Washington in 1898 as the Yellowstone Park Railway Company of Spokane, where it had its headquarters, but was incorporated in Montana at the same time. The 90-mile line was capitalized at $1,500,000 and was authorized to build the following lines: A line from Brisbin via Trail Creek, Bozeman, and Ferris Hot Springs and up the West Gallatin River and up Dodge Creek[25]; from a point near Ferris Hot Springs to a point near Flat Head Pass in the Bridger Mountains; and from a point near Ferris Hot Springs to a point at or near Three Forks, along with any other branch lines as deemed necessary[26]. This route would have taken the line north of Yellowstone National Park, although it was planned not only to haul coal but to transport tourists to the park. In 1899 the first carload of coal was shipped from the mines on the 11.3-mile line which had been constructed to the coal mines on Trail Creek[27].

Other Lines

Numerous other rail lines were proposed and discussed over the years. Typical was the suggestion in 1883 by Wyoming Territorial Governor William Hale for a railroad from the Union Pacific main line via Fort Washakie. In the same year the Livingston newspaper reported proposals for a railroad from the Union Pacific to the park via Togwotee Pass or the Stinking Water Pass[28]. In 1889 the Illinois Central was reported to be backing a survey from Pierre, South Dakota to Puget Sound. The line was to run through Wyoming and Yellowstone Park to Idaho and Oregon[29]. This line, like many others, was never built.

In 1907 the U.S. Forest Service Supervisor at St. Anthony noted that a railroad survey was being performed in the Squirrel Creek Meadows east of Marysville. He had no idea what railroad they were working for, but noted they were headed for Conant Pass. Between 1904 and 1910 local newspapers also reported that the Chicago, Burlington and Quincy Railroad, the Rock Island, the Wyoming Railroad, and the Chicago and North Western Railway were all going to build to the park and Jackson Hole[30]. None of them was ever built, however.

The travelers to the park passed under this arch on their way from the Gallatin Gateway Inn to the Gallatin Canyon and the park. AUTHOR'S COLLECTION

Chapter Twelve

Railroads in Yellowstone National Park

Over the years there were numerous proposals to build railroads into and through Yellowstone National Park, and their history is an interesting side note to the history of the park. Although the transcontinental railroads built branch lines to the park specifically for the tourist traffic, there were also proposals over the years to build through the park to reach the mines near the park, in particular those in the Cooke City area. Other lines were proposed for mines in the park, to haul out lumber from the park and the surrounding areas, and to transport tourists through the park. Although some of these railroads were incorporated, none of them was built to or in the park. There were several times when these interests nearly succeeded, but House and Senate bills authorizing their construction died in conference. These efforts continued through 1919, when improved roads and declining mining activities made it obvious that there was no need for a railroad in the park.

The First Proposals for a Railroad in the Park

Support for a railroad in the park was expressed as early as 1872, the year the park was established. Park Superintendent Langford accompanied the Hayden survey party in 1872 and stated that the exploration and surveys had shown that a railroad into the park was practical. A line could run through the Firehole Basin to the Falls and along the canyon to Mammoth Hot Springs. This would bring in thousands of tourists, as routes from both Idaho and Montana were practical[1]. F. V. Hayden issued a report titled "Means of Access to the Yellowstone National Park by Railroads[2]".

The next report of a railroad in the park was for the Utah and Northern Railway, which built a narrow gauge railroad line from Ogden, Utah north to Butte and Garrison in Montana. In 1879 a survey party for the Utah and Northern was laying out a route from its Red Rock Station through Virginia City into the park[3], even before the main line had been completed to Butte. Seeing the potential for beating the Northern Pacific to the park, the company found a route up the Madison River to the geysers basins, and Park Superintendent Norris discussed the rail line in his 1879 annual report. This did not sit well with the Bozeman populace, and they successfully opposed development of this route[4]. Norris' successor, Park Superintendent Conger, protested that any railroad into the park would be damaging. Robert E. Strahorn was a promoter hired by the Union Pacific, which controlled the Utah and Northern Railway, and his 1880 book, *To the Rockies and Beyond,* showed a proposed branch from the Utah & Northern main line at Beaver Cañon to the park. His map labeled it the "Yellowstone Park Branch"[5].

In December 1881, the Yellowstone Park superintendent wrote that the Northern Pacific had reached Miles City and that it planned to continue construction to the park. The report went on to state that:

"The Utah Northern Railroad ... is now engaged in surveying the route of a branch by way of Ruby Valley, Virginia City, and the Upper Madison, to the Forks of the Fire Holes, a distance of about 140 or 150 miles from the main line at Dillon. With little doubt, one or both of these roads will enter the park within two to three years hereafter, and ultimately a connection by the latter, through the valleys and cañoned branches of the Madison and the Gallatin, skirt the western border of the Park from the Forks of the Fire Holes to Bozeman, on the line of the Northern Pacific Railroad."[6]

The Oregon Short Line, which controlled the Utah & Northern, organized a survey party in 1882 for a line to be built to and into the park in the summer of 1883[7]. No construction was performed.

There was also interest for a rail line from the Montana side. The New World, or Cooke City Mining District, was discovered in 1872 and gave the impetus for a railroad through the park. The mining district was located in Park County, on the north boundary of Yellowstone National Park and was on the route of what is now the Northeast Entrance. Before the arrival of the railroads, Cooke City was a receiving point for freight transported from the steamboats on the Missouri and Yellowstone rivers for forwarding to Cody and through Red Lodge. In 1877 Chief Joseph and his Nez Perce Indians passed through Cooke City, burning down the gold mills. A smelter was built by the Eastern Montana Mining and Smelting Company in the same year[8], but the transportation costs made it uneconomical to process the bullion. When the mills were rebuilt, the ores were too poor to be mined economically, and the miners left for richer fields[9]. The miners knew they needed a railroad to be able to operate their mines, and that railroad would have to run through the park.

In 1882 some of the surrounding area was ceded from the Crow Indian Reservation and there was a stampede to make mining claims. Fourteen hundred and fifty mining claims were quickly staked in the New World District, although most of them lapsed within a year. The post office opened in the same year, and the town was named for Jay Cooke Jr., who was a miner in the area. Reportedly the son of Jay Cooke, he promised to promote the area and to bring in a railroad. Following financial difficulties his mining claims reverted to the original owners. The townsite was platted in 1883, although it took eight years to complete surveying the townsite due to the irregular mining claims. By that time Cooke City had a population of 227 voters, two smelters, two sawmills, three general stores, two hotels, two livery stables, and a meat market[10].

The Republic Mining Company in Cooke City was organized in 1882 and spent over $300,000 developing its properties, but had to shut down due to lack of transportation[11]. Local miners stated that the drayage costs for the ores were $25 a ton by wagon, but that a railroadwould bring the cost down to $5 a ton[12]. Despite the lack of a railroad, mining continued on a small scale into the twentieth century, with miners bringing out gold, silver, lead and copper.

Various proposals for a railroad through the park arose in 1883, supported by businessmen in Cooke City and Livingston, Washington, D.C., and New York City. This was not surprising since the railroad was the only means of taking out the ore and bringing in equipment, and this was a time when railroads were being built throughout the country. Support was received from other groups who wanted to mine or log in the park, and the need for stronger legislation to protect the park quickly became obvious. Although the railroad interests nearly succeeded several times, a railroad was never built in the park. Some bills passed the Senate or the Senate and House, only to die in the conference committee when the session ended. These railroads were intended for freight business more than for tourist traffic, although they would also have generated revenues from the tourists

In 1882 it was reported that the Northern Pacific had surveyed a route south through Yellowstone Park to Jackson Hole when it was exploring for a route from Livingston to Cinnabar. Although this line was completed to Cinnabar in 1882 and to Gardiner, at the north edge of the park in 1902, it was never built into the park. These surveyors were apparently the ones encountered by Lieutenant Sheridan in 1882 on the Lewis River in the park[13]. Sheridan was adamantly opposed to the construction of any rail line in the park.

A Summary of the Initial Bills for a Railroad in the Park

It was in the early 1880s that the first proposals were introduced into Congress to authorize the construction of a railroad in the park. There was intense debate in Congress related to the construction of a railroad into and through the park, most of it related to the Cooke City mining district. The names of the railroad changed over the years, and included the Cinnabar & Clarks Fork Railroad Company, the Cinnabar Railroad, and the Montana Mineral Railroad Company. These lines were to go from Cinnabar, the end of the Northern Pacific line which eventually ran to Gardiner, to the Lamar River, up to Soda Butte Creek, and to Cooke City and the New World Mining District. Some supporters of the railroads proposed that the northeast section of the park be removed from the park and placed back in the public domain[14]. Others simply asked for a right-of-way 100 to 160 feet wide through the park, while some asked to have everything north of the Lamar River and east of theYellowstone be taken out of the park[15]. Some organizations vigorously opposed the construction of any rail line in the park, and fought these proposals, despite the efforts of the mining interests to hide authorizations in bills which would expand the park boundaries[16].

There were also congressmen who felt strongly that the park should remain intact with no railroads allowed. Park supporters included General Philip Sheridan, Park Engineer Captain Chittenden, George

Bird Grinnell, editor of *Forest and Stream*, Senator Vest of Missouri, and Representative Lacey of Iowa[17]. Senator Vest worked long and hard for many years opposing the construction of a railroad in the park and successfully prevented a railroad being built. The westerners supported a railroad, while the eastern interests were interested in preserving the integrity of the park. There was also an anti-railroad mood in the country at this time, which prevented some support for the proposed railroads[18].

On January 30, 1882, in the First Session of the Forty-Seventh Congress, Representative Samuel S. Cox of New York introduced a bill to protect the park. The bill proposed the park be under the jurisdiction of the War Department, but hidden in the proposal was authorization for right-of-way for any "existing Railroad Company" duly chartered to build in the park. The bill was referred to the Public Lands Committee and was not reported. Ironically, in the same session of Congress a bill was introduced to build a military road from Fort Washakie to the park, but it was adversely reported out of the Military Affairs Committee[19]. No bills were introduced in the Second Session of the Forty-Seventh Congress.

The Bullion Railroad Company, to be capitalized at $1 million, was incorporated to build a narrow gauge line through the park from Cinnabar to Cooke City. This line was secretly backed by the Northern Pacific. George Haldorn, an attorney for the Northern Pacific, was known to be connected with the line[20]. In the First Session of the Forty-Eighth Congress, however, the Montana Legislature requested that the mining district be excluded from the park, which would have made the construction of a railroad to Cooke City easier. In early 1884 Representative Maginnis of Montana introduced a bill for the Cinnabar & Clarks Fork Railroad. This was referred to the Committee on Pacific Railroads. At the same time Senator McMillan of St. Paul, Minnesota introduced a bill to grant a right-of-way in the park to the Cinnabar & Clarks Fork Railroad. Representative Rosecrans of California also introduced a bill to incorporate the Yellowstone Park Railroad, but nothing more was heard of this proposal[21].

At the same time, in 1883-84, the Livingston newspaper expressed its support for a railroad in the park. Controlled by the government, the railroad would connect all entrances and allow a trip through the park in one day instead of the five needed for travel by stage. However, this idea, too, was opposed by others and the line was not built[22].

With no action on the proposals by Congress, Representative John Toole of Montana introduced a bill for the Cinnabar & Clarks Fork Railroad Company in the First Session of the Forty-Ninth Congress in early 1886, and Senator McMillan again introduced a bill for the same railroad. The citizens of Cooke also submitted a petition to Congress for a wagon road between Cooke City and Cinnabar[23]. Special Agent Phillips submitted a report at the request of Congress in February 1886, and it recommended opposition to a railroad in the park[24]. General Sheridan expressed his opposition by stating *"A railroad though any portion of the park is not in harmony with the objects for which this reservation was created.[25]"*

In the First Session of the Fiftieth Congress, during the summer of 1888, there was a House Report on the Cinnabar & Cooke City Railroad. There was additional activity on the proposed railroad in the Second Session[26]. In the First Session of the Fifty-First Congress, a Senate bill was reported in the House to authorize the construction of the Cinnabar Railroad. After Minnesota Representative Dunnell expressed his opposition, the discussion of a railroad ended for the session of Congress[27]. The Second Session authorized the Montana & Wyoming Railroad through the Crow Indian Reservation. There was discussion relating to how close to the park the railroad should be allowed to construct its line, with an amendment stating it should be built no closer than one mile, although Senator Hale wanted a distance of three miles[28].

The legislative activity continued in the Fifty-First Congress, and in the First Session there was more discussion on a proposed railroad in the park. In the Second Session, the Senate passed a bill in February 1891 authorizing the Montana & Wyoming Railroad near the park. The Montana Legislature also submitted a memorial requesting the Senate grant permission to the Montana Mineral Railroad Company through the park in the same month[29]. This resulted in a bill being introduced by Senator Carlisle of Kentucky to authorize the construction of the Montana Mineral Railroad Company through the park[30].

The Fifty-Second Congress marked the high point of the railroad lobbying to build a rail line into the park. In the First Session of the Fifty-Second Congress bills were introduced in December 1891 by Mississippi Representative Stockdale and Kentucky Senator Carlisle to grant the right-of-way for the

Montana Mineral Railroad Company. It was proposed that the northern boundary of the park become the state line, so that the land in Montana could be used for the rail line to Cooke City. Expressing support for the railroad, Virginia Representative Tucker stated *"Cooke City, or the New World mining district, is pronounced by mining experts the most valuable and extensive mining district in the world. There are now registered over 1,500 mining claims awaiting the vitalizing touch of a railroad to be developed into enormous wealth...."* Senator Vest, an ardent park supporter, replied *"the aggressive action of a lobby that for years have been endeavoring to put a railroad into the park in order to sell it for a large sum to the Northern Pacific."*[31] By the end of 1892 the Northern Pacific gave up, and Northern Pacific President Oakes said that his railroad had evaluated the Cooke City mines and determined there was no need to build a rail line to them. Three years later the Northern Pacific's "Sketches of Wonderland" stated support for expansion of the park[32].

In September 1892 in the First Session of the Fifty-Third Congress Senator Shoup of Idaho introduced a bill to authorize the construction of an electric railroad in the park, using power generated by the Falls of the Yellowstone River. At the same time Representative Doolittle of Washington also introduced a bill to authorize construction of an electric railroad by David B. May[33]. This was done at the request of the Yellowstone Park Association, which was backed by the Northern Pacific, in order to make travel in the park easier and more convenient[34]. However, Hiram Chittenden, First Lieutenant of Engineers in the park, surveyed travelers in the park, and found that a large majority opposed the introduction of an electric railroad into the park[35].

In the Second Session Representative Coffeen introduced a bill to authorize the extension of the Burlington railroad by the construction of the Grand Island - Wyoming Railroad to improve travel to, in, and from the park. This was adversely reported by Representative Hare of Ohio, based on reports from Secretary Lamar, Park Superintendent Captain Anderson, and General Sheridan[36]. Anderson wrote that the railroad was *"unneeded, undesirable, vicious"*,[37] and went on to say that *"Six months from the entrance of the first locomotive within the limits of the Park there will not be left one acre of its magnificent forests unburned."*[38] The House proposal for the railroad also received an adverse report by Iowa Representative Lacey[39].

There was another proposal in the Second Session of the Fifty-Third Congress to change the park boundaries. Captain Anderson wrote that *"It is claimed that the north part is needed as a right of way for a railroad to Cooke City. The whole wealth of Cooke would not pay running expenses on one train a year, and there is not the slightest chance of such a railroad even being built....The bill is purely in the interest of private greed and that too not of a very high order*[40]. By this time the House and Senate were both giving only adverse reports to any proposals to encroach on the park boundary and for the construction of any railroad in the park.

Idaho Senator Shoup again submitted a bill to authorize the construction of an electric railroad in the park in December 1895, during the First Session of the Fifty-Fourth Congress. It was again adversely reported by Senator Davis in April[41].

Other Proposals in Following Years

There was no significant activity for several years, although the Union Pacific incorporated the Idaho and Wyoming Railroad in 1905 to build a line to the south edge of the park. A bill was introduced into the Sixty-Fifth Congress (1917-1919) to allow the Union Pacific to build a Teton-Yellowstone line. The bill never passed, although Interior Secretary Lane felt that were positive aspects to the proposal[42]. With the failure of this bill, the Idaho and Wyoming charter was allowed to lapse.

In 1900 the Yellowstone Park Railroad was proposed to run from Bridger through Cooke City to Livingston, in large part to serve the coal mines. Talks continued for several years, and the Bear Creek Coal Company began developing its properties. Finally, with backing from eastern capitalists, the Yellowstone Park Railroad Company was incorporated in Maine on May 17, 1905 and in Montana on August 30, with Frank A. Hall of Belfry as president, S.N. Mumma of Lancaster, Pennsylvania, vice president, and George J. Atkins of Chicago secretary-treasurer. The line was to run from Bridger 125 miles to the coal fields and mines in the Cooke City area. Three million dollars in stocks and bonds were authorized, and a small portion of this money was issued to build the line from Bridger to Bear Creek. The balance was to be used for the extension to Cooke City with the line to Cooke City following the Clarks Fork River from Belfry. The line was officially completed to Belfry and the mines at Bear Creek on August 23, 1906. Due to financial difficulties foreclosure was performed on the line in June 1907, and the line reorganized as the Montana, Wyoming & Southern Railroad in New Jersey on June 30, 1909. The Montana, Wyoming and Southern Railroad took over the Yellowstone Park Railroad on September 1, 1909. There was no serious discussion of extending the line to Cooke City. After World War II coal traffic decreased to the point it was no longer profitable, and the Montana, Wyoming & Southern Railroad was abandoned in May, 1954.

In the same time period, the Western Smelting and Power Company requested permission to use the road in the park to Cooke City. Robert McKay of the Buffalo Mining Company in Cooke City went so far as to travel to Washington, D.C. to propose building a rail line from Gardiner to Cooke City, but his request was denied[43]. This was effectively the end of any serious proposals to build a railroad in the park. A few other proposals continued over the years. In 1918 it was reported that the Cooke County Transit Company had been incorporated to build a 1.5 mile line from the Lamar River to Soda Butte Creek. It was backed by businessmen from Lewistown, Montana[44].

Although the Cooke City mines were never very profitable, mining did continue through the 1950s. In 1989 a gold mine at Jardine, near Gardiner was reopened, and there have been other proposals to open gold mines near Cooke City. In 1989 attempts to use the Cooke City road through the park to haul out timber burned in the fires of the previous year were unsuccessful. Mining in the vicinity of Yellowstone National Park continues to be controversial.

Although railroads in the park were never approved, there are some photos which show that short, narrow-gauge lines were built during the construction of various roads. These railroads were used to transport fill and materials at the construction site and were only temporary. There is also a location known as "Narrow Gauge Terrace" and "Narrow Gauge Springs" at Mammoth Hot Springs. It was given this name at some time because it resembled a narrow-gauge roadbed, ready to receive ties and rails[45].

Although there were several proposals for a rail line in Yellowstone National Park, none was ever built. "Narrow Gauge Terrace" and "Narrow Gauge Springs" at Mammoth Hot Springs are references to the fact that the terrace looks as though it was ready for a narrow gauge rail line to be built on it. AUTHOR'S PHOTO

Railroad Travel to Yellowstone National Park Today

Five different railroads served the five park entrances over the course of almost 100 years. The Northern Pacific began taking tourists to the park through the North Entrance, followed by the Chicago, Burlington and Quincy through the East Entrance and the Union Pacific through the West Entrance. Due to its convenience and the markets the railroads served, the West Entrance was the most popular, followed by the Northern Pacific's North Entrance. The Cody gateway through the East Entrance was a distant third. The Chicago and North Western made a feeble attempt to bring in travelers through Lander to the South Entrance, and the Northern Pacific promoted the new Northeast Entrance through Red Lodge, while the Union Pacific offered service through Victor to the South Entrance. None of these was very successful. The Milwaukee Road's service through the Gallatin Gateway was also not successful, in part due to the late date it began offering the service. The various rail lines, however, all provided the traveler with a wide variety of ways to reach and see the park, and were responsible for its increasing popularity.

Although all passenger service to the park ended in 1960 and the rails to the west and north entrances have been removed, there are still ways to visit the park on a train. The *American Orient Express*, a luxury cruise train, recently renamed The GrandLuxe Rail Journeys takes travelers to the park on luxury buses from its train. The operations have varied over the years since it started offering visits to Yellowstone and Grand Teton national parks in 1997. The first year the train traveled up the former Yellowstone Branch of the Union Pacific to St. Anthony, where a transfer was made to buses. Since then the train has continued to either travel up to St. Anthony or stops at Idaho Falls, and the travelers spend one night in the park on their tour. For several years another train reached the park from the north. Originally known as the *Montana Rockies Rail Tour*, it traveled between Sandpoint, Idaho and Livingston, but this train was discontinued in the 2005 season.

It is interesting that, although the railroads were prevented from running through the park in the end of the nineteenth century, there are proposals to build a rail line at another national park. A light rail line is being built on the south edge of the Grand Canyon due to the high number of visitors, and other national parks also offer mass transit to reduce air pollution and traffic.

Although a railroad will most likely never be built in Yellowstone National Park, there are efforts and proposals to encourage use of mass transit. Previous railroad service to the park, in the meantime, is a memory of the time when all travel was by rail.

Left: The log Gardiner station was replaced with the one-story wooden building on the left after passenger service was discontinued. The building is now used by the town of Gardiner for a variety of purposes. The Roosevelt Arch and the road to Mammoth Hot Springs are on the right. Right: Union Pacific's shield is on a pylon at the edge of the park at West Yellowstone, a reminder of the time when tourists arrived by train at the nearby depot. AUTHOR'S PHOTOS

Appendix A

A Brief Chronology of Yellowstone

Some of the significant dates associated with Yellowstone National Park and the railroads are as follows:

- 1803: Park land is part of Louisiana Purchase
- 1807-08: John Colter, member of the Lewis and Clark Expedition, is the first white man to see the park.
- 1859-1860: Captain W.F. Raynold leads a party which includes Dr. F.V. Hayden and Jim Bridger, to explore the park, but they are blocked by snow.
- 1869: Charles W. Cook makes a prospecting trip through the park.
- 1870: The Expedition of 1870 is headed by Surveyor General H.D. Washburn. It explores the park regions.
- 1871: Dr. F.V. Hayden heads up a U.S. Geological expedition, the first official government exploration of the park. William H. Jackson takes the first photographs, and Thomas Moran makes paintings on the trip.
- 1872: President Ulysses S. Grant establishes the park on March 1.
- 1873: Captain W.A. Jones leads a party through the park, and they discover Togwotee Pass.
- 1877: Chief Joseph and several hundred Nez Perce Indians are pursued through the park by General O.O. Howard. The army builds the first wagon road, a primitive path. General Sheridan makes his first trip through the park.
- 1878: Norris Road from Mammoth to Lower Geyser Basins is built by Park Superintendent Norris. Hayden continues exploration and mapping in the park.
- 1879: The park has 90 miles of roads which can be traveled by wagons.
- 1880: Mammoth Hot Springs post office opens.
- 1881: Frank Jay Haynes drives a wagon to and through the park.
- 1883: Northern Pacific completes line to Cinnabar. Yellowstone Park Improvement Company is organized.
    Mammoth Hotel partially completed.
    Dr. Arnold Hague of the U.S. Geological Survey studies the park.
    President Chester A. Arthur visits the park.
    Henry Villard, president of Northern Pacific, visits the park with his party of guests as part of the celebration for the completion of Northern Pacific's transcontinental line
- 1884: George W. Wakefield establishes a stage line using Concord coaches which begins operating in the park.
- 1886: Yellowstone Park Association acquires leases of the Yellowstone National Park Improvement Company, completing Mammoth Hotel, building a hotel at Norris, and operating tent hotels at the lower and upper geyser basins.
    Haynes and Wakefield operate the Concord coaches under the name of Wakefield & Haynes, Yellowstone Park Stage Company.
- 1890: Construction of Fort Yellowstone started.
    Construction of road from Yellowstone Lake to Cody started but is not opened until 1903.
    Construction of Cody Road started.
- 1891: Fountain Hotel built by Yellowstone Park Association.
- 1892: The Yellowstone Park Transportation Company starts operations.
- 1894: Act of May 7, 1894 passed by Congress to protect the birds and animals in the park.
- 1896: William W. Wylie granted franchise to conduct tourists through the park and house them at permanent tent camps.
- 1897: Fort Yellowstone enlarged.
    First travel over road from West Thumb via the South Gate to Jackson Lake.

- 1898: Monida & Yellowstone State Company, organized by F.J. Haynes, begins operating between Monida and the West Entrance.
- 1901: H.W.Child assumes management of the companies managing hotels and transportation in the park from the North Entrance.
- 1903: Northern Pacific Railway extends line from Cinnabar to Gardiner.
  Entrance from Cody opened.
  President Theodore Roosevelt dedicates arch at North Entrance
  Old Faithful Inn under construction
- 1904: Old Faithful Inn completed, Lake Hotel enlarged.
- 1906: Wylie's franchise taken over by the Wylie Permanent Camping Company.
- 1907: Union Pacific Railroad completes its line to West Yellowstone, begins offering passenger service the following summer.
  Yellowstone Park Boat Company succeeds Yellowstone Lake Coat Company.
  Yellowstone Park Hotel Company succeeds Yellowstone Park Association.
- 1908: Union Pacific Railroad begins operating passenger trains to what is now West Yellowstone.
- 1909: Stone buildings at Mammoth Hot Springs completed.
- 1911: Canyon Hotel enlarged.
  Gallatin road between Bozeman and West Yellowstone completed.
- 1912: First rail passenger pass through East Entrance from Cody over Chicago, Burlington and Quincy Railroad.
- 1913: Monida & Yellowstone Stage Company reorganized to the Yellowstone-Western Stage Company.
  Shaw & Powell Camping Company granted franchise to transport tourists and operate tent camps in the park.
- 1915: Effective August 1, automobiles allowed into park.
  Season record of 20,151 tourists carried by the Yellowstone-Western Stage Company in horse-drawn vehicles.
- 1916: National Park Service created.
  U.S. Army leaves Yellowstone National Park.
  Cody-Sylvan Pass Motor Company, with President F.J. Haynes, starts operation between Cody and Yellowstone Lake, the first motor line in the park.
- 1917: Yellowstone Park Transportation Company motorizes its operations, and use of all horse-drawn passenger vehicles terminates.
  Yellowstone Park Camping Company acquires Wylie Permanent Camping Company and Shaw & Powell Camping Company.
- 1918: U.S. Army troops removed from the park.
  All hotels and some permanent camps closed due to World War I.
- 1919: Yellowstone Park Camping Company name changed to Yellowstone Parks Camping Company.
- 1921: Opening of the south road from Lander is celebrated at Togwotee Pass.
- 1922: Chicago and North Western Railway begins offering service to park through South Entrance.
- 1923: President Harding visits the park.
  Mammoth Lodge completed, construction started in 1922.
- 1924: Yellowstone Parks Company name changed to Yellowstone Park Lodge and Camps Company.
- 1926: Chicago, Milwaukee and St. Paul Railway begins offering service to park through West Entrance from Three Forks.
- 1927: Opening of Gallatin Gateway Inn on June 17. Chicago, Milwaukee and St. Paul Railway begins offering service to West Entrance from the inn.
  North Wing of Old Faithful Inn built.
  The Fountain and Norris hotels razed. They had been closed shortly after motorized vehicles were permitted in the park.
  President Calvin Coolidge visits the park.

- 1929: Grand Teton National Park established.
  Union Pacific Railroad begins offering service to South Entrance through Victor.
- 1931: William Morse Nichols becomes president of Yellowstone Park Transportation Company, Yellowstone Park Hotel Company, and Yellowstone Park Boat Company.
- 1934: Construction of a large wing of the Canyon hotel, started in 1930, completed.
- 1935: Air service to West Yellowstone introduced. First air service to any of the park entrances.
- 1936: Consolidation of Yellowstone Park Transportation Company, Yellowstone Park Hotel Company, and Yellowstone Park Boat Company into Yellowstone Park Company.
  Road from Red Lodge through Cooke City to Northeast Entrance opens
- 1937: President Franklin Delano Roosevelt and his wife visit the park for two days.
  Northern Pacific Railway begins offering service to park through Northeast Entrance via Red Lodge.
- 1941: All facilities except Mammoth Lodge and Lake Hotel are open.
- 1942: Old Faithful Inn, Mammoth Hot Spring Hotel, Canyon Hotel and a few other facilities remain open. The rest are closed due to World War II.
- 1943: Tourist Cabins at Old Faithful and Fishing Bridge and some other facilities remain open.
- 1946: Most of park facilities open following end of World War II.
- 1947: Lake Hotel reopened. Closed since 1941.
- 1948: Last year of scheduled passenger service to Gardiner by Northern Pacific Railway.
- 1953: Last year of scheduled passenger service to Cody by Chicago, Burlington & Quincy Railroad.
- 1960: Last year of scheduled passenger service to West Yellowstone by Union Pacific Railroad.

Union Pacific Railroad Train #45, the *Yellowstone Special*, has arrived at West Yellowstone in this view taken about 1930. The railroad took care to maintain the station grounds, as indicated by the sign telling the arriving tourists to stay off the lawn. AUTHOR'S COLLECTION

Appendix B
Rail Travel to Yellowstone National Park

For many years the Annual Report of the Superintendent of Yellowstone National Park listed the number of visitors arriving by rail, starting in 1920. They were first listed by entrance, but after 1934, they simply reported the number of rail visitors without categorizing them by entrance. This was, of course, due to the decreasing number and lesser importance of rail visitors. After World War II, the Park Service did not list the number of rail visitors at all. The following is information taken from annual reports for the years as indicated.

Year	- North - Gardiner (NP)	- East - Cody (CB&Q)	- West - Union Pacific/ The Milwaukee Road	- Northeast - C&NW	Total Rail Visitors	Total Park Visitors
1920	9,717	4,075	14,268	N/A	28,060	81,651
1921	— — — — — — — — information not available — — — — — — — —					
1922	10,861	5,304	17,094	99	33,358	98,225
1923	14,117	7,407	23,116	167	44,806	138,352
1924	13,439	6,999	20,409	207	41,054	144,158
1925	17,007	7,267	20,287	225	44,786	154,282
1926	14,127	7,611	18,138 (UP) 813 (Milw. from Three Forks)	271	40,960	187,807
1927	13,772	7,588	17,157 (UP) 2,788 (Milw- GG Inn) 271 (NP- Bozeman)	109	41,685	200,825
1928	13, 021	7,567	17,408 (UP) 3,337 (Milw.- GG Inn) 256 (NP- Bozeman)	108	41,697	230,984
1929	12, 243	7,233	14,520 (UP) 3,128 (Milw.- GG Inn) 401 (NP- Bozeman)	261 (C&NW) 29 (UP- Victor)	38,979 (Includes 1,164 temporary employees)	260,697
1930	9,209	4,585	10,271 (UP) 1,637 (Milw.- GG Inn) 383 (NP- Bozeman)	90	26,845 (Includes 670 temporary employees)	227,901

- Year -	- North -	- East -	- West -	- Northeast -	- Total Rail -	- Total Park -
1931	6,693	3,203	6,657 (UP) 1,261 (Milw.–GG Inn) 331 (NP–Bozeman) (Plus 623 temp. employees)	121 (C&NW) 40 (UP–Victor)	18,929 (Includes 623 temporary employees)	221,248
1932	3,242	1,524	2,271 (UP) 590 (Milw.–GG Inn) 33 (NP–Bozeman) (Plus 402 temp. employees)	27 (C&NW) 33 (UP–Victor)	8,572 (Includes 402 temporary employees)	147,747
1933	2,955	966	2,146 (UP) 328 (Milw.–GG Inn) 20 (NP–Bozeman) (Plus 353 temp. employees)	8 (C&NW) 11 (UP–Victor)	6,787 (Includes 353 temporary employees)	154,017
1934 (Oct. 1, 1933–June 30, 1934)	590	237	518 (UP) 58 (Milw.–GG Inn) 5 (NP–Bozeman)	4 (C&NW) 3 (UP–Victor)	1,415	60,090
1947[1]	na	na	7,751 (UP)	238 (UP)	na	na
1948[2]	na	na	7,820 (UP)	390 (UP)	na	na

*na-not available

The National Park Service changed its reporting year effective 1934 so that the statistics were no longer related to the park season, but to the government fiscal year of July 1 to June 30 the following year.

The archives at the Yellowstone Heritage and Research Center at Gardiner, Montana have reports from the Yellowstone Park Transportation Company. These reports give the number of passengers transported on its buses over the years. These numbers are lower than those reported by the Park Service, which included all rail passengers to the park, not just those arriving on YPTC buses. The following are the numbers from the reports submitted to the National Park Service.

1924: 37,351	1932: 7,195	1940: 16,909	1952: 17,386
1925: 42,248	1933: 5,366	1941: 18,322	1953: 23,023
1926: 38,192	1934: 12,384	1946: 14,964	1954: 17,818
1927: 39,276	1935: 15,991	1947: 19,846	1955: 17,981
1928: 38,750	1936: 18,297	1948: 18,839	1956: 16,889
1929: 35,811	1937: 19,251	1949: 17,496	1957: 18,862
1930: 24,474	1938: 17,144	1950: 19,000	1959: 12,931
1931: 16,906	1939: 16,279	1951: 15,705	1960: 14,594

1941 through 1960 reports include train, bus and plane arrivals. Prior years were, for all practical purposes, all train arrivals.

Footnotes

Introduction
1. The only national park in the country which was on the main line of a railroad was Glacier National Park, which was reached by the Great Northern Railway.

Chapter One
Yellowstone National Park – A Brief History
1. Idaho in 1863 became a territory, Montana in 1864, and Wyoming in 1868. Montana became a state in 1889, and Wyoming and Idaho were both admitted as states in 1890.

Chapter Two
The Road to Yellowstone National Park
1. Aubrey L. Haines, The Yellowstone Story, Vol. I (Niwot: University Press of Colorado, 1997, 1996 edition), pp. 141-144. The Union Pacific and Central Pacific transported the men and equipment for the Hayden Expedition, at no cost, over their lines.
2. F.V. Hayden, The Yellowstone National Park, and the Mountain Regions of Portions of Idaho, Nevada, Colorado and Utah (Boston: L. Prang and Company 1876. 1997 reprint by the Thomas Gilcrease Museum Association, Tulsa, OK), pp. 2-3.
3. Richard A. Bartlett, Yellowstone, A Wilderness Besieged (Tucson: The University of Arizona Press 1985), p. 12. Clawson's trip is described in his book A Ride to the Infernal Region - Yellowstone's First Tourists (Helena: Riverbend Publishing), 2003. This book collects his reports as published in The New North-West (Deer Lodge, Montana) newspaper describing his trip. Bartlett states there were five men, and Clawson lists six men on the trip.
4. Haines, p. 195, and Clawson, p. 13.
5. Clawson, ix.
6. "Historic Document Donated to Archives", Wonderland News,, Yellowstone Historic Center, April 1, 2004.
7. Kenneth L. Diem and Lenore L. "A Community of Scalawags, Renegades, Discharged Soldiers and Predestined Stinkers" (Moose: Grand Teton Natural History Association, 1998), p. 9. In his report, "Reconnaissance of the Yellowstone River. Report of a Reconnaissance in WY and MT Territories", he stated that "I am led to believe that a practicable road possibly a railroad can be constructed from Yellowstone Lake south to Snake River on the direction of the Tetons....."
8. Haines, pp. 191-192.
9. Clawson, Calvin C. A Ride to the Infernal Region - Yellowstone's First Tourists, Helena: Riverbend Publishing, 2003, p. 105.
10. Diem, p. 10.
11. Eagle Rock was renamed to Idaho Falls in 1890. The Utah & Northern Railway was at what is now Pocatello when this report was written and reached Eagle Rock in the spring of 1879.
12. "Report of the Secretary of the Interior, Yellowstone National Park", dated December 10, 1878, p. 995, available at the Yellowstone Heritage and Research Center, Yellowstone National Park.
13. Diem, p. 9.

Chapter Three
The Park Tour
1. The tourists would wear dusters and hats to keep their clothes clean, since the roads were dusty and rough.
2. Robert Goss, *Yellowstone - The Chronology of Wonderland*, (Second Edition, 2002) ,p. 72.
3. Robert Goss, *Making Concessions in Yellowstone* (Second Edition, 2002), p. 70.
4. Goss, *Making Concessions in Yellowstone*, p. 67
5. Goss, *Making Concessions in Yellowstone*, p. 67.
6. Goss, *Making Concessions in Yellowstone*, 71.
7. Copy on file at the Yellowstone Heritage and Research Center, Yellowstone National Park.
8. The Milwaukee Road served Gallatin Gateway, while the Northern Pacific served Bozeman, and both tours routes went through Gallatin Canyon.
9. Correspondence on file at the Yellowstone Heritage and Research Center, Yellowstone National Park.

Chapter Four
Train Travel to Yellowstone National Park

1. Edward Frank Allen, editor. *A Guide to the National Parks of America,* (McBride, Nast & Company: New York), 1915, pp. 2-3.
2. The four entrances were the North, West, East, and South. The five railroads were the Chicago, Burlington & Quincy, the Chicago & North Western, The Milwaukee Road, the Northern Pacific, and the Union Pacific. The Northeast Entrance did not open to automobiles until 1936, and the Northern Pacific did not offer service to the park from Red Lodge through the Northeast Entrance until the following year.
3. In mixed train service the passengers rode in the caboose or a passenger car on the end of the freight train. On the West Yellowstone line the railroad would offer this mixed train service from one to three days a week in the spring and fall months. The trains were slow since freight cars were switched in and out of the train along the route.
4. Peter T. Maiken, *Night Trains,* (Beloit: Lakme Press, 1989), p. 289.
5. Craig Reese, *The Gardiner Gateway to Yellowstone,* "The Mainstreeter" (The Northern Pacific Railway Historical Association), Vol. 15, No. 2, Spring, 1996, pp. 1-21.
6. Union Pacific advertisement for the year 1931, Collection of the Yellowstone Heritage Center, West Yellowstone, Montana.
7. *Idaho Register* (Idaho Falls), September 3, 1915 advertisement.
8. "Each of two or more trains running on the same timetable schedule at intervals...", [*Railway Age's Comprehensive Railroad Dictionary*, (Omaha: Simmons-Boardman), 1984 (1992 edition), p.128].
9. Sometimes the railroad had to run more than two sections. The June 11, 1915 issue of *Idaho Register* (Idaho Falls) reported that the railroad was making plans so it could operate 5 sections of the first *Yellowstone Special* of the season, scheduled for June 15.
10. *Teton Peak-Chronicle* (St. Anthony), July 10, 1924.
11. Correspondence on file at the Union Pacific Museum in Council Bluffs, Iowa, with copies at the Yellowstone Historic Center, West Yellowstone, Montana.
12. Correspondence on file at the Union Pacific Museum in Council Bluffs, Iowa, with copies at the Yellowstone Historic Center, West Yellowstone, Montana.
13. *Union Pacific Bulletin,* June 1942. This was a monthly publication issued to ticket agents to inform them of the services the Union Pacific offered.
14. *Union Pacific Bulletin,* May 1943. The bulletin noted that no bus service was available at Yellowstone, Teton, and Glacier and the Southern Utah national parks. It also noted that the Awahnee Hotel in Yosemite had been taken over by the Navy for rest and recuperation.
15. Correspondence on file at the Union Pacific Museum in Council Bluffs, Iowa, with copies at the Yellowstone Historic Center, West Yellowstone, Montana.
16. Annual Report of Yellowstone National Park for the year 1937, p. 2.
17. Annual Report of Yellowstone National Park for the year 1936, p. 8.
18. Annual Report of Yellowstone National Park for the year 1938, p. 2.
19. Annual Report of Yellowstone National Park for the year 1939, p. 2.
20. Annual Report of Yellowstone National Park for the year 1940, p. 4.
21. Aubrey L. Haines, *The Yellowstone Story, Vol. II,* (Niwot: University Press of Colorado), 1977, 1996 edition, pp. 372-373.
22. *The Union Pacific Magazine*, August, 1931, p. 23.
23. *The Union Pacific Magazine*, May, 1925, p. 8.
24. Al Richmond, *Cowboys, Miners, Presidents and Kings, The Story of the Grand Canyon Railway,* (Flagstaff: The Grand Canyon Pioneers Society, Inc.), 1985, p. 113.
25. *Pocatello Tribune*, July 30, 1921.
26. Copies of the timetables for the "Savage Special" for the 1952 and 1953 summer seasons are on file at the Yellowstone Heritage and Research Center.
27. Train orders on file at the Yellowstone Historic Center, West Yellowstone, Montana.
28. This trip is described in *President Arthur in Yellowstone National Park* by Thomas C. Reeves in "Montana - the magazine of Western History" (Montana Historical Society, Helena, Montana, Vol. XIX, No. 3, July, 1969), pp. 18-29, and *The President Travels by Train*, by Bob Withers, (Lynchburg: TLC Publishing, 1996), p. 54.
29. This trip is described in *Twice Told on the Upper Yellowstone, Vol. 1*, by Doris Whithorn, pp. 1-42.
30. Bob Withers, *The President Travels by Train* (Lynchburg: TLC Publishing, 1996), pp. 109-111.
31. *Haynes Guide - Yellowstone National Park* (Bozeman: Haynes Studios Inc., 1949 edition), p. 166.

Chapter Five
Visiting Wonderland – Promotion of Rail Travel to the Park

1. There was a slight increase in the costs for travel through Lander due to the long stage ride.
2. Robert W. Rydell, *All the World's a Fair*, Chicago: The University of Chicago Press, 1984, p. 227.
3. The *Wonderland* series started in 1886 and were intially based on the *Alice in Wonderland* book. They continued through 1906. Bill & Jan Taylor, *Rails to Gold and Silver*. (Missoula: Pictorial Histories Publishing Co.), 1999, pp. 33-34.
4. Lecture – Yellowstone National Park, Northern Pacific notes, in files of the Yellowstone Heritage and Research Center, Yellowstone National Park.
5. Pamphlet – "Department of Tours - 1917," written by Hazen H. Hunkins for the C&NW Ry and the UP RR. Available at the Yellowstone Heritage and Research Center, Yellowstone National Park.
6. *The Union Pacific Magazine*, December 1923, p. 17.
7. *A Trip to Yellowstone National Park over the Union Pacific* by Richard Henry Little describes a trip to the park through West Yellowstone in 1909, when the route was first opened. This book is on file at the Yellowstone Heritage and Research Center.
8. *The Union Pacific Magazine*, May 1924, p. 34.
9. Available at the Yellowstone Heritage and Research Center, Yellowstone National Park.
10. The Union Pacific Railroad employee magazine, *The Union Pacific Magazine*, was published in the 1920s through the early 1930s and often included articles on destinations on the railroad.
11. "Summer School and Rocky Mountain Tours for School Boys" pamphlet, in the files of the Yellowstone Heritage and Research Center, Yellowstone National Park.-
12. "Through Yellowstone Park on a Bicycle," in the files of the Yellowstone Heritage and Research Center, Yellowstone National Park.
13. *Annual Report of Yellowstone National Park for the Year 1923*, p. 20.
14. "The Tourists' Wonderland," published in 1884 by the Chicago, Milwaukee & St. Paul Railway. A copy is on file at the Yellowstone Heritage and Research Center.
15. Craig Reese, *The Gardiner Gateway to Yellowstone*, ("The Mainstreeter" The Northern Pacific Railway Historical Association, Vol. 15, No. 2, Spring 1996), p. 21.
16. Jack E. Haynes, *Haynes Guide*, p. 150.
17. Some of the Union Pacific bear poster advertisements promoted stopovers to the park when there was a fair. In 1939, when world's fair's were held in both San Francisco and New York, the railroad offered special fares for side trips to Yellowstone National Park. These posters are on file at the Union Pacific Museum in Council Bluffs, Iowa.
18. *Teton Peak-Chronicle*, June 21, 1923.
19. *The Union Pacific Magazine*, August 1927.
20. *Annual Report of Yellowstone National Park for the year 1923*, p. 62.
21. *Annual Report of Yellowstone National Park for the year 1924*, p. 35.
22. *Annual Report of Yellowstone National Park for the year 1925*, p. 41, and *The Union Pacific Magazine*, August 1925, p. 51.
23. *Annual Report of Yellowstone National Park for the year 1926*, pp. 3, 37.
24. *Annual Report of Yellowstone National Park for the year 1927*, p. 1.
25. *Annual Report of Yellowstone National Park for the year 1928*, p. 1.
26. *Annual Report of Yellowstone National Park for the year 1929*, p. 2.
27. *Annual Report of Yellowstone National Park for the year 1930*, p. 2.
28. *The Union Pacific Magazine*, September 1925, p. 51.
29. *The Official Guide of the Railways*, December 1937, p. 1268.
30. *The Official Guide of the Railways*, May 1945, p. 11292.

Chapter Six
"Yellowstone Park Line" – Northern Pacific Railway to Gardiner, Red Lodge, and Bozeman, Montana

1. The Northern Pacific Rail<u>road</u> Company built the transcontinental line across Montana in 1883 and the line to Cinnabar in the same year. The railroad entered bankruptcy in 1893 and was reorganized as the Northern Pacific Rail<u>way</u> Company in 1896. The Northern Pacific Railway became part of the Burlington Northern Railroad Company when the Burlington Northern was organized in March 1970. The Burlington Northern became part of the Burlington Northern and Santa Fe Railway Company when the Burlington Northern merged with the Atchison, Topeka & Santa Fe Railway in 1997.
2. This story is discussed in *Myth and History in the Creation of Yellowstone National Park*, by Paul Schullery and

Lee Whittlesey, (Lincoln: University of Nebraska), 2003.

3. Aubrey L. Haines, *The Yellowstone Story, Vol. I*, (Niwot: University Press of Colorado), 1997 (1996 edition), pp. 105, 137-138.

4. Haines, *Vol. I*, p. 142.

5. Articles of incorporation for the Rocky Mountain Railroad Company of Montana, on file with the Montana Secretary of State. Interestingly, the articles were not forfeited until 1985 for failure to pay annual reports and fees. This was after the abandonment of the line between Livingston and Gardiner.

6. Taylor, p. 29.

7. Kenneth L.. Diem and Lenore L. "*A Community of Scalawags, Renegades, Discharged Soldiers and Predestined Stinkers*", Moose: Grand Teton Natural History Association, 1998, p. 10.

8. A history of the town of Cinnabar can be found in the draft manuscript by Lee Whittlesey, "*They're Going to Build a Railroad!*": *Cinnabar, Stephens Creek, and the Game Ranch Addition to Yellowstone National Park*, dated March 9, 1995 and available at the Yellowstone Heritage and Research Center, Yellowstone National Park.

9. Taylor, p. 31.

10. Reese, p. 5.

11. Reese, pp. 5-6.

12. Taylor, p. 31.

13. Renz, p. 112.

14. Taylor, p. 31.

15. Renz, p. 112.

16. Taylor, p. 32.

17. A wye is "*used to describe a track arrangement shaped like the letter "Y" but with a connecting segment between the two upper legs. This track layout is often used in small yards ... to enable equipment to be turned without a turntable.*" [*Railway Age's Comprehensive Railroad Dictionary*, (Omaha: Simmons-Boardman), 1984 (1992 edition), p. 159]. The Northern Pacific had more space at Gardiner, so they built a "balloon" track, which allowed the trains to make a complete loop in front of the depot so that the train was facing back towards Livingston when the it was ready to depart.

18. Reese, p. 7.

19. This weight of rail was used on main lines at this time, suitable for the heavy and fast trains of the era. Railroads today typically use rail weighing 133 pounds a yard.

20. Reese, p. 12.

21. Reese, p. 12.

22. Reese, p. 13.

23. Reese, p. 14.

24. Reese, p. 15.

25. Reese, 15.

26. Haines, *The Park Branch Line*.

27. Roberta C. Cheney, *Names on the Face of Montana*, Missoula: Mountain Press Publishing Company, 1983 (1992 edition), p. 111, and *The WPA Guide to 1930s Montana*, Compiled and written by the Work Projects Administration for the State of Montana, Tucson: University of Arizona Press, 1994, p. 274.

28. Craig Reese, *The Gardiner Gateway to Yellowstone*, "The Mainstreeter" (The Northern Pacific Railway Historical Association), Vol. 15, No. 2, Spring, 1996, p. 6.

29. Cheney, p. 111.

30. *The Park Branch Line*, Unpublished manuscript by Aubrey Haines, written in 1963. In the files of the Yellowstone Heritage and Research Center.

31. This was noted in the 1896 issue of the *Wonderland '98*, published in 1898 by the Northern Pacific to promote travel on the line to Yellowstone National Park.

32. Haines, *Vol. II*, p. 230.

33. Reese, p. 9.

34. Reese, p. 11.

35. Reese, p. 15.

36. Bill and Jan Taylor. *Rails to Gold and Silver*, (Missoula: Pictorial Histories Publishing Co.), 1999, pp. 9, 32, 34.

37. Reese, pp. 11-12.

38. *Travelers' Official Guide of the Railway and Steam Navigation Line in the United States and Canada, June, 1893*, p. 478. This guide was published monthly and listed the passenger train schedules for all of the railroads in the United States, Canada, Mexico, and Cuba.

39. Reese, p. 19.

40. *The Official Railway Guide,*, June, 1921, pp. 918, 925. There was also a through sleeping car from St. Paul through Billings to Cody, Wyoming on the Burlington line.

41. Reese, p. 19.
42. Reese, p. 19.
43. *The Official Railway Guide,* August, 1940, p. 1052.
44. Reese, p. 19.
45. Reese, p. 15.
46. Reese,15.
47. Reese, p. 13.
48. Taylor, p. 36.
49. Reese, p. 15.
50. 1993 Montana State Rail Plan Update, Montana Department of Transportation, Rail and Transit Division, p. 2-17.
51. In 1987 Montana Rail Link took over the operations of the BN line through Livingston.
52. Reese, p. 15.
53. www.ceic.commerce.state.mt.us
54. Janet Greenstein Potter. *Great American Railroad Stations*, New York: John Wiley & Sons, 1996, pp. 504-505, and Reese, p. 10.
55. "*Unique Passenger Station on the Northern Pacific*", The Railroad Gazette, April 29, 1904.
56. Reese, p. 8.
57. Taylor, p. 34.
58. For a more thorough look at the life and works of Robert Reamer, see *Weaver of Dreams* by Ruth Quinn, published by Leslie & Ruth Quinn, Gardiner, Montana, 2004, and *The Inn: Centennial of a Beloved Landmark* by Ruth Quinn, Yellowstone Science, Vol. 12 #2, Spring 2004, pp. 5 -45.
59. *Boston Evening Transcript*, May 11, 1912.
60. Leavengood, pp. 495-499.

The Northeast Entrance-The Northern Pacific to Red Lodge, Montana

61. *Astonishing Yellowstone*, advertising brochure published by the Northern Pacific Railway for the 1938 season. Collection of the author.
62. Richard A. Bartlett, *Yellowstone, A Wilderness Besieged,* Tucson: The University of Arizona Press, 1985, p. 33.
63. Mary Shivers Culpin, *The History of the Construction of the Road System in Yellowstone National Park, 1872-1966, Historic Resource Study, Volume I,* National Park Service, Rocky Mountain Region, Division of Cultural Resources, No. 5, 1994, p. 311.
64. Shirley Zupan and Harry J. Owens. *Red Lodge - Saga of a Western Area,* (Red Lodge: Carbon County Historical Society), p. 20.
65. Zupan, p. 129.
66. Zupan, p. 19.
67. Cheney, p. 92.
68. Zupan, p. 129.
69. Zupan, p. 130.
70. Bonnie Christensen, *Red Lodge and the Mythic West.* Lawrence: University of Kansas Press, 2002, p. 24.
71. Zupan, p. 39. Billings Avenue was named for Frederick Billings, a former president of the Northern Pacific Railroad; Hauser Avenue was named for Samuel Hauser, one of the founders of the mines and former territorial governor; Villard Avenue was named for Henry Villard of the Northern Pacific Railroad;. Other street names also had associations with some of the businessmen and first residents in the area.
72. Zupan, pp. 39-40.
73. Zupan, p. 29.
74. Zupan, p. 31.
75. Zupan, p. 14.
76. Zupan, p. 41.
77. Zupan, p. 31.
78. Zupan, p. 32.
79. Zupan, p. 31.
80. Zupan, p. 35.
81. Christensen, p. 128.
82. Zupan, pp. 274-275.
83. Mary Shivers Culpin, *The History of the Construction of the Road System in Yellowstone National Park, 1872-1966, Historic Resource Study, Volume I,* National Park Service, Rocky Mountain Region, Division of Cultural Resources, No. 5, 1994, p. 320.
84. Zupan, p. 278,and Schwieterman, Joseph S., *When the Railroad Leaves Town - Western United States*, Kirksville:

Truman State University Press, 2004, p. 173. It was the most expensive highway built in the country at the time.
85. Zupan, p. 278.
86. Culpin, p. 321.
87. Culpin, p. 320.
88. *Annual Report of Yellowstone National Park* for the year 1939, p. 3.
89. *Annual Report of Yellowstone National Park* for the year 1937, p. 5.
90. Articles of incorporation for the Rocky Fork and Cooke City Railway Company on file in the offices of the Montana Secretary of State.
91. Louis Tuck Renz, *The History of the Northern Pacific Railroad*, Fairfield: Ye Galleon Press, pp. 157-158.
92. Christensen, p. 48.
93. Articles of incorporation for the Billings, Clark's Fork and Cooke City Railroad Company on file in the offices of the Montana Secretary of State.
94. Renz, p. 158.
95. Renz, p. 158.
96. Thomas T. Taber, *The Histories of the Independently Operated Railroads in Montana,* unpublished manuscript, 1960, pp. 11, 26.
97. *Travelers' Official Guide of the Railways and Steam Navigation Lines in the United States and Canada,* June, 1893, p. 479.
98. *The Official Guide of the Railways and Steam Navigation Line of the United States"*, January, 1910, p. 597.
99. Renz, p. 198.
100. Ira Swett, *Montana's Trolleys - III.* Vol. 27, No. 1, (South Gate: Interurbans Magazine), 1970, p. 102.
101. Ira Swett, p. 98.
102. Zupan, pp. 51-52.
103. Zupan, p. 48.
104. Zupan, p. 248.
105. *The Official Guide,* February, 1901, p. 529.
106. *The Official Guide of the Railways,* January, 1910, p. 597.
107. *The Official Guide of the Railways,* February, 1926, p. 1079. This guide was published monthly and listed the passenger train schedules for all of the railroads in the United States, Canada, Mexico, and Cuba.
108. Craig Reese, *The Gardiner Gateway to Yellowstone,* "The Mainstreeter" (The Northern Pacific Railway Historical Association), Vol. 15, No. 2, Spring, 1996, p. 19.
109. *The Official Guide of the Railways,* June, 1941, p. 1063.
110. Schwieterman, Joseph S., *When the Railroad Leaves Town - Western United States,* (Kirksville: Truman State University Press), 2004, p.174.
111. Schwieterman, Joseph S., *When the Railroad Leaves Town - Western United States,* (Kirksville: Truman State University Press), 2004, p. 174.
112. Schwieterman, p. 174.
113. Zupan, p. 51.
114. Schwieterman, P. 174
115. 1993 Montana State Rail Plan Update, Montana Department of Transportation, Rail and Transit Division, pp. 2-17.
116. *Historic Self-Guided Walking Tour* brochure published by the Carbon County Historical Society.
117. This information was obtained from an E-mail from the Peaks to Plains Museum in Red Lodge and in the Red Lodge Visitors Guide, 1999-2000, published by the *Carbon County News.*
118. Schwieterman, p. 174.

The Bozeman Entrance
119. *Annual Report for Yellowstone National Park* for the year 1927, p. 5.
120. *Annual Report for Yellowstone National Park* for the year 1928, p. 4.
121. *Annual Report for Yellowstone National Park* for the year 1929, p. 8.
122. *Annual Report of Yellowstone National Park* for the year 1930, p. 9.
123. *Annual Report of Yellowstone National Park* for the year 1931, p. 4.
124. *Annual Report of Yellowstone National Park* for the year 1932, p. 5.
125. *Annual Report of Yellowstone National Park* for the year 1933, p. 8 .
126. *Annual Report of Yellowstone National Park* for the year 1934, p. 7.
127. Correspondence from the files of the Union Pacific Museum in Council Bluffs, Iowa and on file at the Yellowstone Historic Center, West Yellowstone, Montana, dated 1927.

Chapter Seven
"The National Park Route"-Union Pacific Railroad to West Yellowstone, Montana and Victor, Idaho

1. The railroad's slogan was "The Overland Route" for many years, but in the 1920s the railroad used "The National Park Route" slogan to promote travel on its passenger trains. The Union Pacific went on to use the slogan "Route of the Streamliners" in the 1940s and 1950s (*Pacific RailNews*, June, 1996), p. 58. The railroad offered service to many of the nation's western national parks, including Grand Canyon National Park, Zion National Park, and Cedar Breaks National Monument in southern Utah, Rainier National Park, Yosemite National Park, and Rocky Mountain - Estes National Park.
2. *The Union Pacific Magazine,* June, 1930, p. 6. This publication was the railroad's employee magazine and often featured articles on Yellowstone National Park.
3. A mixed train carried both freight and passengers. The passengers either rode in the caboose or in a passenger car at the end of the train. A mixed train would switch freight cars along the route, so was slower than a passenger train.
4. *Colorado Rail Annual No. 15.* (Golden: Colorado Railroad Museum, 1981), p. 60.
5. The Fountain Hotel was at the Lower Geyser Basin, a short distance north of the Upper Geyser Basin, where Old Faithful and the Old Faithful Inn were located.
6. Bartlett, pp. 15-17
7. Bartlett, p. 154.
8. Betty and Brigham Madsen, *North to Montana,* (Salt Lake City: Utah State University Press), 1980 (1998 edition), p. 241.
9. F.E. Shearer, *The Pacific Tourist,* (New York: Adams & Bishop, 1884. 1970 edition published by Crown Publishers), pp. 157-159.
10. George W. Wingate, *Through the Yellowstone on Horseback* (Moscow: University of Idaho, 1999, reprint of 1886 edition), p. 15.
11. Merrill D. Beal, *Intermountain Railroads* (Caldwell: Caxton Printers, 1962), pp. 102-103.
12. Stanley Wood, *Over the Range to the Golden Gate,* Chicago: R.R. Donnelly & Sons, 1904 edition, pp. 307-308.
13. Correspondence on file at the Yellowstone Heritage and Research Center, Yellowstone National Park. Monida & Yellowstone Stage Company letter to Captain Brown, Assistant Superintendent, Yellowstone National Park, dated September 16, 1899.
14. The letter to the Secretary of the Interior, dated October 14, 1902, stated that the Union Pacific or Oregon Short Line was considering building a road in conjunction with the Monida Stage Company from Monida to Dwelles, and to use automobiles to transport passengers to the west entrance. Army Records, Letters Sent, Vol. XII, 242-244. In the files of the Yellowstone Heritage and Research Center.
15. Typical of these advertisements was one for the 1923 season. The advertisement boasted that 51-6/10% of rail travelers to the park arrived through West Yellowstone. Originals of the advertisement on file at the Union Pacific Museum in Council Bluffs, Iowa and copies are in the collection of the Yellowstone Heritage and Research Center.
16. The maps of the era showed "Canyon" spelled either "Canon" or "Canôn".
17. *Colorado Rail Annual,* p. 51. This map was taken from Strahorn's book *To the Rockies and Beyond*. Robert Strahorn was a promoter and publicist for the railroad in this time period.
18. Maury Klein. *Union Pacific - Birth of a Railroad, 1862-1893,* Garden City: Doubleday & Company, 1987, p. 24.
19. Klein, pp. 523-524.
20. The Utah & Northern Railroad was consolidated with several other railroads to form the Oregon Short Line & Utah Northern Railroad, which was incorporated on August 1, 1889. Receivers were appointed on October 13, 1893 and the properties of the OSL & UN were deeded to the Oregon Short Line Railroad Company on February 23, 1897. The Oregon Short Line was operated by the Union Pacific, but was a separate corporate entity until it was leased to the Union Pacific Railroad on December 30, 1935.
21. Amended articles of incorporation for the Oregon Short Line & Utah Northern, on file in the offices of the Idaho Secretary of State, Boise, Idaho.
22. Haines, Aubrey L. *The Yellowstone Story, Vol. II*, Niwot: University Press of Colorado, 1977 (1996 edition), p. 48.
23. Klein, p. 524. To give an idea of the value of this amount of money, in 1899 the Oregon Short Line advertised a rate of $105 for rail travel from Chicago to Monida, an 8-day stage trip to and through the park, and return, rail and transportation only. The same rate from Portland was $96, and $47.75 from Pocatello. Exit through Cinnabar was also offered.(*Where Gush the Geysers* advertising brochure for the 1899 season, published by the Oregon Short Line Railroad. From the files of the Yellowstone Heritage and Research Center, Yellowstone National Park.)

24. "People's Railroad Committee Material", in the Historical Department, The Church of Jesus Christ of Latter-Day Saints, Salt Lake City, Utah, and David L.. Crowder *Rexburg, Idaho, The First One Hundred Years, 1883-1983*, Caldwell: Caxton Printers, 1983, pp. 83-85.
25. *Corporate History of the Oregon Short Line Railroad Company as of June 30th, 1916*, prepared in accordance with Valuation Order No. 20 of the Interstate Commerce Commission, p. 53.
26. Donald B. Robertson, *Encyclopedia of Western Railroad History, Volume II - The Mountain States*, Dallas: Taylor Publishing Company, 1991, p. 230.
27. Patricia L. Scott. *The Hub of Eastern Idaho: A History of Rigby, Idaho, 1885-1976*, City of Rigby, 1976, p. 54.
28. Robertson, p. 230
29. *Annual Report to the Interstate Commerce Commission of the United States for the Year Ending June 30, 1908*. On file at the Nebraska Historical Society, Lincoln, Nebraska.
30. *Corporate History*, p. 53.
31. *Corporate History*, p. 53.
32. Corporate notes for the St. Anthony Railroad Company, collection of the author.
33. Robertson, p. 230.
34. *Teton Peak-Chronicle*, June 18., 1908.
35. Letter from F.H. Knickerbocker to D.S. Spencer dated January 30, 1926, in the files of the Yellowstone Heritage and Research Center.
36. Articles of incorporation for the St. Anthony Railroad Company, on file in the offices of the Idaho Secretary of State, Boise, Idaho.
37. Corporate notes for the Yellowstone Park Railroad Company, collection of the author.
38. The magazine often spelled the towns and settlements incorrectly, in part because they were new and not on any maps of the time. The town referenced was actually Marysville.
39. Brochure on file at the Yellowstone Historic Center.
40. *Corporate History*, p. 63.
41. Robertson, p. 244.
42. Correspondence on file at the Yellowstone Heritage and Research Center, File #7878, letter from W. H. Bancroft to Major John Pitcher, dated September 24, 1906.
43. Sam Eagle and Ed, *West Yellowstone's 70th Anniversary: 1908 - 1978*, West Yellowstone: Eagle Company, 1978, pp. 2-14.
44. A geological description of the Yellowstone Branch is contained in United States Geological Survey Bulletin 612, *Guidebook of the Western United States, Part B. The Overland with a Side Trip to Yellowstone Park*, by Willis T. Lee, Ralph Stone, Hoyt Gale and Others, Washington: GPO, 1915.
45. Eagle, p. 1-2.
46. Mary Shivers Culpin, *The History of the Construction of the Road System in Yellowstone National Park, 1872-1966, Historic Resource Study, Volume I*, National Park Service, Rocky Mountain Region, Division of Cultural Resources, No. 5, 1994, p. 363.
47. Letter from D.H. Prater to D.S. Spencer, dated January 9, 1916, in the files of the Yellowstone Heritage and Research Center.
48. Eagle, p. 3-7.
49. *The Post-Register* (Idaho Falls), March 13, 1988, and Aubrey L.Haines, *The Yellowstone Story, Vol. II*, Niwot: University Press of Colorado, 1977, 1996 edition, pp. 52-53.
50. The railroad right-of-way map shows that the Oregon Short Line Railroad received the deed for this land on May 27, 1921. Map in collection of the author.
51. *Environmental Assessment for the Grizzly Discovery and Conservation Center*, Montana Department of Fish, Wildlife and Parks.
52. *USGS Bulletin # 612*, p. 144, and *Annual Report, Union Pacific System, Year Ended June 30, 1916*.
53. *Pocatello Tribune*, June 9, 1908.
54. Notes from Sam Eagle to C.R. Davidson, dated April 19, 1984, in the files of the Yellowstone Historic Center. The Union Pacific did not use this name for the train at this time, and a letter from B.H. Prater to D.S. Spencer, dated January 9, 1929, in the files of the Yellowstone Heritage and Research Center.
55. *Pocatello Tribune* (Pocatello, Idaho), June 11, 1908.
56. Conversation with former Union Pacific employee Ken Marler (deceased), who was a ticket agent at West Yellowstone in the summer of 1960. It was common for the employees to bring their families with them to West Yellowstone for the summer, and the railroad provided housing for the families. Some of this housing, on the tail of the wye, had running water, but the toilet facilities were outside. At this time bears were common in the area, and Ken's son, Loran, told the author that when they had to use the facilities in the middle of the night they would put the dog outside to see if there were any bears in the area before they would go outside.
57. *Teton Peak - Chronicle* (St. Anthony, Idaho), May 11, 1922.

58. Correspondence on file at the Yellowstone Heritage and Research Center, Monida & Yellowstone Stage Company to Frank Pierce, Department of the Interior, April 20, 1908, #7996.
59. Correspondence on file at the Yellowstone Heritage and Research Center, Monida & Yellowstone Stage Company to Frank Pierce, Department of the Interior, April 20, 1908, #7996.
60. Eagle, p. 2-8.
61. Advertising brochure *Yellowstone National Park*, published by the Union Pacific System. The tour packages were sold by the Department of Tours, which was jointly sponsored by the C.& N. W. Ry. and the Union Pacific System. Brochure collection of the author.
62. *Teton Peak - Chronicle*, May 25, 1922.
63. *Teton Peak-Chronicle*, July 10, 1924.
64. Union Pacific travel brochure for the 1961 season, collection of Thornton Waite.
65. *Post-Register*, April 23, 1964.
66. Culpin, p. 363.
67. Culpin, p. 364.
68. Culpin, pp. 363-364.
69. Eagle, p. 2-2.
70. Eagle, p. 2-6.
71. Letter from D.H. Prater to D.S. Spencer, dated January 9, 1916, in the files of the Yellowstone Heritage and Research Center.
72. Eagle, p. 2-14
73. *Annual Report, Union Pacific System, Year Ended December 31, 1922*.
74. *Annual Report, Union Pacific System, Year Ended December 31, 1925*.
75. *The Union Pacific Magazine*, September, 1926, p. 15.
76. *The Union Pacific Magazine*, September, 1925. This was a magazine for Union Pacific employees, and contained notes and information on the operations of the entire railroad system.
77. *Annual Report, Union Pacific System, Year Ended December 31, 1927*, and *The Union Pacific Magazine*, August, 1927, p. 49.
78. ICC Valuation, for the Oregon Short Line Railroad Company, Section 4 - Montana, 572-577.
79. Eagle, p. 2-14.
80. Eagle, p. 2-15.
81. *Post-Register* (Idaho Falls), June 12, 1988.
82. National Register of Historic Places, *West Yellowstone MRA 83001069*.
83. www.census.gov
84. For further information on Gilbert Stanley Underwood, see *Gilbert Stanley Underwood, His Rustic, Art Deco, and Federal Architecture*, by Joyce Zaitlin, Pangloss Press, Malibu, 1989.
85. Zaitlin, pp.169 - 170.

South Entrance, Victor, Idaho
86. National Register of Historic Places Nomination Form for the Victor Railroad Depot, Victor, Teton County, Idaho, #19950427/95000508.
87. *Annual Report for Yellowstone National Park* for the year 1931, p. 4.
88. *Annual Report for Yellowstone National Park* for the year 1932, p. 5.
89. *Annual Report for Yellowstone National Park* for the year 1931, p. 8.
90. *Annual Report for Yellowstone National Park* for the year 1931, p. 7.
91. *Union Pacific Bulletin*, October, 1948. This was a newsletter published by the Passenger Traffic Department of the Union Pacific Railroad for travel bureaus and ticket agents.
92. *The Official Guide of the Railways*, August, 1963, p. 630.
93. Annual Report of Yellowstone National Park, dated August 15, 1891, p. 11. However, the Fair did not open until 1893.
94. This information is based on correspondence in the files of the Union Pacific Museum, Council Bluffs, Iowa, and available at the Yellowstone Historic Center in West Yellowstone.
95. *The Mixed Train*, published by Camerail, Omaha, Nebraska. Issue 2000-3, p. 3.

Chapter Eight
"The National Park Road"-Chicago, Burlington & Quincy Railroad to Cody, Wyoming
1. *Magic Yellowstone* advertising brochure, published by the Northern Pacific for the 1928 season.
2. Mae Urbanek, *Wyoming Place Names*, Missoula: Mountain Press Publishing Company, 1988, p. 181.
3. National Register of Historic Places Nomination Form for the "Irma Hotel", Cody, Park County, Wyoming, #19730403/73001936

4. Urbanek, 41.
5. Paul Fees, *Buffalo Bill's Town in the Rockies: A Pictorial History of Cody, Wyoming*. Virginia Beach: The Donning Company, 1996, pp. 13-15.
6. Fees, p. 15.
7. Fees, p. 13.
8. Fees, p. 46.
9. Fees, pp. 13, 52.
10. *Wyoming - A Guide to its History, Highways, and People*, Writers' Program of the Work Projects Administration, New York: Oxford University Press, 1941, p. 336.
11. Fees, p. 13.
12. "Irma Hotel"
13. Fees, p. 51.
14. Fees, p. 73.
15. An excellent article on the newspaper and Cody's support for the newspaper can be found in *Preacher's Son on the Loose in Buffalo Bill Country*, by Charles Towne in "Montana - the magazine of Western History", Volume XVIII, No. 4, Autumn 1968, pp. 40-55.
16. Richard A. Bartlett, *Yellowstone, A Wilderness Besieged*. Tucson: The University of Arizona Press, 1985, p. 81.
17. Fees, p. 15.
18. Urbanek, p. 151.
19. Website "Yellowstone Genealogy Forum: Burlington Railroad - Pryor Gap", www.rootsweb.com
20. A description of the construction of this line can be found in the article "Reminiscences of an Early-Day Railroad Civil Engineer in Northwestern Wyoming", *Annals of Wyoming*, Vol. 13, #1, January, 1941, pp. 48-57.
21. T.A. Larson, *History of Wyoming*, Lincoln: University of Nebraska Press, 1965 (Second edition, revised 1978), p. 339. Other sources indicate construction started in 1899.
22. From the files of the Park County Archives, Cody, Wyoming.
23. *Stampede Edition*, Cody Enterprise, 1977 edition.
24. Website "Yellowstone Genealogy Forum: Burlington Railroad - Pryor Gap", www.rootsweb.com
25. *Stampede Edition*, Cody Enterprise, 1977 edition.
26. From the files of the Park County Archives, Cody, Wyoming.
27. Fees, pp. 58, 59.
28. Website "Yellowstone Genealogy Forum: Burlington Railroad - Pryor Gap", www.rootsweb.com. The CB&Q had acquired control of the Colorado & Southern in 1908.
29. Fees, p. 110.
30. Charles W. Towne, *Preacher's Son on the Loose in Buffalo Bill Country*, Montana - the magazine of Western History, Volume XVIII, No. 4, Autumn 1968, pp. 43-44.
31. *The Official Guide of the Railways*, June, 1921, pp. 823-824. This guide was published monthly and listed the passenger train schedules for all of the railroads in the United States, Canada, Mexico, and Cuba.
32. *The Official Guide*, p. 836.
33. *The Official Guide*, September, 1930, p. 1109.
34. Austin, p. 4.
35. *Stampede Edition*, Cody Enterprise, 1977 edition.
36. Fees, p. 130.
37. *Annual Report of Yellowstone National Park* for the year 1937, p. 5.
38. The railroad would add a second, or "helper" locomotive when there were too many cars for one locomotive to handle.
39. Lucius Beebe, and Charles Clegg. *The Trains We Rode, Vol. 1,* Berkeley: Howell-North, 1965, pp. 154-155.
40. Yellowstone advertising brochure published by the Northern Pacific for the 1928 season. Collection of Thornton Waite, and *Night Trains* by Peter Maiken, p. 198.
41. *The Official Railway Guide,*, January, 1938, p. 1983. This guide was published monthly and listed the passenger train schedules for all of the railroads in the United States, Canada, Mexico, and Cuba.
42. Craig Reese, *The Gardiner Gateway to Yellowstone*, "The Mainstreeter" (The Northern Pacific Railway Historical Association), Vol. 15, No. 2, Spring, 1996, p. 19.
43. Reese, p. 19.
44. *The Official Railway Guide*, June, 1954, p. 1035.
45. Lee Whiteley. *The Yellowstone Highway*, Boulder: Lee Whiteley, 2001, p. 142.
46. Mary Shivers Culpin. *The History of the Construction of the Road System in Yellowstone National Park, 1872-1966, Historic Resource Study, Volume I,* National Park Service, Rocky Mountain Region, Division of Cultural Resources, No. 5, 1994, p. 90.

47. For more information on the road see *The Yellowstone Highway* by Lee Whiteley, Boulder: Lee Whiteley, 2001.
48. Fees, p. 66.
49. Private autos were not allowed to enter the park until August 1, 1915, and the concessionaires began utilizing trucks and buses immediately after this date. Horses were no longer used starting with the 1917 season due to the dangers of having automobiles and horses on the roads at the same time.
50. Bruce Austin, Robert Goss, and Gerard Pesman. *Yellowstone Park Transportation Company*, Motor Coach Today, April-June 2000, p. 4.
51. Austin, p. 4.
52. Fees, p. 90.
53. Rocky Mountain National Park, Yellowstone National Park, and Glacier National Park.
54. Haines, Aubrey L. *The Yellowstone Story, Vol. II*, Niwot: University Press of Colorado, 1977 (1996 edition), p. 372.
55. Bartlett, p. 92.
56. *Stampede Edition,* Cody Enterprise, 1977 edition.
57. "Irma Hotel".
58. www.census.gov

Chapter Nine
"Where Rails End and Trails Begin–Chicago & North Western Railway to Lander, Wyoming

1. "Teton Mountain Route to Yellowstone National Park" advertising brochure for the Chicago & North Western Railway for the 1925 season, Gadamus Collection, Yellowstone Historic Center, West Yellowstone, Montana.
2. Mae Urbanek, *Wyoming Place Names*, Missoula: Mountain Press Publishing Company, 1988, pp.117-118.
3. Urbanek, p. 76.
4. Candy Moulton, *Roadside History of Wyoming,* Missoula: Mountain Press Publishing Company, 1995, p. 195.
5. Urbanek, p. 118.
6. Gary L. Ecelbarger, *Frederick W. Lander - The Great Natural American Soldier,* Baton Rouge: Louisiana State University Press, 2000, pp. 39-40. His work is also discussed in the National Register of Historic Places Nomination Form "Lander Downtown Historic District", #19870505/87000700.
7. Moulton, pp. 50-51.
8. Moulton, p. 197.
9. Urbanek, p. 118.
10. National Register of Historic Places Nomination Form "Lander Downtown Historic District", #19870505/87000700.
11. "Lander Downtown Historic District".
12. "Lander Downtown Historic District".
13. Moulton, p. 196.
14. *Wyoming - A Guide to its History, Highways, and People* (Writers' Program of the Work Projects Administration) New York: Oxford University Press, 19451, pp. 313-314. These pages give a brief summary of the history of Lander and what it looked like in the Depression years.
15. *County and City Data Book,* U.S. Department of Commerce, U.S. Census Bureau, pp. 65, 981.
16. Brigham D. Madsen, *Corinne - The Gentile Capital of Utah* (Salt Lake City: Utah State Historical Society), 1980, pp. 185-187, and Enoch Bryan, *Orient Meets Occident,* Pullman: The Student Book Corporation, 1936, pp. 133-134.
17. Enoch Bryan, *Orient Meets Occident*, Pullman: The Student Book Corporation, 1936, pp. 133-134.
18. Madsen, pp. 185-186. The company also purchased 200,000 feet of lumber and surveyed a route along the Snake River before running out of money.
19. *The Railway Age,* September 27, 1907.
20. *The Railway Age,* January 3, 1908.
21. Donald B. Robertson, *Encyclopedia of Western Railroad History, Volume II -The Mountain States*. Dallas: Taylor Publishing Company, 1991, p. 114.
22. Robertson, p. 406.
23. Robertson, p. 396.
24. Robertson, p. 405. The articles of incorporation for The Wyoming & North Western Railway Company are on file with the office of the Secretary of State, State of Wyoming.
25. The articles of incorporation for The Wyoming and Northwestern Railway Company are on file with the office of the Secretary of State, State of Wyoming.
26. Robertson, p. 405.
27. This date is recorded on the articles of incorporation for the Wyoming and Northwestern Railway Company, on file with the office of the Secretary of State, State of Wyoming.

28. This date was obtained from the website www.thecbandqinwyoming.com/Timeline.
29. *The September 17, 1909 issue of Railway Age* reported that surveys had been made by the Chicago & North Western west from Lander, paralleling the branch of the Oregon Short Line which ran to Yellowstone Park. The October 1, 1909, issue stated that the report was positively denied by an office of the company.
30. This was reported in the May 16, 1915 issue the *Idaho Falls Register* (Idaho Falls, Idaho). The newspapers at this time were always optimistically reporting on proposals for rail lines through their areas, even if the rumors were improbable.
31. The train schedule was taken from the January 1910 issue of *The Official Guide of the Railways.* This guide was published monthly and listed the passenger train schedules for all of the railroads in the United States, Canada, Mexico and Cuba. In addition to showing the passenger train schedule to Lander the timetable listed the fares and departure times for the stage connections at Lander.
32. *The Lander-Yellowstone Transportation Company*, Wind River Mountaineer, April-June 1993, published by the Museum of the American West, p. 8. This issue gives a thorough history of the Lander-Yellowstone Transportation Company.
33. "Lander Downtown Historic District".
34. Urbanek, p. 207.
35. *The Lander-Yellowstone Transportation Company*, p. 8.
36. Moulton, p. 194.
37. *The Lander-Yellowstone Transportation Company*, pp. 8-9.
38. *The Lander-Yellowstone Transportation Company*, p. 9.
39. *The Lander-Yellowstone Transportation Company*, p. 9, and John Daughtery, *A Place Called Jackson Hole.* Moose: Grand Teton National Park, 1999, p. 181.
40. *The Lander-Yellowstone Transportation Company*, p. 7.
41. *The Lander-Yellowstone Transportation Company*, pp. 11-12.
42. *The Lander-Yellowstone Transportation Company*, p. 13.
43. *The Lander-Yellowstone Transportation Company*, p. 9.
44. Mary Shivers Culpin, *The History of the Construction of the Road System in Yellowstone National Park, 1872-1966, Historic Resources Study, Volume 1.* National Park Service, Rocky Mountain Region, Division of Cultural Resources, No. 5, 1994. pp. 355-356.
45. Culpin, pp. 355-356.
46. Correspondence in the files of the Yellowstone Historic Center, West Yellowstone, Montana, copied from the files of the Union Pacific Railroad. The differential fare was discussed in letters to W.S. Basinger of the Union Pacific Railroad from the C&NW Passenger Traffic Manager, dated June 22, 1922; July 20, 1922; and July 25, 1922.
47. The timetable was listed in the *Travelers Railway Guide, Western Edition,* for December 1916, p. 309.
48. *The Official Guide of the Railways,* June 1921. Apparently the schedule did not vary much between summer and winter since this issue of the Guide listed the schedule for August, 1920.
49. *The Lander-Yellowstone Transportation Company*, p. 13.
50. *The Lander-Yellowstone Transportation Company*, pp. 13-14. The Union Pacific and the Chicago & North Western continued to jointly promote travel to West Yellowstone, but these advertisements did not mention the Lander route. Correspondence from the Union Pacific files, available at the Yellowstone Historic Center in West Yellowstone, indicated that the Union Pacific was concerned about losing traffic if the route through Lander was included in the advertisements.
51. *The Lander-Yellowstone Transportation Company*, p. 14.
52. *The Lander-Yellowstone Transportation Company*, p. 24.
53. *The Lander-Yellowstone Transportation Company*, p. 24.
54. *The Lander-Yellowstone Transportation Company*, p. 15, and the National Register of Historic Places Nomination Form for "Brooks Lake Lodge", Fremont County, Wyoming, #19820929/82004333.
55. *The Lander-Yellowstone Transportation Company*, p. 16.
56. *The Lander-Yellowstone Transportation Company*, pp. 16,24.
57. *The Lander-Yellowstone Transportation Company*, p. 18.
58. *The Lander-Yellowstone Transportation Company*, p. 22.
59. *The Lander-Yellowstone Transportation Company*, pp.22, 24.
60. Daugherty, p. 263.
61. *Annual Report for Yellowstone National Park for the year 1922,* p. 6.
62. *The Lander-Yellowstone Transportation Company*, p. 214.
63. *The Lander-Yellowstone Transportation Company*, p. 25.
64. *The Lander-Yellowstone Transportation Company*, p. 25.
65. Correspondence in the files of the Yellowstone Historic Center, West Yellowstone, Montana, obtained from

the Union Pacific Museum in Council Bluffs, Iowa, dated 1921 and 1922. Letters were written by the businessmen in Pinedale and the State of Wyoming Board of Immigration to the National Park Service and the Union Pacific to promote development of this route. There was also a letter from the Lions Club in Rock Springs in1929 promoting the route through their town.

66. *The Lander-Yellowstone Transportation Company*, p. 25.
67. *The Lander-Yellowstone Transportation Company*, p. 26.
68. *The Lander-Yellowstone Transportation Company*, pp. 26-27.
69. Copy of the agreement between the Lander-Yellowstone Transportation Company and J.T. Gratiot, dated June 21, 1930. From the archives of the Chicago & North Western Historical Society.
70. This letter is in the Gadamus Collection at the Yellowstone Historic Center in West Yellowstone, Montana.
71. *The Lander-Yellowstone Transportation Company*, p. 27.
72. "*Teton Mountain Route to Yellowstone Park*", published by the Chicago & North Western Line for the 1925 season. Collection of the Chicago & North Western Historical Society.
73. "*Manual for Railroad Visitors -Time-Tables Yellowstone Park Tours: (June 20 -September 19, 1929)*", on file at the Yellowstone Heritage and Research Center, Yellowstone National Park.
74. *Annual Report for Yellowstone National Park for the year 1923*, p. 22.
75. *Annual Report for Yellowstone National Park for the year 1924*, pp. 3,5.
76. *Annual Report for Yellowstone National Park for the year 1925*, p. 5.
77. *Annual Report for Yellowstone National Park for the year 1926*, p. 6.
78. *Annual Report for Yellowstone National Park for the year 1927*, p. 5.
79. *Annual Report for Yellowstone National Park for the year 1928*, p. 4.
80. *Annual Report for Yellowstone National Park for the year 1929*, p. 10.
81. *Annual Report for Yellowstone National Park for the year 1930*, p.10. This year the Park Service did not break out the number of visitors arriving through the South Entrance by the different railroads.
82. *Annual Report for Yellowstone National Park for the year 1931*, p. 1.
83. *Annual Report for Yellowstone National Park for the year 1932*, p. 5.
84. *Annual Report for Yellowstone National Park for the year 1933*, p. 9.
85. *Annual Report for Yellowstone National Park for the year 1934*, p. 7.
86. Chicago & North Western timetable dated August 1, 1934, Table 83. From the files of the Chicago & North Western Historical Society.
87. *The Lander-Yellowstone Transportation Company*, p. 28.
88. "Yellowstone National Park", National Park Service brochure for the 1941 season. Collection of the author.
89. Chicago & North Western brochure for the 1927 season, from the files of the Chicago and North Western Historical Society.
90. Brochure from the files of the Chicago & North Western Historical Society, A-820-27.
91. "Wyoming Wild West Ranches", (1928), from the files of the Chicago and North Western Historical Society.
92. *The Lander-Yellowstone Transportation Company*, p. 13.
93. Letter dated June 26, 1922, from W.S. Basinger to H.M. Adams, from the files at the Yellowstone Historic Center, West Yellowstone, Montana, and copied from the files of the Union Pacific Museum in Council Bluffs, Iowa.
94. *The Lander-Yellowstone Transportation Company*, p. 15, and "Brooks Lake Lodge".
95. "Brooks Lake Lodge".
96. "Brooks Lake Lodge".
97. Daugherty, p. 303.
98. Advertisement from the *Casper Tribune* dated February 18, 1951, from the files of the Chicago & North Western Historical Society.
99. *The Official Guide of the Railways*, January 1938, pp. 765 and 778.
100. *The Official Guide of the Railways*, June 1941, p. 782, timetable dated June 10, 1939.
101. This date was obtained from the website www.thecbandqinwyoming.com timeline.
102. *The Official Guide of the Railways*, May 1945, p. 746.
103. *Chronological History of Abandoned, Sold and Leased Lines*, www.up.com/uprr/facvts-fig/abandon/
104. *Chronological History of Abandoned, Sold and Leased Lines*, www.up.com/uprr/facvts-fig/abandon/
105. Don Strack and Jim Ehernberger, *Cabooses of the Union Pacific Railroad*, Cheyenne: Union Pacific Historical Society, 2002, p. 235.
106. E-mail from Eugene Lewis dated November 26, 2003, as part of the rlhsgroup website.
107. William Kratville, *The Union Pacific Streamliners*, Omaha: Kratville Publications, 1074, (1980 edition), p. 327.

Chapter Ten
The Historic Scenic Route-The Milwaukee Road to Gallatin Gateway

1. "New Gallatin Gateway into Yellowstone Park. The Historic-Scenic Route", advertising brochure distributed by the Chicago, Milwaukee and St. Paul Railway for the 1926 season. Gadamus Collection, Yellowstone Heritage Center, West Yellowstone, Montana.
2. At the turn of the century the Chicago, Milwaukee & St. Paul Railway ran from Chicago to Minneapolis and Omaha, and had numerous branch lines in the Midwest. Since it was dependent on the other transcontinental railroads to reach the West Coast, the company decided to build an extension to the Pacific Coast in 1905. When it was completed in 1909 the construction had cost more than anticipated. Combined with the loss of business due to the opening of the Panama Canal in 1914, the railroad entered receivership in 1925. The company was reorganized as the Chicago, Milwaukee, St. Paul & Pacific Railroad in 1928. The company again entered bankruptcy in 1935, and reorganized in 1945. The company again went into bankruptcy in 1977 and in 1982 abandoned all lines west of Ortonville, Minnesota. Some of these lines were taken over by other railroads, but most of the track, including the line to Gallatin Gateway, was pulled up. (Drury, George H., *The Historical Guide to North American Railroads*. Milwaukee: Kalmbach Publishing, 1985, pp. 83-84).
3. Ira Swett, *Montana's Trolleys - III*, (Vol. 27, No. 1, South Gate: Interurban Magazine, 1970), p. XXX; Thomas T. Taber, *The Histories of the Independently Operated Railroads in Montana*, (unpublished manuscript, 1960, Montana Historical Society); GV RY, p. 1, and Milton Clark, *The Milwaukee's Gallatin Valley Line*, (The Milwaukee Railroader, Second Quarter 1994), p. 1.
4. Milton Clark, *The Milwaukee's Gallatin Valley Line* (The Milwaukee Railroader, Second Quarter 1994), p. 5.
5. *Taber*, GV RY, p. 1.
6. The Gallatin River, which enters the Missouri River at Three Forks, was named by Lewis and Clark in 1805 for Albert Gallatin, Secretary of the Treasury. Gallatin County, which includes the towns of Bozeman, West Yellowstone and Gallatin Gateway (originally known as Salesville), was one of the original nine counties in the Territory of Montana and was named for the river. Roberta C. Cheney, *Names on the Face of Montana*, (Missoula: Mountain Press Publishing Company, 1983, (1992 edition), p. 110.
7. Louis Tuck Renz. *The History of the Northern Pacific Railroad*, Fairfield: Ye Galleon Press, 1980, p. 112.
8. Taber, GV RY, p. 1.
9. Swett, pp. 27, 31.
10. Clark, p. 6.
11. Swett, pp. 27, 31.
12. Swett, pp. 27, 31, and Taber, *GV RY, p. 2.*
13. Clark, p. 6.
14. Clark, p. 6.
15. Swett, pp. 27, 31, and Taber, *GV RY, p. 3.*
16. August Derleth, *The Milwaukee Road - Its First Hundred Years* (Iowa City: University of Iowa Press, 1948, 2002 edition), p. 187.
17. Derleth, p. 187.
18. Derleth, p. 187.
19. Swett, p. 36.
20. Derleth, 36.
21. Clark, p. 9.
22. Clark, p. 9.
23. Swett, p. 39.
24. Swett, p. 39.
25. Swett, p. 36.
26. Taber, GV RY, p. 2.
27. Swett, p. 39.
28. Clark, p. 9.
29. "Report on Survey for Wagon Road in Yellowstone National Park", Letter from the Secretary of War, House of Representatives, 60th Congress, 1st Session, Document No. 502, available at the Yellowstone Heritage and Research Center, Yellowstone National Park.
30. Mary Shivers Culpin, *The History of the Construction of the Road System in Yellowstone National Park, 1872-1966, Historic Resource Study, Volume I*, (National Park Service, Rocky Mountain Region, Division of Cultural Resources, No. 5, 1994), p. 375.
31. Culpin, p. 377.
32. Culpin, pp. 382-384.
33. Christine Barnes, *Great Lodges of the National Parks* (Bend: W.W. West, 2002), p. 56. Tourist traffic to the Paradise Inn in Mount Rainier National Park increased following World War I, breaking all records in the 1924 season. The

Rainier National Park Company had 14 buses to transport tourists between the Ashford depot and the inn.
34. Michael P. Malone, *The Gallatin Canyon and the Tides of History* (Montana History, Montana Historical Society, Helena, Montana, July, 1973), p. 11.
35. Stan Cohen, *Montana's Grandest - Historic Hotels and Resorts of the Treasure State* (Missoula: Pictorial Histories Publishing Company, 2004), p. 160.
36. Janet Cronin and Dorothy Vick, *Montana's Gallatin Canyon,* (Missoula: Mountain Press Publishing Company, 1992), p.195.
37. Linda Flint McClelland, *Building the National Parks* (Baltimore: John Hopkins Press, 1998), p. 125. The Mount Rainier entrance was built using western red cedar logs and this design was used at for the park's other entrances into the 1930s. It was an actual gateway, with a pair of log gates which could be used to close the road.
38. Culpin, p. 383.
39. *Annual Report of Yellowstone National Park for the year 1926*, p. 5.
40. Cohen, p. 31, and Clark, p. 11.
41. National Register of Historic Places Nomination Form for the "Gallatin Gateway Inn", Gallatin County, Montana, #19800124/80002417. Reports of the cost for the inn have varied from $260,000 to over $300,000. The latter number is noted in an advertising brochures titled "New Gallatin Gateway into Yellowstone Park", published by the Milwaukee Road for the 1927 season. Available in the files of the Gadamus Collection, Yellowstone Historic Center, West Yellowstone, Montana.
42. Clark, p. 10.
43. National Register of Historic Places Nomination Form for the "Gallatin Gateway Inn", Gallatin County, Montana, #19800124/80002417.
44. Undated newspaper clipping titled "Gallatin Gateway Inn, Magnificent Hotel of the Milwaukee Road, Commanding New Scenic Entrance to Yellowstone, courtesy of Marion Schenck. It was possibly the June 12, 1927 issue of the *Anaconda Standard*.
45. Cohen, p. 33.
46. Undated newspaper clipping titled "Gallatin Gateway Inn, Magnificent Hotel of the Milwaukee Road, Commanding New Scenic Entrance to Yellowstone, courtesy of Marion Schenck. It was possibly the June 12, 1927 issue of the *Anaconda Standard*.
47. Undated newspaper clipping titled "Gallatin Gateway Inn, Magnificent Hotel of the Milwaukee Road, Commanding New Scenic Entrance to Yellowstone, courtesy of Marion Schenck. It was possibly the June 12, 1927 issue of the *Anaconda Standard*.
48. "Gateway Inn Opens Today", *Bozeman Daily Chronicle,* June 17, 1928, courtesy of Marion Schenck.
49. Present-day Montana State University.
50. *Undated newspaper clipping titled "Gallatin Gateway Inn, Magnificent Hotel of the Milwaukee Road, Commanding New Scenic Entrance to Yellowstone, courtesy of Marion Schenck. It is possibly the June 12, 1927 issue of the Anaconda Standard.*
51. Stan Johnson, *The Milwaukee Road Olympian: A Ride to Remember* (Coeur d'Alene: Museum of North Idaho, 2001), p. 184.
52. William Hoy, *Railroad Stations in the Gallatin Area, Montana* (Bozeman: Gallatin County Historical Society/School of Architecture, Montana State University, 1998), 94.
53. Clark, p. 7.
54. Cheney, p. 238.
55. "Gallatin Gateway Inn", and the *Bozeman Daily Chronicle,* June 17, 1977.
56. Malone, p. 11.
57. *Hoy, p. 82.*
58. *Hoy, p. 82.*
59. This statement can be found on many of the brochures distributed by The Milwaukee Road to promote travel on their rail line. For many years the timetables had a heading ""The Electrified Route to Yellowstone Park".
60. Bus drivers in the park have always been known as "gear-jammers", and not all of the drivers may have shifted the buses as smoothly as advertised. The quote is from an advertising brochure from the collection of Marion Schenck.
61. *Annual Report of Yellowstone National Park for the year 1926*, p. 6.
62. The Milwaukee Road reported it had 5,200 passengers use its line in the 1927 season in a letter sent to Secretary Work, Secretary of the Interior. This number differs from the numbers reported by the National Park Service in its annual report. (Richard A. Bartlett, *Yellowstone, A Wilderness Besieged,* Tucson: The University of Arizona Press, 1985. p. 93).
63. *Annual Report of Yellowstone National Park for the year 1927*, p. 5.
64. *Annual Report of Yellowstone National Park for the year 1928*, p. 4.
65. Correspondence discussing the arrangements is in the files of the Yellowstone Historic Center at West Yellowstone. The copies were obtained from the Union Pacific Museum files in Council Bluffs, Iowa.

66. *Annual Report of Yellowstone National Park for the year 1929*, p. 1.
67. *Annual Report of Yellowstone National Park for the year 1929*, p. 1, and correspondence from Marion Schenck, daughter of Yellowstone National Park Superintendent Horace Albright.
68. *Annual Report of Yellowstone National Park for the year 1930*, p. 8.
69. *Annual Report of Yellowstone National Park for the year 1931*, pp. 20-21.
70. This train schedule was taken from the September 1930 issue of *The Official Guide of the Railways,* p. 1077. This guide was published monthly and listed the passenger train schedules for all of the railroads in the United States, Canada, Mexico, and Cuba.
71. *Annual Report of Yellowstone National Park* for the year 1931, p. 20.
72. Correspondence discussing the arrangements is in the files of the Yellowstone Historic Center at West Yellowstone. The copies were obtained from the files at the Union Pacific Museum in Council Bluffs, Iowa.
73. *The Milwaukee's Gallatin Valley Line*, p. 11.
74. *Annual Report of Yellowstone National Park for the year 1932*, p. 5.
75. *Annual Report of Yellowstone National Park for the year 1932*, p. 8.
76. *Annual Report of Yellowstone National Park for the year 1934*, p. 7.
77. Advertising brochure published by The Milwaukee Road for the 1938 season, from the Gadamus collection at the Yellowstone Historic Center.
78. *National Geographic*, March, 1941.
79. *The Milwaukee's Gallatin Valley Line*, p. 11.
80. Undated newspaper clipping from the *Bozeman Daily Chronicle,* discussing renovation of the inn by Hillard, courtesy of Marian Schenck.
81. *The Milwaukee's Gallatin Valley Line*, p. 11.
82. *The Milwaukee's Gallatin Valley Line*, p. 11.
83. This brochure is in the Gadamus Collection, from the files at the Yellowstone Historic Center.
84. *National Geographic*, March, 1957.
85. Clark, p. 11.
86. Undated newspaper clipping from the *Bozeman Daily Chronicle*, from the collection of Marion Schenck.
87. *Bozeman Daily Chronicle*, "History Lives on at Gateway Inn, August 10, 1986, courtesy of Marion Schenck.
88. Steve McCarter, *Guide to The Milwaukee Road in Montana* (Helena: Montana Historical Society, 1992), p. 84.
89. Clark, p. 11, and www.historic-hotels.com website.
90. "Gallatin Gateway Inn"
91. National Register of Historic Places Nomination Form for the Sacajawea Hotel, Three Forks, Gallatin County, Montana, #19800124/80002418. The Sacajawea Hotel was also closely connected with The Milwaukee Road.
92. Clark, p. 11.
93. Clark, pp. 11, 14.

Chapter Eleven
Proposed Railroads to Yellowstone National Park

1. Ira Swett, *Montana's Trolleys - III.* Vol. 27, No. 1, South Gate: Interurbans Magazine, 1970, p. 95.
2. Articles of Incorporation for The Billings & Cooke City Railway Company, on file in the offices of the Montana Secretary of State.
3. Swett, p. 95.
4. Fort Ellis was located near present-day Bozeman.
5. This proposed line is shown on a map on display at the Golden Spike National Historic Site at Promontory, Utah. The map was dated September, 1882, and showed lines which had been constructed and which were proposed.
6. Swett, p. 98.
7. Swett, p. 101.
8. *Record Journal (Douglas County, Colorado)*, December 2, 1910.
9. *The Railway Age.* July 27, 1906, and articles of incorporation on file in the office of the Idaho Secretary of State.
10. Louis Cramton, *Early History of Yellowstone National Park*, USGPO, 1932, p. 67.
11. Articles of incorporation for the Idaho & Wyoming, on file in the offices of the Idaho Secretary of State, and notes from the collection of the author.
12. Robert M. Orme, *Railroads and the Rockies*, Denver: Sage Books, 1963, p. 286.
13. *An Illustrated History of North Idaho,* Chicago: Western Historical Publishing Company, 1903, pp. 76-77.

14. Stephen L. Carr, and Robert W. Edwards. *Utah Ghost Rails,* Salt Lake City: Western Epics, 1989, p. 26. This was also reported in the June 23, 1916 issue of *The Pocatello Tribune.*
15. Articles of incorporation on file in the offices of the Idaho Secretary of State.
16. Although the commonly accepted spelling today is Gros Ventre, the articles used the Grosventre spelling.
17. This is the spelling used in the articles of incorporation.
18. Articles of incorporation on file in the offices of the Idaho Secretary of State.
19. Articles of incorporation for the Three Forks, Helena and Madison Valley Railroad Company, on file with the Montana Secretary of State.
20. Tilliston Papers, Stanford University Special Collections. The information was obtained from the 1911-12 and 1913-14 annual reports of the Montana Railroad Commissioners, and the April 13, 1912, August 21, 1915 and October 2, 1915 issues of the *Electric Railway Journal.*
21. *Idaho Register,* Idaho Falls, Idaho, December 8, 1914.
22. Taber, Thomas T., *The Histories of the Independently Operated Railroads in Montana*, unpublished manuscript, 1960, White Sulphur Springs and Yellowstone Park Railroad; and Baker, Don, *The Montana Railroad*, privately published, 1990, pp. 81-94.
23. Articles of incorporation on file in the office of the Montana Secretary of State.
24. Taber, Thomas T. *The Histories of the Independently Operated Railroads in Montana,* unpublished manuscript, 1960, MW&S.
25. Brisbin was on the Northern Pacific line between Livingston and Gardiner. Ferris Hot Springs is known today as Bozeman Hot Springs. Dodge Creek is now known as Taylor Fork.
26. Articles of incorporation on file in the office of the Montana Secretary of State.
27. Taber, Thomas T. *The Histories of the Independently Operated Railroads in Montana,* unpublished manuscript, 1960, Yellowstone Park Railway.
28. Kenneth L. Diem and Lenore L. "*A Community of Scalawags, Renegades, Discharged Soldiers and Predestined Stinkers*", (Moose: Grand Teton Natural History Association, 1998, p. 10).
29. *Winona Daily Republican*, May 8, 1889.
30. Diem, pp. 13-14.

Chapter Twelve
Railroads in Yellowstone National Park

1. Hugh D. Galusha, "*Railroads, Politics, and the Early History of Yellowstone National Park*", p. 10, unpublished manuscript in the files of the Yellowstone Heritage and Research Center.
2. Kenneth L. Diem,. and Lenore L. "*A Community of Scalawags, Renegades, Discharged Soldiers and Predestined Stinkers*", Moose: Grand Teton Natural History Association, 1998, p. 180, and *U.S. Geological Survey of the Territories, 6th Annual Report* This report was authored by R. Hering and printed by the G.P.O. in Washington D.C. in 1873.
3. Merrill D. Beal, *Intermountain Railroads*, Caldwell: Caxton Printers, 1962, pp. 82-83, and *Colorado Rail Annual No. 15,* Golden: Colorado Railroad Museum, 1981, p. 45.
4. Aubrey L. Haines, *The Yellowstone Story, Vol. I,* Niwot: University Press of Colorado, 1997 (1996 edition), p. 255.
5. *Colorado Rail Annual No. 15*, p. 51.
6. "Annual Report of the Superintendent", Yellowstone National Park, dated December 1, 1881, p. 68. Available at Yellowstone Heritage and Research Center, Yellowstone National Park.
7. Philip Sinclair Nicholson, editor. *Steel Rails and Territorial Trails,* Boise: Limberlost Press, 1994, p. 85.
8. Helen Fitzgerald Sanders, *A History of Montana*, Chicago: The Lewis Publishing Company, 1913, p. 467.
9. *The WPA Guide to 1930s Montana,* Compiled and written by the Work Projects Administration for the State of Montana, Tucson: University of Arizona Press, 1994, p. 346, and Roberta C. Cheney, *Names on the Face of Montana,* p. 61, (Missoula: Mountain Press Publishing Company, 1983 (1992 edition)).
10. Internet site www.cookecitychamber.com and Cheney, p. 61,
11. Sanders, pp. 467-468.
12. Richard A.Bartlett, *Yellowstone, A Wilderness Besieged,* Tucson: The University of Arizona Press, 1985, 310.
13. Diem, p. 10.
14. Bartlett, p. 310.
15. Bartlett, p. 310.
16. John Reiger, *American Sportsmen and the Origin of Conservation*. Norman: University of Oklahoma, 1986, p. 126.
17. Bartlett, p. 311.

18. A more detailed discussion of this battle is discussed in chapter 11, "The Railroaders and the Poachers", *Yellowstone, A Wilderness Besieged* by Richard Bartlett, (Tucson: The University of Arizona Press, 1985) and Chapter 13, "The Railroad Bogey", *The Yellowstone Story, Vol. II*, by Aubrey Haines (Niwot: University Press of Colorado, 1997, (1996 edition).
19. Louis Cramton, *Early History of Yellowstone National Park*, USGPO, 1932, p. 62.
20. Haines, *Vol.* II, p. 34.
21. Cramton, pp. 43, 63.
22. Diem, p. 10.
23. Cramton, p. 64.
24. Cramton, p. 44.
25. Cramton, p. 50.
26. Cramton, p. 65.
27. Cramton, pp. 46, 65.
28. Cramton, pp. 47, 65.
29. Cramton, p. 65.
30. Cramton, p. 66.
31. *Cramton, p. 47.*
32. Craig Reese, *The Gardiner Gateway to Yellowstone*, "The Mainstreeter" (The Northern Pacific Railway Historical Association), Vol. 15, No. 2, Spring, 1996, p. 8.
33. Cramton, p. 67.
34. Haines, p. 46.
35. Diem, p. 12.
36. Cramton, p. 67.
37. Cramton, p. 49.
38. Diem, p. 12.
39. Cramton, p. 68.
40. *Cramton, p. 49.*
41. Cramton, p. 68.
42. Bartlett, p. 316
43. Mary Shivers Culpin, *The History of the Construction of the Road System in Yellowstone National Park, 1872-1966, Historic Resource Study, Volume I,* National Park Service, Rocky Mountain Region, Division of Cultural Resources, No. 5, 1994, pp. 316-317.
44. Tilliston Papers, Special Collections at the Stanford University Library, from the *Electric Railway Journal,* May 11, 1918.
45. Lee Whittlesey, *Yellowstone Place Names*, Helena: Montana Historical Society, 1988, p. 110.

Appendix B
Rail Travel to Yellowstone National Park

1. *Union Pacific Bulletin,* October 1948. This was a newsletter published by the Union Pacific Railroad for travel bureaus and ticket agents.
2. *Ibid.*

References

Allen, Edward Frank, editor. *A Guide to the National Parks of America,* McBride, Nast & Company: New York, 1915.

An Illustrated History of North Idaho, Chicago: Western Historical Publishing Company, 1903.

Austin, Bruce, Robert Goss and Gerard Pesman. "Yellowstone Park Transportation Company", *Motor Coach Today,* April-June 2000.

Barnes, Christine, *Great Lodges of the National Parks,* Bend: W.W. West, 2002.

Bartlett, Richard A., *Yellowstone, A Wilderness Besieged,* Tucson: The University of Arizona Press, 1985.

Bates, Grace, *Gallatin County, Places & Things, Present & Past,* Second Edition, privately published, 1994.

Beal, Merrill D. *Intermountain Railroads,* Caldwell: Caxton Printers, 1962

Beebe, Lucius, and Charles Clegg, *The Trains We Rode, Vol. 1,* Berkeley: Howell-North, 1965.

Bryan, Enoch. *Orient Meets Occident,* Pullman: The Students Book Corporation, 1936.

Carr, Stephen L., and Robert W. Edwards. *Utah Ghost Rails,* Salt Lake City: Western Epics, 1989.

Cheney, Roberta C. *Names on the Face of Montana,* Missoula: Mountain Press Publishing Company, 1983 - 1992 edition.

Christensen, Bonnie. *Red Lodge and the Mythic West,* Lawrence: University of Kansas Press, 2002.

Clark, Milton, "The Milwaukee's Gallatin Valley Line", *The Milwaukee Railroader,* Second Quarter 1994.

Clawson, Calvin C. *A Ride to the Infernal Region - Yellowstone's First Tourists,* Helena: Riverbend Publishing, 2003.

Cohen, Stan. *Montana's Grandest - Historic Hotels and Resorts of the Treasure State,* Missoula: Pictorial Histories Publishing Company, 2004.

Colorado Rail Annual No. 15, Golden: Colorado Railroad Museum, 1981.

Cook, Jeannie, and Lynn J. Houze, Bob Edgar, Paul Fees. *Buffalo Bill's Town in the Rockies,* Virginia Beach: The Downing Company, 1996.

Corporate History of the Oregon Short Line Railroad Company as of June 30th, 1916, prepared in accordance with Valuation Order No. 20 of the Interstate Commerce Commission.

County and City Data Book: 2000, 13th edition. U.S. Department of Commerce, U.S. Census Bureau, USGPO.

Cramton, Louis. *Early History of Yellowstone National Park,* USGPO, 1932.

Cronin, Janet, and Dorothy Vick, *Montana's Gallatin Canyon,* Missoula: Mountain Press Publishing Company, 1992.

Crowder, David L. *Rexburg, Idaho, The First One Hundred Years, 1883-1983,* Caldwell: Caxton Printers, 1983.

Culpin, Mary Shivers. "The History of the Construction of the Road System in Yellowstone National Park, 1872-1966," *Historic Resource Study, Volume I,* National Park Service, Rocky Mountain Region, Division of Cultural Resources, No. 5, 1994.

Daugherty, John. *A Place Called Jackson Hole,* Moose: Grand Teton National Park, 1999.

Derleth, August, *The Milwaukee Road - Its First Hundred Years,* Iowa City: University of Iowa Press, 1948, 2002 edition.

Diem, Kenneth L. and Lenore L. *"A Community of Scalawags, Renegades, Discharged Soldiers and Predestined Stinkers"*, Moose: Grand Teton Natural History Association, 1998.

Drury, George H., *The Historical Guide to North American Railroads,* Milwaukee: Kalmbach Publishing, 1985.

Eagle, Sam and Ed, *West Yellowstone's 70th Anniversary: 1908 - 1978,* West Yellowstone: Eagle Company, 1978.

Ecelbarger, Gary L., *Frederick W. Lander - The Great Natural American Soldier,* Baton Rouge: Louisiana State University Press, 2000.

Ehernberger, James L., and Francis Gschwind. *Union Pacific Steam: Northwestern District,* Callaway: E. & G. Publications, 1966.

Fees, Paul. *Buffalo Bill's Town in the Rockies: A Pictorial History of Cody, Wyoming,* Virginia Beach: The Donning Company, 1996.

Galusha, Hugh D., *"Railroads, Politics, and the Early History of Yellowstone National Park",* unpublished manuscript in the files of the Yellowstone Heritage and Research Center.

Goss, Robert V. *Making Concessions in Yellowstone,* self-published, Second Edition, 2002.

-------------, *Yellowstone - The Chronology of Wonderland,* self-published, Second Edition, 2002.

Haines, Aubrey L. *The Yellowstone Story, Vol. I and Vol. II,* Niwot: University Press of Colorado, 1977, 1996 edition.

-------------*The Park Branch Line,* unpublished manuscript written in 1963. In files of the Yellowstone Heritage and Research Center.

Hampton, H. Duane. *How the U.S. Cavalry Saved our National Parks,* Bloomington: Indiana University Press, 1971.

Hayden, F.V. *The Yellowstone National Park, and the Mountain Regions of Portions of Idaho, Nevada, Colorado and Utah,* Boston: L. Prang and Company, 1876. 1997 reprint by the Thomas Gilcrease Museum Association, Tulsa, OK.

Haynes Guide - Yellowstone National Park, Bozeman: Haynes Studios Inc., 1949 edition and 1958 editions.

Hoy, William, *Railroad Stations in the Gallatin Area, Montana,* Bozeman: Gallatin County Historical Society/ School of Architecture, Montana State University, 1998.

Johnson, Stan. *The Milwaukee Road Olympian: A Ride to Remember,* Coeur d'Alene: Museum of North Idaho, 2001.

Klein, Maury. *Union Pacific - Birth of a Railroad, 1862-1893,* Garden City: Doubleday & Company, 1987.

Kratville, William, and Harold Ranks. *The Union Pacific Streamliners,* Omaha: Kratville Publications, 1974, 1980 edition.

Kratville, William W., *Steam, Steel & Limiteds,* Omaha: Kratville Publications, 1967.

"The Lander-Yellowstone Transportation Company," *Wind River Mountaineer,* April-June, 1993, The Museum of the American West.

Larson, T.A. *History of Wyoming,* Lincoln: University of Nebraska Press, 1965 (Second edition, revised 1978)

Leavengood, David. *A Sense of Shelter: Robert C. Reamer in Yellowstone National Park,* Pacific Historical Review, 1985, pp. 495 - 513.

Madsen, Brigham D. *Corinne - The Gentile Capital of Utah,* Salt Lake City: Utah State Historical Society, 1980.

Madsen, Betty and Brigham D. Madsen. *North to Montana!,* Salt Lake City: Utah State University Press, 1980 (1998 edition).

Maiken, Peter T. *Night Trains,* Beloit: Lakme Press, 1989.

Malone, Michael P. *The Gallatin Canyon and the Tides of History,* Montana History, July, 1973.

McCarter, Steve, *Guide to The Milwaukee Road in Montana,* Helena: Montana Historical Society, 1992.

McClelland, Linda Flint, *Building the National Parks,* Baltimore: Johns Hopkins Press, 1998.

Moulton, Candy, *Roadside History of Wyoming,* Missoula: Mountain Press Publishing Company, 1995.

Nicholson, Philip Sinclair, editor. *Steel Rails and Territorial Trails,* Boise: Limberlost Press, 1994.

Orme, Robert M., *Railroads and the Rockies,* Denver: Sage Books, 1963.

Overton, Richard C. *Burlington Route - A History of the Burlington Lines,* Lincoln: University of Nebraska, 1965.

Potter, Janet Greenstein. *Great American Railroad Stations,* New York: John Wiley & Sons, 1996.

Railway Age's Comprehensive Railroad Dictionary, Omaha: Simmons-Boardman, 1984 (1992 edition).

Reese, Craig. "The Gardiner Gateway to Yellowstone," *The Mainstreeter* (The Northern Pacific Railway Historical Association), Vol. 15, No. 2, Spring, 1996, pp. 1-21.

Reeves, Thomas C. "President Arthur in Yellowstone National Park," *Montana - The Magazine of Western History* (Montana Historical Society), Vol. XIX, No. 3, July, 1969, pp. 18-29

Reiger, John. *American Sportsmen and the Origin of Conservation,* Norman: University of Oklahoma, 1986.

Renz, Louis Tuck. *The History of the Northern Pacific Railroad,* Fairfield: Ye Galleon Press, 1980.

Richmond, Al. *Cowboys, Miners, Presidents and Kings, The Story of the Grand Canyon Railway,* Flagstaff: The Grand Canyon Pioneers Society, Inc., 1985.

Robertson, Donald B., *Encyclopedia of Western Railroad History, Volume II - The Mountain States,* Dallas: Taylor Publishing Company, 1991.

Runte, Alfred. *Trains of Discovery,* Niwot: Roberts Rinehart Publisher, 1990, 1994 edition.

Rydell, Robert W. *All the World's a Fair,* Chicago: The University of Chicago Press, 1984.

Sanders, Helen Fitzgerald. *A History of Montana,* Chicago: The Lewis Publishing Company, 1913.

Schwieterman, Joseph S., *When the Railroad Leaves Town - Western United States,* Kirksville: Truman State University Press, 2004.

Scott, Patricia L. *The Hub of Eastern Idaho: A History of Rigby, Idaho, 1885-1976,* City of Rigby, 1976.

Shearer, F.E. *The Pacific Tourist,* New York: Adams & Bishop, 1884. 1970 edition published by Crown Publishers.

Smith, Phyllis, *Bozeman and the Gallatin Valley, A History,* Helena: Two Dot, 1996.

Strack, Don, and Jim Ehernberger. *Cabooses of the Union Pacific Railroad,* Cheynne: Union Pacific Historical Society, 2002.

Swett, Ira. "*Montana's Trolleys - III.*" Vol. 27, No. 1, South Gate: *Interurbans Magazine*, 1970.

Taber, Thomas T. *The Histories of the Independently Operated Railroads in Montana,* unpublished manuscript, 1960.

Taylor, Bill & Jan. *Rails to Gold and Silver,* Missoula: Pictorial Histories Publishing Co., 1999.

Towne, Charles W. "Preacher's Son on the Loose in Buffalo Bill Country," *Montana - The Magazine of Western History,* Volume XVIII, No. 4, Autumn 1968, pages 40-55.

Travelers Railway Guide, Chicago: The American Railway Guide Company, December, 1916.

"Unique Passenger Station on the Northern Pacific", *The Railroad Gazette,* April 29, 1904, pages 316-317.

Urbanek, Mae. *Wyoming Place Names,* Missoula: Mountain Press Publishing Company, 1988.

Waite, Thornton. *The Yellowstone Branch of the Union Pacific Railroad,* Missouri: Bruehhenjohann/Reese, 1997.

Whiteley, Lee. *The Yellowstone Highway,* Boulder: Lee Whiteley, 2001.

Whittlesey, Lee. *Yellowstone Place Names,* Helena: Montana Historical Society, 1988.

Wingate, George W. *Through the Yellowstone on Horseback,* Moscow: University of Idaho, 1999, reprint of 1886 edition.

Withers, Bob. *The President Travels by Train,* Lynchburg: TLC Publishing, 1996.

Whithorn, Doris. *Twice Told on the Upper Yellowstone, Vol. 1,* Livingston: Doris Whithorn, 1994.

Wood, Stanley. *Over the Range to the Golden Gate,* Chicago: R.R. Donnelly & Sons, 1904 edition.

The WPA Guide to 1930s Montana, compiled and written by the Work Projects Administration for the State of Montana, Tucson: University of Arizona Press, 1994.

Wyoming - A Guide to its History, Highways, and People, Writers' Program of the Work Projects Administration, New York: Oxford University Press, 1941.

Zaitlin, Joyce. *Gilbert Stanley Underwood: His Rustic, Art Deco, and Federal Architecture,* Malibu: Pangloss Press, 1989.

Zupan, Shirley and Harry J. Owens. *Red Lodge - Saga of a Western Area,* Red Lodge: Carbon County Historical Society, 1979.

Other sources include:
- Annual Reports for Yellowstone National Park from the files at the Yellowstone Heritage and Resource Center, Yellowstone National Park.
- Files at the Yellowstone Historic Center in West Yellowstone, Montana.
- ICC Valuation, Bureau of Valuation, for the Union Pacific Railroad.
- Idaho Secretary of State Office (Articles of incorporation)
- Issues of *The Official Guide of the Railways,* New York: National Railway Publication Company.
- Information from the archives of the Chicago & Northwestern Railway Historical Society.
- Montana Secretary of State Office (Articles of incorporation)
- Nomination Forms from the National Register of Historic Places, as noted.
- *The Mixed Train,* the publication of Camerail, Omaha, Nebraska.
- *Pacific RailNews*
- 1993 Montana State Rail Plan Update, Montana Department of Transportation, Rail and Transit Division

The Northern Pacific Railway published this 64-page booklet in 1938 to promote travel to Yellowstone National Park. The back cover had a photo of a bear, a prime attraction for tourists to the park. AUTHOR'S COLLECTION

After touring Yellowstone National Park, tourists would eat dinner in the Union Pacific Railroad's Dining Lodge at West Yellowstone and then board the *Yellowstone Special* for their return trip home. AUTHOR'S COLLECTION

First section of a Northern Pacific Special Train, taken from the stone wall, which is an extension from the west pillar of the Roosevelt Arch at the north entrance to Yellowstone National Park. Note steam plume in the distance from the second section of this special train, circa 1952. COURTESY KENT E. WATSON

About the Author

Thornton Waite is a project manager for Battelle Energy Alliance at the Idaho National Laboratory. He lives in Idaho Falls, Idaho, with his wife, Susan. They have a married daughter in Nampa and another daughter attending the University of Idaho. Other books by Thornton Waite include *Union Pacific: Montana Division, Route of the* Butte Special; *Yellowstone Branch of the Union Pacific, Route of the* Yellowstone Special; and *"Get Off and Push", The Story of the Gilmore & Pittsburgh Railroad* as well as numerous articles on the history and operation of railroads.

COURTESY BOB NITSCHKE

168